T0114341

EASTERTIDE

PRAYERS FOR LENT
THROUGH EASTER
FROM *THE DIVINE HOURS*™

Ephesians 5:19 and 20
Sing psalms and hymns and inspired songs among yourselves,
singing and chanting to the Lord in your hearts, always and everywhere giving
thanks to God who is our Father in the name of our Lord Jesus Christ.

EASTERTIDE

PRAYERS FOR LENT
THROUGH EASTER
FROM *THE DIVINE HOURS*™

Compiled and with a Preface by

Phyllis Tickle

Galilee

New York   London   Toronto   Sydney   Auckland

A GALILEE BOOK
PUBLISHED BY DOUBLEDAY
a division of Random House, Inc.

GALILEE and DOUBLEDAY are registered trademarks of Random House, Inc., and the portrayal of a ship with a cross above a book is a trademark of Random House, Inc.

First Galilee edition published March 2004

The Divine Hours™ Tickle, Inc.

Excerpted material contained herein previously appeared in *The Divine Hours: Prayers for Springtime,* published by Doubleday in 2001.

The Library of Congress has cataloged the hardcover edition of *The Divine Hours* as follows: The Divine Hours: Prayers for Springtime: a manual for prayer / compiled and with a preface by Phyllis Tickle
p. cm.
Includes index.
1. Divine office—Texts. 2. Spring—Prayer-books and devotions—English.
I. Tickle, Phyllis.
BV199.D3 D58 2001
264'.15—dc21

ISBN-13: 978-0-385-51128-5

Copyright © 2004 Tickle, Inc.

Contents

"Whoever sings, prays twice."

—ST. AUGUSTINE

An Introduction to
This Manual

Despite its title, the book you are holding in your hand is not a book of prayers in the usual sense of that term. That is, while this is indeed a collection of prayers and while the ancient words it contains are intended for use during the five weeks of Lent and Holy Week, it is neither a random collection of Psalms, hymns, scripture, and prayers, nor is it arranged for random or casual use. Rather, this is a manual—a manual for doing fixed-hour prayer during the holy weeks of springtime.

Sometimes called "keeping the daily offices" or "observing the divine hours," fixed-hour prayer, together with the hallowing of the Sabbath and the celebration of Communion, is the oldest and most authentic form of Christian spiritual practice. Like Sabbath observance and participation in the communal Passover meal, it comes to us out of ancient Judaism and by way of the devout, practicing Jews who were first Jesus' disciples and then, after the Resurrection, His evangelists and missionaries. Through them and through the early regimens of the Church, all three— Sabbath, Communion, and fixed-hour prayer—were passed to us and have remained with us as central, though adapted, parts of Christian discipline and Christian worship.

For me, and based on my own years of "praying the hours," fixed-hour prayer is best understood as a kind of free, widely windowed, and open passageway between two places—one very physical and the other very virtual. Put more concretely, observing the hours allows our human awareness or mental focus to move back and forth on a daily basis and in a disciplined way, from attending to the necessary bustle of each day of our lives to attending to the eternal timelessness and magnificence of divine life.

By the time of Our Lord, the hours for such praying had become "fixed" into a regimen almost identical to that followed by the Christian Communion today. The hours of six and nine in the morning, noon, three in the afternoon, sunset, retirement, and sometimes midnight were, as they still are, the ones when the faithful—either alone or together—stopped what they were doing, invoked the presence of God, praised Him with the beloved hymns of two or three appointed Psalms, meditated on a piece of holy scripture, sang another hymn, and returned to the workaday world aware of the God to Whom they belonged and of the privilege of worship that had just been granted them.

While we do not have in the Gospels any record of Our Lord's keeping fixed-hour prayer, we must assume that as a devout Jew, He did. We certainly know that the disciples did. Thus, the Spirit fell as tongues of fire upon them on Pentecost while, as we are told in Acts, they were gathered for prayer "at the third hour of the day"—that is, at nine o'clock in the morning. Christianity spread beyond the confines of Judaism primarily because of a vision granted Peter early in the faith's history. That vision involved a sheet filled with unclean or forbidden, but edible, creatures and a heavenly voice instructing Peter to kill and eat. Three times Peter refused, saying that he had never broken halakah or Jewish dietary law in his life; and three times the voice answered by saying, "What God has called holy, humankind must not call profane." Just as the sheet and voice withdrew for the third time, there came a knock at the door below. A Gentile, the servant of a Gentile, was there to beg Peter "to come over into Macedonia" and instruct them in this new way of salvation. It is a story we all remember. What we often forget to remember is that the knock of Cornelius's servant came from downstairs only because Peter was upstairs. That is, the story says, he had gone up to the rooftop at twelve o'clock for what? For noonday prayers. In the same way, of course, the first healing miracle after Jesus' Ascension occurred on the steps of the Temple as Peter and John, on their way to ninth hour (three o'clock) prayers, passed and took pity upon a cripple begging there.

Because the words and hymns of the divine hours are ancient and because they are the hallowed verbal heritage of our faith, their use is not subject to much modification and/or license. Because they are words, however, and because the words appointed for each fixed hour vary not only from each other but also in accord with the place of their observance in each day in the Church's calendar (thus Lent's offices differ in content from one another and from those of Easter), they require a degree of literacy. One must be able to read at some more or less fundamental level in order to follow the changing course of each fixed hour.

As Rome grew increasingly weaker, eventually falling into disrepair, and as the known world spun down into the Dark Ages, so too did literacy retreat from the citizenry of Europe, becoming instead the often rote possession of certain communities of monks. Thus, while the peasant faithful could observe the Sabbath without reading and could attend the Mass without being literate, they could no longer "pray" the divine hours; and the observation of the offices passed, along with literacy, into the monasteries. Up until fairly recently, many American Christians, especially Protestant ones, thought of the offices almost entirely as something that monks did and that involved rote, albeit glorious, Gregorian chant. Even Protestants whose faith resonated with that of the praying couple in Jean-François Millet's popular painting of *The Angelus* failed to perceive any identity between themselves and the artist's subject, between their own history and that vestigial and humble fragment of what had once been part of the office of sundown.

During the last decades of the twentieth century, however, that sense of alienation began to diminish, and lay Christians of every persuasion started to reclaim the divine hours as the third and missing piece in original Christian practice. This manual, like the larger ones from which it is abstracted, was born out of the urgency of that return. Using it requires no instruction beyond that printed on each page itself, save for three things.

First, many Christians—especially Protestant ones who are accustomed to singing the fixed words of their worship—find themselves more comfortable singing both the time-honored and fixed words of the Psalter and the beloved hymns of the vesper office. There is, in the midst of each line of the Psalms, a small asterisk that was originally set there as pointing in the Jewish psalter. On the last syllable before this asterisk, the singer will want to raise his or her monotonal pitch by a single note, just as the last syllable before the end of a line is lowered a note. Your ear will carry you from there to some of the nuisances that lie beyond this primary rule.

Second, a wise rabbi once told me that it is not how many prayers we don't say that matters to God, but rather how many we do. That is important for all of us, but especially for beginners. If this is your first attempt to return to this most ancient of Christian practices, it is wise to remember that you are entering into a discipline and that, like all disciplines, this one sits hard and heavy upon one at times. There are hours you will miss and/or some that you can't even begin to figure out how to observe. That is all right, for either the joy will carry you into greater joy and transmute the discipline into privilege, or you will find yourself simply the wiser and the richer for such experience as you have had. As the rabbi said, that is what matters ultimately.

And last as well as most central, perhaps, is this: Though most contemporary Christians of necessity will observe many offices alone—that is, without the participation in real place and time of other Christians—there are always those fortunate ones of us and/or those blessed occasions in our daily lives when the office can be kept in company with others. When that happens, the pronouns may, and should, be changed from singular to plural. Many of us make that change at all times, however, because (and this is perhaps the most obvious gift of the divine hours) when one prays the hours, one is using the exact words, phrases, and petitions that have informed our faith for centuries. In addition, we are also using the exact words, phrases, and petitions that were offered just an hour earlier by our fellow Christians in the prior time zone and that, in an hour, will be picked up and offered again by our fellow believers in the next time zone. The result is a constant cascade before the throne of God of the "unceasing prayer" to which St. Paul urged us. The result also is the communion of the saints fully realized in words both horizontally through the ages and vertically within this day and hour.

Even so, come, Lord Jesus

The Symbols and Conventions Used in This Manual

NJB: New Jerusalem Bible

KJV: King James Bible

BCP: Book of Common Prayer †

❖:   a medley or hymning of the canonical Psalms as assembled by Dr. Fred Bassett

§:   from the work of St. Augustine

†:   adapted from the Book of Common Prayer

*:   indicate the poetic breaks in the original Hebrew

EASTERTIDE

PRAYERS FOR LENT
THROUGH EASTER
FROM *THE DIVINE HOURS*™

Ephesians 5:19 and 20
Sing psalms and hymns and inspired songs among yourselves,
singing and chanting to the Lord in your hearts, always and everywhere giving
thanks to God who is our Father in the name of our Lord Jesus Christ.

The Gloria

Glory be to God the Father, God the Son, and God the Holy Spirit. As it was
in the beginning, so it is now and so it shall ever be, world without end.
Alleluia*. *Amen.*

The Lord's Prayer

Our Father, who art in heaven, hallowed be your Name.
May your kingdom come, and your will be done, on earth as in heaven.
Give us today our daily bread.
Forgive us our sins as we forgive those who sin against us.
Lead us not into temptation, but deliver us from evil;
for yours are the kingdom and the power and the glory
forever and ever. *Amen.*

Compline Prayers for Holy Week and Easter Are Located on Page 239.

*The Gloria is omitted during Lent by many Christian communities.

"Alleluia" is always omitted from every part of the Church's worship during Lent.
The use of both is restored at Easter.

Lent

The Morning Office

**To Be Observed on the Hour or Half Hour
Between 6 and 9 a.m.**

The Call to Prayer
Give praise, you servants of the LORD;* praise the Name of the LORD.

Psalm 113:1

The Request for Presence
Test me, O LORD, and try me;* examine my heart and mind.

Psalm 26:2

The Greeting
All your works praise you, O LORD,* and your faithful servants bless you.
They make known the glory of your kingdom* and speak of your power.

Psalm 145:10–11

The Refrain for the Morning Lessons
Those who sowed with tears* will reap with songs of joy.
Those who go out weeping, carrying the seed,* will come again with joy,
   shouldering their sheaves.

Psalm 126:6–7

A Reading
Jesus taught us, saying: "Be careful not to parade your uprightness in public to
   attract attention; otherwise you will lose all reward from your Father in
   heaven. So when you give alms, do not have it trumpeted before you; this is
   what the hypocrites do in the synagogues and in the streets to win human
   admiration. In truth I tell you, they have had their reward. But when you give
   alms, your left hand must not know what your right hand is doing; your almsgiving must be secret, and your Father who sees all that is done in secret will
   reward you."

Matthew 6:1–6

The Refrain
Those who sowed with tears* will reap with songs of joy.
Those who go out weeping, carrying the seed,* will come again with joy, shoul-
   dering their sheaves.

The Morning Psalm   *Who Is Like You, O God?*
Your righteousness, O God, reaches to the heavens;* you have done great things;
   who is like you, O God?
You have showed me great troubles and adversities,* but you will restore my life
   and bring me up again from the deep places of the earth.
You strengthen me more and more;* you enfold and comfort me,
Therefore I will praise you upon the lyre for your faithfulness, O my God;* I will
   sing to you with the harp, O Holy One of Israel.
My lips will sing with joy when I play to you,* and so will my soul, which you
   have redeemed.

My tongue will proclaim your righteousness all day long,* for they are ashamed
and disgraced who sought to do me harm.

Psalm 71:19–24

The Refrain
Those who sowed with tears* will reap with songs of joy.
Those who go out weeping, carrying the seed,* will come again with joy, shoul-
dering their sheaves.

The Cry of the Church
Christ, have mercy.
Lord, have mercy.
Christ, have mercy.

The Lord's Prayer

The Prayer Appointed for the Week
Almighty and everlasting God, you hate nothing you have made and forgive the
sins of all who are penitent: Create and make in me a new and contrite heart,
that I, worthily lamenting my sins and acknowledging my wretchedness, may
obtain of you, the God of all mercy, perfect remission and forgiveness; through
Jesus Christ our Lord, who lives and reigns with you and the Holy Spirit, one
God, for ever and ever. †

The Concluding Prayer of the Church
Lord God, almighty and everlasting Father, you have brought me in safety to this
new day: Preserve me with your mighty power, that I may not fall into sin, nor
be overcome by adversity; and in all I do direct me to the fulfilling of your purpose; through Jesus Christ my Lord. *Amen.* †

The Midday Office
**To Be Observed on the Hour or Half Hour
Between 11 a.m. and 2 p.m.**

The Call to Prayer
"Come now, let us reason together," says the Lord.

The Request for Presence
Hear the voice of my prayer when I cry out to you,* when I lift up my hands to
your holy of holies.

Psalm 28:2

The Greeting
Who is like you, LORD God of hosts?* O mighty LORD, your faithfulness is all
around you.

Psalm 89:8

The Refrain for the Midday Lessons
But it is good for me to be near God;* I have made the Lord GOD my refuge.

Psalm 73:28

A Reading

Blow the ram's horn in Zion, sound the alarm on my holy mountain! Let everybody in the country tremble, for the Day of Yahweh is coming, yes, it is near. Day of darkness and gloom, Day of cloud and blackness. Like the dawn, across the mountains spreads a vast and mighty people, such as has never been before, such as will never be again to the remotest ages. . . . 'But now—declares Yahweh—come back to me with all your heart, fasting, weeping, mourning.' Tear your hearts and not your clothes, and come back to Yahweh your God, for he is gracious and compassionate, slow to anger, rich in faithful love . . .

Joel 2:1–2, 12–13

The Refrain

But it is good for me to be near God; I have made the Lord GOD my refuge.

The Midday Psalm   *I Will Thank You with an Unfeigned Heart*

Happy are they whose way is blameless,* who walk in the law of the LORD!
Happy are they who observe his decrees* and seek him with all their hearts!
Who never do any wrong,* but always walk in his ways.
You laid down your commandments,* that we should fully keep them.
Oh, that my ways were made so direct* that I might keep your statutes!
Then I should not be put to shame,* when I regard all your commandments.
I will thank you with an unfeigned heart,* when I have learned your righteous judgments.
I will keep your statutes;* do not utterly forsake me.

Psalm 119:1–8

The Refrain

But it is good for me to be near God;* I have made the Lord GOD my refuge.

The Cry of the Church

Christ, have mercy.
Lord, have mercy.
Christ, have mercy.

The Lord's Prayer

The Prayer Appointed for the Week

Almighty and everlasting God, you hate nothing you have made and forgive the sins of all who are penitent: Create and make in me a new and contrite heart, that I, worthily lamenting my sins and acknowledging my wretchedness, may obtain of you, the God of all mercy, perfect remission and forgiveness; through Jesus Christ our Lord, who lives and reigns with you and the Holy Spirit, one God, for ever and ever. †

The Concluding Prayer of the Church

Almighty and eternal God, ruler of all things in heaven and earth: Mercifully accept my prayers, and strengthen me to do your will; through Jesus Christ our Lord. *Amen.* †

The Vespers Office

To Be Observed on the Hour or Half Hour Between 5 and 8 p.m.

The Call to Prayer
Create in me a clean heart, O God,* and renew a right spirit within me.

Psalm 51:11

The Request for Presence
Exalt yourself above the heavens, O God,* and your glory over all the earth.

Psalm 57:11

The Greeting
May God give us his blessing,* and may all the ends of the earth stand in awe of him.

Psalm 67:7

Litany of Penance
Most holy and merciful Father:
I confess to you and to the whole communion of saints
in heaven and on earth,
that I have sinned by my own fault
in thought, word, and deed;
by what I have done, and by what I have left undone.

I have not loved you with my whole heart, and mind, and strength. I have not loved my neighbors as myself. I have not forgiven others, as I have been forgiven. Have mercy on me, Lord.

I have been deaf to your call to serve, as Christ served us. I have not been true to the mind of Christ. I have grieved your holy spirit. Have mercy on me, Lord.

I confess to you, Lord, all my past unfaithfulness: the pride, hypocrisy, and impatience of my life.
I confess to you, Lord.

My self-indulgent appetites and ways, and my exploitation of other people, I confess to you, Lord.

My anger at my own frustration, and my envy of those more fortunate than I, I confess to you, Lord.

My intemperate love of worldly goods and comforts, and my dishonesty in daily life and work,
I confess to you, Lord.

My negligence in prayer and worship, and my failure to commend the faith that is in me,
I confess to you, Lord.

Accept my repentance, Lord, for the wrongs I have done: for my blindness to human need and suffering, and my indifference to indulgence and cruelty, Accept my repentance, Lord.

For all false judgments, for uncharitable thoughts toward my neighbors, and for my prejudice and contempt towards those who differ from me, Accept my repentance, Lord.

For my waste and pollution of your creation, and my lack of concern for those who come after us, Accept my repentance, Lord.
Restore me, good Lord, and let your anger depart from me, Favorably hear me for your mercy is great.
Accomplish in me and all of your church the work of your salvation, That I may show forth all your glory in the world.

By the cross and passion of your Son, our Lord, Bring me with all your saints to the joy of his resurrection. †

The Refrain for the Vespers Lessons
Let your ways be known upon earth,* your saving health among all nations.

Psalm 67:2

The Vespers Psalm   *Summon Me by Night*
Weigh my heart, summon me by night,* melt me down; you will find no impurity in me.
I give no offense with my mouth as others do;* I have heeded the words of your lips.
My footsteps hold fast to the ways of your law;* in your paths my feet shall not stumble.
I call upon you, O God, for you will answer me;* incline your ear to me and hear my words.
Show me your marvelous loving-kindness,* O Savior of those who take refuge at your right hand from those who rise up against them.
Keep me as the apple of your eye;* hide me under the shadow of your wings.

Psalm 17:3–8

The Refrain
Let your ways be known upon earth,* your saving health among all nations.

The Cry of the Church
Christ, have mercy.
Lord, have mercy.
Christ, have mercy.

The Lord's Prayer

The Prayer Appointed for the Week
Almighty and everlasting God, you hate nothing you have made and forgive the
sins of all who are penitent: Create and make in me a new and contrite heart,
that I, worthily lamenting my sins and acknowledging my wretchedness, may
obtain of you, the God of all mercy, perfect remission and forgiveness; through
Jesus Christ our Lord, who lives and reigns with you and the Holy Spirit, one
God, for ever and ever. †

The Concluding Prayer of the Church
Almighty and eternal God, ruler of all things in heaven and earth: Mercifully
accept the prayers of your people everywhere, and strengthen each of us to do
your will; through Jesus Christ my Lord. *Amen.* †

The Morning Office **To Be Observed on the Hour or Half Hour**
Between 6 and 9 a.m.

The Call to Prayer
The Lord is King; let the people tremble;* he is enthroned upon the cherubim; let
the earth shake.

Psalm 99:1

The Request for Presence
Be seated on your lofty throne, O Most High;* O Lord, judge the nations.

Psalm 7:8

The Greeting
Save us, O Lord our God, and gather us from among the nations,* that we may
give thanks to your holy Name and glory in your praise.

Psalm 106:47

The Refrain for the Morning Lessons
Let all the earth fear the Lord;* let all who dwell in the world stand in awe of him.

Psalm 33:8

A Reading
Jesus taught us, saying: "So when you give alms, do not have it trumpeted before
you; this is what the hypocrites do in the synagogues and in the streets to win
human admiration. In truth I tell you, they have had their reward. But when
you give alms, your left hand must not know what your right is doing; your
almsgiving must be secret, and your Father who sees all that is done in secret
will reward you."

Matthew 6:2–4

The Refrain
Let all the earth fear the Lord;* let all who dwell in the world stand in awe of him.

The Morning Psalm *The Just Shall Not Put Their Hands to Evil*
Those who trust in the Lord are like Mount Zion,* which cannot be moved, but
stands fast for ever.

The hills stand about Jerusalem;* so does the LORD stand round about his people,
from this time forth for evermore.
The scepter of the wicked shall not hold sway over the land allotted to the just,* so
that the just shall not put their hands to evil.

Psalm 125:1–3

The Refrain

Let all the earth fear the LORD;* let all who dwell in the world stand in awe of him.

The Small Verse

"I am the Alpha and the Omega," says the Lord God, who is, who was, and who is
to come, the Almighty.

Revelation 1:8

The Lord's Prayer

The Prayer Appointed for the Week

Almighty and everlasting God, you hate nothing you have made and forgive the
sins of all who are penitent: Create and make in me a new and contrite heart,
that I, worthily lamenting my sins and acknowledging my wretchedness, may
obtain of you, the God of all mercy, perfect remission and forgiveness; through
Jesus Christ our Lord, who lives and reigns with you and the Holy Spirit, one
God, for ever and ever. †

The Concluding Prayer of the Church

Lord God, almighty and everlasting Father, you have brought me in safety to this
new day: Preserve me with your mighty power, that I may not fall into sin, nor
be overcome by adversity; and in all I do direct me to the fulfilling of your purpose; through Jesus Christ my Lord. *Amen.* †

The Midday Office

**To Be Observed on the Hour or Half Hour
Between 11 a.m. and 2 p.m.**

The Call to Prayer

Sing to the LORD, you servants of his;* give thanks for the remembrance of his
holiness.
For his wrath endures but the twinkling of an eye,* his favor for a lifetime.

Psalm 30:4–5

The Request for Presence

Look upon your covenant;* the dark places of the earth are haunts of violence.

Psalm 74:19

The Greeting

O LORD, your love endures for ever;* do not abandon the works of your hands.

Psalm 138:9

The Refrain for the Midday Lessons

He has not dealt with us according to our sins,* nor rewarded us according to our
wickedness.

Psalm 103:10

A Reading

With what shall I enter YAHWEH's presence and bow down before God All-high?
Shall I enter with burnt offerings, with calves one year old? Will he be pleased
with rams by the thousand, with ten thousand streams of oil? Shall I offer my
eldest son for my wrong-doing, the child of my own body for my sin? You have
already been told what is right and what YAHWEH wants of you. Only this, to
do what is right, to love loyalty and to walk humbly with your God.

Micah 6:6–8

The Refrain

He has not dealt with us according to our sins,* nor rewarded us according to our
wickedness.

The Midday Psalm   *How Exalted Is Your Name*

O LORD our Governor,* how exalted is your Name in all the world!

Out of the mouths of infants and children* your majesty is praised above the heavens.

You have set up a stronghold against your adversaries,* to quell the enemy and
the avenger.

When I consider your heavens, the work of your fingers,* the moon and the stars
you have set in their courses,

What is man that you should be mindful of him?* the son of man that you should
seek him out?

You have made him but little lower than the angels;* you adorn him with glory
and honor;

You give him mastery over the works of your hands;* you put all things under his
feet:

All sheep and oxen,* even the wild beasts of the field,

The birds of the air, the fish of the sea,* and whatsoever walks in the paths of the sea.

O LORD our Governor,* how exalted is your Name in all the world!

Psalm 8

The Refrain

He has not dealt with us according to our sins,* nor rewarded us according to our
wickedness.

The Cry of the Church

Christ, have mercy.
Lord, have mercy.
Christ, have mercy.

The Lord's Prayer

The Prayer Appointed for the Week

Almighty and everlasting God, you hate nothing you have made and forgive the
sins of all who are penitent: Create and make in me a new and contrite heart,
that I, worthily lamenting my sins and acknowledging my wretchedness, may
obtain of you, the God of all mercy, perfect remission and forgiveness; through
Jesus Christ our Lord, who lives and reigns with you and the Holy Spirit, one
God, for ever and ever. †

The Concluding Prayer of the Church
Almighty God, to whom our needs are known before we ask: Help me to ask only
what accords with your will; and those good things which I dare not, or in my
blindness cannot ask, grant for the sake of your Son Jesus Christ our Lord.
Amen. †

The Vespers Office   **To Be Observed on the Hour or Half Hour**
                                          Between 5 and 8 p.m.

The Call to Prayer
Rejoice in the LORD, you righteous,* and give thanks to his holy Name.

Psalm 97:12

The Request for Presence
Send forth your strength, O God;* establish, O God, what you have wrought for us.

Psalm 68:28

The Greeting
One generation shall praise your works to another* and shall declare your power.

Psalm 145:4

The Hymn
> My song is love unknown,
>> my Savior's love to me,
> love to the loveless shown
>> that they might lovely be.
>>> O who am I
>>>> that for my sake
>>>> my Lord should take
>>> frail flesh, and die?

> In life no house, no home
>> my Lord on earth might have;
> in death no friendly tomb
>> but what a stranger gave.
>>> What may I say?
>>>> Heaven was his home;
>>>> but mine the tomb
>>> wherein he lay.

> Here might I stay and sing,
>> no story so divine:
> never was love, dear King,
>> never was grief like thine.
>>> This is my friend,
>>>> in whose sweet praise
>>>> I all my days
>>> could gladly spend.

Samuel Crossman

The Refrain for the Vespers Lessons

The hills stand about Jerusalem;* so does the LORD stand round about his people,
   from this time forth for evermore.

Psalm 125:2

The Vespers Psalm   *Your Love Is Ever Before My Eyes*

Test me, O LORD, and try me;* examine my heart and my mind.

For your love is before my eyes;* I have walked faithfully with you.

I have not sat with the worthless,* nor do I consort with the deceitful.

I have hated the company of evildoers;* I will not sit down with the wicked.

I will wash my hands in innocence, O LORD,* that I may go in procession round
   your altar,

Singing aloud a song of thanksgiving* and recounting all your wonderful deeds.

Psalm 26:2–7

The Refrain

The hills stand about Jerusalem;* so does the LORD stand round about his people,
   from this time forth for evermore.

The Small Verse

But if you will not serve the Lord, choose today whom you wish to serve, whether
   the gods that your ancestors served beyond the River, or the gods of the
   Amorites in whose land you are now living. As for me and my House, we will
   serve YAHWEH.

Joshua 24:15

The Lord's Prayer

The Prayer Appointed for the Week

Almighty and everlasting God, you hate nothing you have made and forgive the
   sins of all who are penitent: Create and make in me a new and contrite heart,
   that I, worthily lamenting my sins and acknowledging my wretchedness, may
   obtain of you, the God of all mercy, perfect remission and forgiveness; through
   Jesus Christ our Lord, who lives and reigns with you and the Holy Spirit, one
   God, for ever and ever. †

The Concluding Prayer of the Church

Lord God Almighty, you have made all the peoples of the earth for your glory, to
   serve you in freedom and in peace: Give to the people of our country a zeal for
   justice and the strength of forbearance, that we may use our liberty in accor-
   dance with your gracious will; through Jesus Christ our Lord, who lives and
   reigns with you and the Holy Spirit, one God, for ever and ever. *Amen.* †

The Morning Office   **To Be Observed on the Hour or Half Hour**
Between 6 and 9 a.m.

The Call to Prayer

Proclaim the greatness of the LORD our God and worship him upon his holy hill;*
   for the LORD our God is the Holy One.

Psalm 99:9

The Request for Presence
Be pleased, O Lord, to deliver me;* O Lord, make haste to help me.

Psalm 40:14

The Greeting
But you, O Lord my God, oh, deal with me according to your Name;* for your
tender mercy's sake, deliver me.
For I am poor and needy,* and my heart is wounded within me.

Psalm 109:20–21

The Refrain for the Morning Lessons
The Lord is full of compassion and mercy,* slow to anger and of great kindness.

Psalm 103:8

A Reading
Jesus taught his disciples, saying: "And indeed, which of you here, intending to build
a tower, would not first sit down and work out the cost to see if he had enough to
complete it? Otherwise if he laid the foundation and then found himself unable to
finish the work, everyone who saw it would start making fun of him and saying,
'Here is someone who started to build and was unable to finish.' "

Luke 14:28–30

The Refrain
The Lord is full of compassion and mercy,* slow to anger and of great kindness.

The Morning Psalm   *The Lord Preserves All Those Who Love Him*
The Lord is near to those who call upon him,* to all who call upon him faithfully.
He fulfills the desire of those who fear him;* he hears their cry and helps them.
The Lord preserves all those who love him,* but he destroys all the wicked.

Psalm 145:19–21

The Refrain
The Lord is full of compassion and mercy,* slow to anger and of great kindness.

The Cry of the Church
Christ, have mercy.
Lord, have mercy.
Christ, have mercy.

The Lord's Prayer

The Prayer Appointed for the Week
Almighty and everlasting God, you hate nothing you have made and forgive the
sins of all who are penitent: Create and make in me a new and contrite heart,
that I, worthily lamenting my sins and acknowledging my wretchedness, may
obtain of you, the God of all mercy, perfect remission and forgiveness; through
Jesus Christ our Lord, who lives and reigns with you and the Holy Spirit, one
God, for ever and ever. †

The Concluding Prayer of the Church

Lord God, almighty and everlasting Father, you have brought me in safety to this new day: Preserve me with your mighty power, that I may not fall into sin, nor be overcome by adversity; and in all I do direct me to the fulfilling of your purpose; through Jesus Christ my Lord. *Amen.* †

The Midday Office **To Be Observed on the Hour or Half Hour**
Between 11 a.m. and 2 p.m.

The Call to Prayer

Come, let us bow down, and bend the knee,* and kneel before the LORD our Maker.

For he is our God, and we are the people of his pasture and the sheep of his hand.

Psalm 95:6–7

The Request for Presence

Hear my prayer, O God;* do not hide yourself from my petition.

Listen to me and answer me.

Psalm 55:1–2

The Greeting

O God, you know my foolishness,* and my faults are not hidden from you.

Answer me, O LORD, for your love is kind;* in your great compassion, turn to me.

Psalm 69:6ff

The Refrain for the Midday Lessons

Our sins are stronger than we are,* but you will blot them out.

Psalm 65:3

A Reading

The Apostle wrote, saying: ". . . we have never failed to remember you in our prayers and ask that through perfect wisdom and spiritual understanding you should reach the fullest knowledge of his will and so be able to lead a life worthy of the Lord, a life acceptable to him in all its aspects, bearing fruit in every kind of good work and growing in knowledge of God."

Colossians 1:9–10

The Refrain

Our sins are stronger than we are,* but you will blot them out.

The Midday Psalm *The LORD Is a Friend to Those Who Fear Him*

Who are they who fear the LORD?* he will teach them the way that they should choose.

They shall dwell in prosperity,* and their offspring shall inherit the land.

The LORD is a friend to those who fear him* and will show them his covenant.

Psalm 25:11–13

The Refrain

Our sins are stronger than we are,* but you will blot them out.

The Cry of the Church
Christ, have mercy.
Lord, have mercy.
Christ, have mercy.

The Lord's Prayer

The Prayer Appointed for the Week
Almighty and everlasting God, you hate nothing you have made and forgive the
sins of all who are penitent: Create and make in me a new and contrite heart,
that I, worthily lamenting my sins and acknowledging my wretchedness, may
obtain of you, the God of all mercy, perfect remission and forgiveness; through
Jesus Christ our Lord, who lives and reigns with you and the Holy Spirit, one
God, for ever and ever. †

The Concluding Prayer of the Church
Almighty God, whose most dear Son went not up to joy before he first suffered
pain, and did not enter into glory before he was crucified: Mercifully grant that
I, walking in the way of the cross, may find it to be none other than the way of
life and peace; through Jesus Christ your Son my Lord. *Amen.* †

The Vespers Office   **To Be Observed on the Hour or Half Hour**
Between 5 and 8 p.m.

The Call to Prayer
I will call upon God,* and the Lord will deliver me.
In the evening, in the morning, and at the noonday, I will complain and lament,*
and he will hear my voice.
He will bring me safely back . . . God, who is enthroned of old, will hear me.

Psalm 55:17ff

The Request for Presence
Teach me your way, O Lord, and I will walk in your truth;* knit my heart to you
that I may fear your Name.

Psalm 86:11

The Greeting
To you, O Lord, I lift up my soul;* my God, I put my trust in you.

Psalm 25:1

The Hymn
Hail, O Star of ocean God's own Mother blessed,
Ever sinless Virgin gate of heavenly rest.

Show yourself a Mother, may the Word divine
Born for us your Infant hear my prayer through thine.

Keep my life all spotless, Make my way secure,
Till I find in Jesus joy that will endure.

Praise to God the Father honor to the Son,
In the Holy Spirit be the glory one.

adapted from The Short Breviary

The Refrain for the Vespers Lessons
As far as the east is from the west,* so far has he removed our sins from us.

Psalm 103:12

The Vespers Psalm   *You Are the Holy One, Enthroned Upon the Praises of Israel*
My God, my God, why have you forsaken me?* and are so far from my cry and
   from the words of my distress?
O my God, I cry in the daytime, but you do not answer;* by night as well, but I
   find no rest.
Yet you are the Holy One,* enthroned upon the praises of Israel.
Our forefathers put their trust in you;* they trusted, and you delivered them.
They cried out to you and were delivered;* they trusted in you and were not put to
   shame.

Psalm 22:1–5

The Refrain
As far as the east is from the west,* so far has he removed our sins from us.

The Cry of the Church
Christ, have mercy.
Lord, have mercy.
Christ, have mercy.

The Lord's Prayer

The Prayer Appointed for the Week
Almighty and everlasting God, you hate nothing you have made and forgive the
   sins of all who are penitent: Create and make in me a new and contrite heart,
   that I, worthily lamenting my sins and acknowledging my wretchedness, may
   obtain of you, the God of all mercy, perfect remission and forgiveness; through
   Jesus Christ our Lord, who lives and reigns with you and the Holy Spirit, one
   God, for ever and ever. †

Concluding Prayers of the Church
Almighty God, who has promised to hear the petitions of those who ask in your
   Son's Name: I beseech you mercifully to incline your ear to me who have made
   my prayers and supplications to you; and grant that those things which I have
   faithfully asked according to your will, may effectually be obtained, to the
   relief of my necessity, and to the setting forth of your glory; through Jesus
   Christ my Lord. *Amen.* †

May the souls of the faithful departed, through the mercy of God, rest in eternal
   peace. *Amen.*

The Morning Office   **To Be Observed on the Hour or Half Hour**
                                          Between 6 and 9 a.m.

The Call to Prayer
Ascribe to the Lord the glory due his Name;* worship the Lord in the beauty of
   holiness.

Psalm 29:2

The Request for Presence
O God, you are my God; eagerly I seek you;* my soul thirsts for you, my flesh
   faints for you, as in barren and dry land where there is no water.

Psalm 63:1

The Greeting
We have heard with our ears, O God, our forefathers have told us,* the deeds you
   did in their days, in the days of old.

Psalm 44:1

The Refrain for the Morning Lessons
Rescue the weak and the poor;* deliver them from the power of the wicked.

Psalm 82:4

A Reading
Jesus taught us, saying: "You have heard how it was said, *You will love your neighbor* and hate your enemy. But I say this to you, love your enemies and pray for
   those who persecute you; so that you may be children of your Father in
   heaven, for he causes his sun to rise on the bad as well as the good, and sends
   down rain to fall on the upright and the wicked alike."

Matthew 5:43–45

The Refrain
Rescue the weak and the poor;* deliver them from the power of the wicked.

The Morning Psalm   ***Whoever Is Wise Will Ponder These Things***
The Lord changed rivers into deserts,* and water-springs into thirsty
   ground,
A fruitful land into salt flats,* because of the wickedness of those who dwell
   there.
He changed deserts into pools of water* and dry land into water-springs.
He settled the hungry there,* and they founded a city to dwell in.
They sowed fields, and planted vineyards,* and brought in a fruitful harvest.
He blessed them, so that they increased greatly;* he did not let their herds
   decrease.
Yet when they were diminished and brought low,* through stress of adversity and
   sorrow,
(He pours contempt on princes* and makes them wander in trackless wastes)
He lifted up the poor out of misery* and multiplied their families like flocks of
   sheep.
The upright will see this and rejoice,* but all wickedness will shut its mouth.

Whoever is wise will ponder these things,* and consider well the mercies of the
    LORD.

Psalm 107:33–43

The Refrain
Rescue the weak and the poor;* deliver them from the power of the wicked.

The Cry of the Church
Christ, have mercy.
Lord, have mercy.
Christ, have mercy.

The Lord's Prayer

The Prayer Appointed for the Week
Almighty and everlasting God, you hate nothing you have made and forgive the
    sins of all who are penitent: Create and make in me a new and contrite heart,
    that I, worthily lamenting my sins and acknowledging my wretchedness, may
    obtain of you, the God of all mercy, perfect remission and forgiveness; through
    Jesus Christ our Lord, who lives and reigns with you and the Holy Spirit, one
    God, for ever and ever. †

The Concluding Prayer of the Church
Lord God, almighty and everlasting Father, you have brought me in safety to this
    new day: Preserve me with your mighty power, that I may not fall into sin, nor
    be overcome by adversity; and in all I do direct me to the fulfilling of your pur-
    pose; through Jesus Christ my Lord. *Amen.* †

The Midday Office   **To Be Observed on the Hour or Half Hour
Between 11 a.m. and 2 p.m.**

The Call to Prayer
Bless God in the congregation;* bless the LORD, you that are of the fountain of
    Israel.

Psalm 68:26

The Request for Presence
I call upon you, O God, for you will answer me;* incline your ear to me and hear
    my words.

Psalm 17:6

The Greeting
You are my God, and I will thank you;* you are my God, and I will exalt you.

Psalm 118:28

The Refrain for the Midday Lessons
The LORD, the God of gods, has spoken;* he has called the earth from the rising of
    the sun to its setting.

Psalm 50:1

A Reading

The Apostle wrote, saying: "I have accepted the loss of all other things, and look
on them all as filth if only I can gain Christ and be given a place in him, with
the uprightness I have gained not from the Law, but through faith in Christ, an
uprightness from God, based on faith, that I may come to know him and the
power of his resurrection."

Philippians 3:8–10

The Refrain

The Lord, the God of gods, has spoken;* he has called the earth from the rising of
the sun to its setting.

The Midday Psalm   *Kingship Belongs to the Lord*

All the ends of the earth shall remember and turn to the Lord,* and all the families
of the nations shall bow before him.

For kingship belongs to the Lord;* he rules over the nations.

To him alone all who sleep in the earth bow down in worship;* who go down to
the dust fall before him.

My soul shall live for him; my descendants shall serve him;* they shall be known
as the Lord's for ever.

They shall come and make known to a people yet unborn* the saving deeds that
he has done.

Psalm 22:26–30

The Refrain

The Lord, the God of gods, has spoken;* he has called the earth from the rising of
the sun to its setting.

The Cry of the Church

Christ, have mercy.

Lord, have mercy.

Christ, have mercy.

The Lord's Prayer

The Prayer Appointed for the Week

Almighty and everlasting God, you hate nothing you have made and forgive the
sins of all who are penitent: Create and make in me a new and contrite heart,
that I, worthily lamenting my sins and acknowledging my wretchedness, may
obtain of you, the God of all mercy, perfect remission and forgiveness; through
Jesus Christ our Lord, who lives and reigns with you and the Holy Spirit, one
God, for ever and ever. †

The Concluding Prayer of the Church

O God, the source of eternal light: Shed forth your unending day upon all of us
who watch for you, that our lips may praise you, our lives may bless you, and
our worship may give you glory; through Jesus Christ our Lord. *Amen.* †

The Vespers Office   To Be Observed on the Hour or Half Hour
Between 5 and 8 p.m.

The Call to Prayer
The LORD is my strength and my shield;* my heart trusts him, and I have been
   helped;
Therefore my heart dances for joy,* and in my song I will praise him.

Psalm 28:8–9

The Request for Presence
Hear, O LORD, and have mercy upon me;* O LORD, be my helper.

Psalm 30:11

The Greeting
Your righteousness, O God, reaches to the heavens;* you have done great things;
   who is like you, O God?

Psalm 71:19

The Hymn
Blessed Jesus, at Your word we are gathered all to hear You;
Let our hearts and souls be stirred now to seek and love and fear You,
      By your teachings sweet and holy,
      Drawn from earth to love You solely.

All our knowledge, sense, and sight lie in deepest darkness shrouded,
Till Your spirit breaks our night with the beams of truth unclouded.
      You alone to God can win us;
      You must work all good within us.

Glorious Lord, Yourself impart! Light of light, from God proceeding,
Open now our ears and heart; help is by Your spirit's pleading;
      Hear the cry your people raises;
      Hear, and bless our prayers and praises.

Tobias Clausnitzer

The Refrain for the Vespers Lessons
Remember me, O LORD, with the favor you have for your people,* and visit me
   with your saving help.

Psalm 106:4

The Vespers Psalm   *Who Can Ascend the Hill of the LORD?*
The earth is the LORD's and all that is in it,* the world and all who dwell therein.
For it is he who founded it upon the seas* and made it firm upon the rivers of the
   deep.
"Who can ascend the hill of the LORD?* and who can stand in his holy place?"
"Those who have clean hands and a pure heart,* who have not pledged themselves
   to falsehood, nor sworn by what is a fraud.
They shall receive a blessing from the LORD* and a just reward from the God of
   their salvation."

Such is the generation of those who seek him,* of those who seek your face, O God of Jacob.

Psalm 24:1–6

The Refrain
Remember me, O LORD, with the favor you have for your people,* and visit me with your saving help.

The Cry of the Church
Christ, have mercy.
Lord, have mercy.
Christ, have mercy.

The Lord's Prayer

The Prayer Appointed for the Week
Almighty and everlasting God, you hate nothing you have made and forgive the sins of all who are penitent: Create and make in me a new and contrite heart, that I, worthily lamenting my sins and acknowledging my wretchedness, may obtain of you, the God of all mercy, perfect remission and forgiveness; through Jesus Christ our Lord, who lives and reigns with you and the Holy Spirit, one God, for ever and ever. †

The Concluding Prayer of the Church
Give me courage to resist, patience to endure, constancy to persevere. Grant, in place of all consolations of the world, the most sweet unction of Thy Spirit, and in place of carnal love, pour into me the love of Thy Name.

Thomas à Kempis

The Morning Office **To Be Observed on the Hour or Half Hour Between 6 and 9 a.m.**

The Call to Prayer
Let the peoples praise you, O God;* let all the peoples praise you.
Let the nations be glad and sing for joy,* for you judge the peoples with equity and guide all nations upon the earth.
Let the peoples praise you, O God;* let all the peoples praise you.

Psalm 67:3–5

The Request for Presence
Hear my voice, O LORD, according to your loving-kindness;* according to your judgments, give me life.

Psalm 119:149

The Greeting
Hosanna, LORD, hosanna!* LORD, send us now success.

Blessed is he who comes in the name of the LORD;* we bless you from the house of the LORD.

Psalm 118:25–26

The Refrain for the Morning Lessons
I was glad when they said to me,* "Let us go to the house of the LORD."

Psalm 122:1

A Reading
Jesus said: "The Sabbath was made for man, not man for the Sabbath; so the Son of man is master even of the Sabbath."

Mark 2:27–28

The Refrain
I was glad when they said to me,* "Let us go to the house of the LORD."

The Morning Psalm   *The LORD Has Ordained a Blessing*
Oh, how good and pleasant it is,* when brethren live together in unity!
It is like fine oil upon the head* that runs down upon the beard,
Upon the beard of Aaron,* and runs down upon the collar of his robe.
It is like the dew of Hermon* that falls upon the hills of Zion.
For there the LORD has ordained the blessing:* life for evermore.

Psalm 133

The Refrain
I was glad when they said to me,* "Let us go to the house of the LORD."

The Cry of the Church
O God, come to my assistance! O Lord, make haste to help me.

The Lord's Prayer

The Prayer Appointed for the Week
O God, the strength of all who put their trust in you: Mercifully accept my prayers; and because in my weakness I can do nothing good without you, give me the help of your grace, that in keeping your commandments I may please you in both will and deed; through Jesus Christ my Lord, who lives and reigns with you and the Holy Spirit, one God, for ever and ever. *Amen.* †

The Concluding Prayer of the Church
Lord God, almighty and everlasting Father, you have brought me in safety to this new day: Preserve me with your mighty power, that I may not fall into sin, nor be overcome by adversity; and in all I do direct me to the fulfilling of your purpose; through Jesus Christ my Lord. *Amen.* †

The Midday Office   **To Be Observed on the Hour or Half Hour**
                                   Between 11 a.m. and 2 p.m.

The Call to Prayer
Worship the LORD in the beauty of holiness;* let the whole earth tremble before him.

Psalm 96:9

The Request for Presence
Hear, O Shepherd of Israel, leading Joseph like a flock;* shine forth, you that are
enthroned upon the cherubim.

Psalm 80:1

The Greeting
Yours is the day, yours also is the night;* you established the moon and the sun.
You fixed all the boundaries of the earth;* you made both summer and winter.

Psalm 74:15–16

The Refrain for the Midday Lessons
The earth, O LORD, is full of your love;* instruct me in your statutes.

Psalm 119:64

A Reading
The past is out of reach, buried deep—who can discover it? But I have reached the
point where, having learned, explored and investigated wisdom and reflection,
I recognize evil as being a form of madness, and folly as something stupid.

Ecclesiastes 7:24–25

The Refrain
The earth, O LORD, is full of your love;* instruct me in your statutes.

The Midday Psalm   *The Righteous Shall Flourish Like a Palm Tree*
LORD, how great are your works!* your thoughts are very deep.
The dullard does not know, nor does the fool understand,* that though the wicked
grow like weeds, and all the workers of iniquity flourish,
They flourish only to be destroyed for ever;* but you, O LORD, are exalted for
evermore.
For lo, your enemies, O LORD, lo, your enemies shall perish,* and all the workers
of iniquity shall be scattered.
But my horn you have exalted like the horns of wild bulls;* I am anointed with
fresh oil.
My eyes also gloat over my enemies,* and my ears rejoice to hear the doom of the
wicked who rise up against me.
The righteous shall flourish like a palm tree,* and shall spread abroad like a cedar
of Lebanon.
Those who are planted in the house of the LORD* shall flourish in the courts of our
God;
They shall still bear fruit in old age;* they shall be green and succulent;
That they may show how upright the LORD is,* my Rock, in whom there is no fault.

Psalm 92:5–14

The Refrain
The earth, O LORD, is full of your love;* instruct me in your statutes.

*The Gloria**

The Lord's Prayer

The Prayer Appointed for the Week

O God, the strength of all who put their trust in you: Mercifully accept my
prayers; and because in my weakness I can do nothing good without you, give
me the help of your grace, that in keeping your commandments I may please
you in both will and deed; through Jesus Christ my Lord, who lives and reigns
with you and the Holy Spirit, one God, for ever and ever. *Amen.* †

The Concluding Prayer of the Church

O God, you make me glad with the weekly remembrance of the glorious resurrection of your Son my Lord: Give me this day such blessing through my worship
of you, that the week to come may be spent in your favor; through Jesus Christ
our Lord. *Amen.* †

The Vespers Office   **To Be Observed on the Hour or Half Hour**
Between 5 and 8 p.m.

The Call to Prayer

Let the Name of the LORD be blessed,* from this time forth for evermore.
From the rising of the sun to its going down* let the Name of the LORD be praised.

Psalm 113:2–3

The Request for Presence

As the eyes of servants look to the hand of their masters,* and the eyes of a maid to
the hand of her mistress,
So our eyes look to you, O LORD our God.

adapted from Psalm 123:2–3

The Greeting

Blessed is the LORD!* for he has heard the voice of my prayer.

Psalm 28:7

The Hymn   *Something for Thee*

Savior, Your dying love you gave to me,
Nothing should I withhold, Dear Lord, from Thee:
　　　In love my soul would bow,
　　　My heart fulfill its vow,
　　　Some offering bring you now,
Something for Thee.

At the blessed mercy seat, pleading for me,
My feeble faith looks up, Jesus, to Thee:
　　　Help me the cross to bear,
　　　Your wondrous love declare,
　　　Some song to raise, or prayer,
Something for Thee.

Give me a faithful heart, likeness to Thee,
That each departing day henceforth may see
　　　Some work of love begun,

Some deed of kindness done,
Some wanderer sought and won,
 Something for Thee.

All that I am and have, Your gifts so free,
In joy, in grief, through life, Dear Lord, for Thee!
 And when your face I see,
 My ransomed soul shall be,
 Through all eternity,
Something for Thee.

Sylvanus Phelps

The Refrain for the Vespers Lessons

For you, O Lord, are good and forgiving,* and great is your love toward all who call upon you.

Psalm 86:5

The Vespers Psalm   More Than Watchmen for the Morning

I wait for the Lord; my soul waits for him;* in his word is my hope.
My soul waits for the Lord, more than watchmen for the morning,* more than watchmen for the morning.

Psalm 130:4–5

The Refrain

For you, O Lord, are good and forgiving,* and great is your love toward all who call upon you.

The Cry of the Church

Lord, have mercy on us. Christ, have mercy on us. Lord, have mercy on us.

The Lord's Prayer

The Prayer Appointed for the Week

O God, the strength of all who put their trust in you: Mercifully accept my prayers; and because in my weakness I can do nothing good without you, give me the help of your grace, that in keeping your commandments I may please you in both will and deed; through Jesus Christ my Lord, who lives and reigns with you and the Holy Spirit, one God, for ever and ever. *Amen.* †

The Concluding Prayer of the Church

In truth God has heard me;* he has attended to the voice of my prayer.
Blessed be God, who has not rejected my prayer,* nor withheld his love from me.

Psalm 66:17–18

The Morning Office   To Be Observed on the Hour or Half Hour Between 6 and 9 a.m.

The Call to Prayer

The Lord is King; let the earth rejoice;* let the multitude of the isles be glad.

Psalm 97:1

The Request for Presence
I long for your salvation, O Lord,* and your law is my delight.
Psalm 119:174

The Greeting
The Lord lives! Blessed is my Rock!* Exalted is the God of my salvation!
Psalm 18:46

The Refrain for the Morning Lessons
The fool has said in his heart, "There is no God."
Psalm 14:1

A Reading
He went back again to the far side of the Jordan to the district where John had been baptizing at first and he stayed there. Many people who came to him said, 'John gave no signs, but all he said about this man was true'; and many of them believed in him.
John 10:40–42

The Refrain
The fool has said in his heart, "There is no God."

The Morning Psalm   *This Is My Prayer to You*
But as for me, this is my prayer to you,* at the time you have set, O Lord:
"In your great mercy, O God,* answer me with your unfailing help.
Save me from the mire; do not let me sink;* let me be rescued from those who hate me and out of the deep waters.
Let not the torrent of waters wash over me, neither let the deep swallow me up;* do not let the Pit shut its mouth upon me.
Answer me, O Lord, for your love is kind;* in your great compassion, turn to me."
Psalm 69:14–18

The Refrain
The fool has said in his heart, "There is no God."

The Cry of the Church
Even so, come Lord Jesus!

The Lord's Prayer

The Prayer Appointed for the Week
O God, the strength of all who put their trust in you: Mercifully accept my prayers; and because in my weakness I can do nothing good without you, give me the help of your grace, that in keeping your commandments I may please you in both will and deed; through Jesus Christ my Lord, who lives and reigns with you and the Holy Spirit, one God, for ever and ever. *Amen.* †

The Concluding Prayer of the Church
Lord God, almighty and everlasting Father, you have brought me in safety to this new day: Preserve me with your mighty power, that I may not fall into sin, nor

be overcome by adversity; and in all I do direct me to the fulfilling of your purpose; through Jesus Christ my Lord. *Amen.* †

The Midday Office   **To Be Observed on the Hour or Half Hour**
Between 11 a.m. and 2 p.m.

The Call to Prayer
Let us make a vow to the LORD our God and keep it;* let all around him bring gifts
to him who is worthy to be feared.

adapted from Psalm 76:11

The Request for Presence
Let the peoples praise you, O God;* let all the peoples praise you.

Psalm 67:3

The Greeting
Happy are the people whose strength is in you!* whose hearts are set on the
pilgrims' way.

Psalm 84:4

The Refrain for the Midday Lessons
All the nations you have made will come and worship you, O LORD,* and glorify
your Name.

Psalm 86:9

A Reading
Who can overcome the world but the one who believes in the Son of God?

I John 5:5

The Refrain
All the nations you have made will come and worship you, O LORD,* and glorify
your Name.

The Midday Psalm   *Great Is Our LORD*
How good it is to sing praises to our God!* how pleasant it is to honor him with
praise!
The LORD rebuilds Jerusalem;* he gathers the exiles of Israel.
He heals the brokenhearted* and binds up their wounds.
He counts the number of the stars* and calls them all by their names.
Great is our LORD and mighty in power;* there is no limit to his wisdom.
The LORD lifts up the lowly,* but casts the wicked to the ground.
Sing to the LORD with thanksgiving;* make music to our God upon the harp.

Psalm 147:1-7

The Refrain
All the nations you have made will come and worship you, O LORD,* and glorify
your Name.

The Small Verse
Give thanks to the LORD, for he is good,* for his mercy endures for ever.
Give thanks to the God of gods,* for his mercy endures for ever.
Give thanks to the Lord of lords,* for his mercy endures for ever.

Psalm 136:1–3

The Lord's Prayer

The Prayer Appointed for the Week
O God, the strength of all who put their trust in you: Mercifully accept my
  prayers; and because in my weakness I can do nothing good without you, give
  me the help of your grace, that in keeping your commandments I may please
  you in both will and deed; through Jesus Christ my Lord, who lives and reigns
  with you and the Holy Spirit, one God, for ever and ever. *Amen.* †

The Concluding Prayer of the Church
Let us bless the Lord God living and true! Let us always render him praise, glory,
  honor, blessing, and all good things! Amen. Amen. So be it! So be it!

St. Francis of Assisi

The Vespers Office **To Be Observed on the Hour or Half Hour**
Between 5 and 8 p.m.

The Call to Prayer
Open my lips, O Lord,* and my mouth shall proclaim your praise.
Had you desired it, I would have offered sacrifice,* but you take no delight in
  burnt-offerings.
The sacrifice of God is a troubled spirit;* and a broken and contrite heart, O God,
  you will not despise.

Psalm 51:16–18

The Request for Presence
Give ear, O LORD, to my prayer,* and attend to the voice of my supplications.

Psalm 86:6

The Greeting
I give you thanks, O God, I give you thanks,* calling upon your Name and declaring
  all your wonderful deeds.

adapted from Psalm 75:1

The Hymn
  Praise the Lord through every nation;
  His holy arm has brought salvation;
      Exalt him on his Father's throne.
  Praise your King, you Christian legions,
  Who now prepares in heavenly regions
      Unfailing mansions for his own:

With voice and minstrelsy
Extol his majesty,
    Raise your anthem now!
His praise shall sound
All nature round,
and hymns on every tongue abound.

Jesus, Lord, our captain glorious,
Over sin and death, and hell victorious,
    Wisdom and might to you belong:
We confess, proclaim, adore you;
We bow the knee, we fall before you;
    Your love henceforth will be our song.
The cross meanwhile we bear,
The crown ere long to wear;
    Raise your anthem now!
Your reign extend
World without end;
Let praise from all to you ascend.

Rhijnvis Feith

The Refrain for the Vespers Lessons

For you are my hope, O Lord GOD,* my confidence since I was young.

Psalm 71:5

The Vespers Psalm

May All the Nations Bless Themselves in Him and Call Him Blessed

Long may he live! and may there be given to him gold from Arabia;* may prayer
  be made for him always, and may they bless him all the day long.
May there be abundance of grain on the earth, growing thick even on the hilltops;*
  may its fruit flourish like Lebanon, and its grain like grass upon the earth.
May his Name remain for ever and be established as long as the sun endures;*
  may all the nations bless themselves in him and call him blessed.

Psalm 72:15–17

The Refrain

For you are my hope, O Lord GOD,* my confidence since I was young.

The Small Verse

The Lord is my shepherd and nothing is wanting to me. In green pastures He has
  settled me.

The Lord's Prayer

The Prayer Appointed for the Week

O God, the strength of all who put their trust in you: Mercifully accept my
  prayers; and because in my weakness I can do nothing good without you, give
  me the help of your grace, that in keeping your commandments I may please

you in both will and deed; through Jesus Christ my Lord, who lives and reigns
with you and the Holy Spirit, one God, for ever and ever. *Amen.* †

The Concluding Prayer of the Church

Visit, I beseech you, O Lord, this dwelling and drive far from it all the snares of the
enemy; let Your holy angels dwell herein, who may keep us in peace, and let
Your blessing always be upon me. Through our Lord Jesus Christ, Your Son,
who lives and reigns with You in the unity of the Holy Spirit, God. World without end. *Amen.*

adapted from THE SHORT BREVIARY

The Morning Office

**To Be Observed on the Hour or Half Hour
Between 6 and 9 a.m.**

The Call to Prayer

Praise the Name of the LORD;* give praise, you servants of the LORD,
Praise the LORD, for the LORD is good;* sing praises to his Name, for it is lovely.
For I know that the LORD is great,* and that our Lord is above all gods.

Psalm 135:1ff

The Request for Presence

Satisfy us by your loving-kindness in the morning;* so shall we rejoice and be glad
all the days of our life.

Psalm 90:14

The Greeting

Out of Zion, perfect in its beauty,* God reveals himself in glory.
Let the heavens declare the rightness of his cause;* for God himself is judge.

Psalm 50:2, 6

The Refrain for the Morning Lessons

Wake up, my spirit; awake, lute and harp;* I myself will waken the dawn.

Psalm 108:2

A Reading

He said again to the crowds, "When you see a cloud looming up in the west you
say at once that rain is coming, and so it does. And when the wind is from the
south you say it's going to be hot, and it is. Hypocrites! You know how to inter-
pret the face of the earth and the sky. How is it you do not know how to inter-
pret these times?"

Luke 12:54–56

The Refrain

Wake up, my spirit; awake, lute and harp;* I myself will waken the dawn.

The Morning Psalm   *Praise Him, All His Host*

Praise the LORD from the earth,* you sea-monsters and all deeps;
Fire and hail, snow and fog,* tempestuous wind, doing his will;

Mountains and all hills,* fruit trees and all cedars;
Wild beasts and all cattle,* creeping things and winged birds;
Kings of the earth and all peoples,* princes and all rulers of the world;
Young men and maidens,* old and young together.
Let them praise the Name of the Lord,* for his Name only is exalted, his splendor
  is over earth and heaven.
He has raised up strength for his people and praise for all his loyal servants,* the
  children of Israel, a people who are near him. Hallelujah!

Psalm 148:6–14

The Refrain
Wake up, my spirit; awake, lute and harp;* I myself will waken the dawn.

The Gloria*

The Lord's Prayer

The Prayer Appointed for the Week
O God, the strength of all who put their trust in you: Mercifully accept my
  prayers; and because in my weakness I can do nothing good without you, give
  me the help of your grace, that in keeping your commandments I may please
  you in both will and deed; through Jesus Christ my Lord, who lives and reigns
  with you and the Holy Spirit, one God, for ever and ever. *Amen.* †

The Concluding Prayer of the Church
Lord God, almighty and everlasting Father, you have brought me in safety to this
  new day: Preserve me with your mighty power, that I may not fall into sin, nor
  be overcome by adversity; and in all I do direct me to the fulfilling of your purpose; through Jesus Christ my Lord. *Amen.* †

The Midday Office **To Be Observed on the Hour or Half Hour
Between 11 a.m. and 2 p.m.**

The Call to Prayer
Worship the Lord in the beauty of holiness;* let the whole earth tremble before
  him.
Tell it among the nations: "The Lord is King!* he has made the world so firm that
  it cannot be moved; he will judge the peoples with equity."

Psalm 96:9–10

The Request for Presence
Be my strong rock, a castle to keep me safe,* for you are my crag and my stronghold; for the sake of your Name, lead me and guide me.

Psalm 31:3

The Greeting
I love you, O Lord of my strength,* O Lord my stronghold, my crag, and my
  haven.

My God, my rock in whom I put my trust,* my shield, the horn of my salvation,
and my refuge; you are worthy of praise.

Psalm 18:1–2

The Refrain for the Midday Lessons
Into your hands I commend my spirit.

Psalm 31:5

A Reading
Here is a saying you can rely on: If we have died with him, then we shall live with
him. If we persevere, then we shall reign with him. If we disown him, then he
will disown us. If we are faithless, he is faithful still, for he can not disown his
own self.

2 Timothy 2:11–13

The Refrain
Into your hands I commend my spirit.

The Midday Psalm   *He Turns the Flint-stone into a Flowing Spring*
When Israel came out of Egypt,* the house of Jacob from a people of strange
speech,
Judah became God's sanctuary* and Israel his dominion.
The sea beheld it and fled;* Jordan turned and went back.
The mountains skipped like rams,* and the little hills like young sheep.
What ailed you, O sea, that you fled?* O Jordan, that you turned back?
You mountains, that you skipped like rams?* you little hills like young sheep?
Tremble, O earth, at the presence of the Lord,* at the presence of the God of Jacob,
Who turned the hard rock into a pool of water* and flint-stone into a flowing
spring.

Psalm 114

The Refrain
Into your hands I commend my spirit.

The Small Verse
I will bless the Lord at all times
And his praise shall be always in my mouth.
Glory to the Father and the Son
And the eternal Spirit.

Traditional

The Lord's Prayer

The Prayer Appointed for the Week
O God, the strength of all who put their trust in you: Mercifully accept my
prayers; and because in my weakness I can do nothing good without you, give
me the help of your grace, that in keeping your commandments I may please
you in both will and deed; through Jesus Christ my Lord, who lives and reigns
with you and the Holy Spirit, one God, for ever and ever. *Amen.* †

The Concluding Prayer of the Church

Heavenly Father, you have promised to hear what we ask in the Name of your
Son: Accept and fulfill my petitions, I pray, not as I ask in my ignorance, nor as
I deserve in my sinfulness, but as you know and love me in your Son Jesus
Christ our Lord. *Amen.* †

The Vespers Office **To Be Observed on the Hour or Half Hour**
Between 5 and 8 p.m.

The Call to Prayer

Sing to the LORD, you servants of his;* give thanks for the remembrance of his
holiness.
For his wrath endures but the twinkling of an eye,* his favor for a lifetime.

Psalm 30:4–5

The Request for Presence

Hear my prayer, O LORD, and give ear to my cry; . . . For I am but a sojourner with
you,* a wayfarer, as all my forebears were.

Psalm 39:13–14

The Greeting

O God, when you went forth before your people* when you marched through the
wilderness,
The earth shook, and the skies poured down rain, at the presence of God, the God
of Sinai* at the presence of God, the God of Israel.
You sent a gracious rain, O God, upon your inheritance;* you refreshed the land
when it was weary.
The Lord gave the word;* great was the company of women who bore the tidings.

Psalm 68:7ff

The Hymn

O for a thousand tongues to sing my dear Redeemer's praise,
The glories of my God and King, the triumphs of his grace!

My gracious Master and my God, assist me to proclaim
And spread through all the earth abroad the honors of your Name.

Jesus! The Name that charms our fears and bids our sorrows cease;
'Tis music in the sinners' ears, 'tis life and health and peace.

He speaks; and, listening to his voice, new life the dead receive,
The mournful broken hearts rejoice, the humble poor believe.

Hear him, you deaf, you voiceless ones, your loosened tongues employ;
You blind, behold, your Savior comes; and leap, you lame, for joy!

Glory to God and praise and love be now and ever given
By saints below and saints above, the Church in earth and heaven.

Charles Wesley

The Refrain for the Vespers Lessons
Weeping may spend the night,* but joy comes in the morning.
Psalm 30:6

The Vespers Psalm   ***Blessed Be the Lord***
Blessed be the Lord!* he has not given us over to be a prey for their teeth.
We have escaped like a bird from the snare of the fowler;* the snare is broken, and
   we have escaped.
Our help is in the Name of the Lord,* the maker of heaven and earth.
Psalm 124:6–8

The Refrain
Weeping may spend the night,* but joy comes in the morning.

*The Gloria**

The Lord's Prayer

The Prayer Appointed for the Week
O God, the strength of all who put their trust in you: Mercifully accept my
   prayers; and because in my weakness I can do nothing good without you, give
   me the help of your grace, that in keeping your commandments I may please
   you in both will and deed; through Jesus Christ my Lord, who lives and reigns
   with you and the Holy Spirit, one God, for ever and ever. *Amen.* †

The Concluding Prayer of the Church
Hear, O Lord, your servants, offering evening praises to your Name. Through the
   silent hours of the night deign to watch over us, whom You have protected in
   all dangers of the day. Through Jesus Christ our Lord. *Amen.*
Anglo-Saxon, Traditional

The Morning Office   **To Be Observed on the Hour or Half Hour**
Between 6 and 9 a.m.

The Call to Prayer
I will call upon God,* and the Lord will deliver me.
In the evening, in the morning, and at the noonday, I will complain and lament,*
   and he will hear my voice.
He will bring me safely back . . . God, who is enthroned of old, will hear me.
Psalm 55:17ff

The Request for Presence
Show us the light of your countenance, O God,* and come to us.
based on Psalm 67:1

The Greeting
In you, O LORD, have I taken refuge; let me never be put to shame;* deliver me in your righteousness.

Psalm 31:1

The Refrain for the Morning Lessons
The same stone that the builders rejected* has become the chief cornerstone.

Psalm 118:22

A Reading
The apostles said to the Lord, 'Increase our faith.' The Lord replied, 'If you had faith like a mustard seed you could say to this mulberry tree, "Be uprooted and planted in the sea," and it would obey you.'

Luke 17:5–6

The Refrain
The same stone that the builders rejected* has become the chief cornerstone.

The Morning Psalm   *A Canticle of the Messiah*
The LORD said to my Lord, "Sit at my right hand,* until I make your enemies your footstool."
The LORD will send the scepter of your power out of Zion,* saying, "Rule over your enemies round about you.
Princely state has been yours from the day of your birth;* in the beauty of holiness have I begotten you, like dew from the womb of the morning."
The LORD has sworn and he will not recant:* "You are a priest for ever after the order of Melchizedek."

Psalm 110:1–4

The Refrain
The same stone that the builders rejected* has become the chief cornerstone.

The Cry of the Church
O God, come to my assistance! O Lord, make haste to help me!

The Lord's Prayer

The Prayer Appointed for the Week
O God, the strength of all who put their trust in you: Mercifully accept my prayers; and because in my weakness I can do nothing good without you, give me the help of your grace, that in keeping your commandments I may please you in both will and deed; through Jesus Christ my Lord, who lives and reigns with you and the Holy Spirit, one God, for ever and ever. *Amen.* †

The Concluding Prayer of the Church
Lord God, almighty and everlasting Father, you have brought me in safety to this new day: Preserve me with your mighty power, that I may not fall into sin, nor be overcome by adversity; and in all I do direct me to the fulfilling of your purpose; through Jesus Christ my Lord. *Amen.* †

The Midday Office   **To Be Observed on the Hour or Half Hour**
                                         Between 11 a.m. and 2 p.m.

The Call to Prayer
Sing to the Lord a new song;* sing his praise in the congregation of the faithful.
Psalm 149:1

The Request for Presence
You are good and you bring forth good;* instruct me in your statutes.
Psalm 119:68

The Greeting
Be exalted, O Lord, in your might;* we will sing and praise your power.
Psalm 21:14

The Refrain for the Midday Lessons
It is better to rely on the Lord* than to put any trust in flesh.
It is better to rely on the Lord* than to put any trust in rulers.
Psalm 118:8–9

A Reading
For *all humanity is grass, and all its beauty like the wildflower's. As grass withers, the
flower fades, but the Word of the Lord remains for ever.* And this Word is the Good
News that has been brought to you.
I Peter 1:24–25

The Refrain
It is better to rely on the Lord* than to put any trust in flesh.
It is better to rely on the Lord* than to put any trust in rulers.

The Midday Psalm   *The Judgments of the Lord Are Sweeter Far Than Honey*
The law of the Lord is perfect and revives the soul;* the testimony of the Lord is
    sure and gives wisdom to the innocent.
The statutes of the Lord are just and rejoice the heart;* the commandment of the
    Lord is clear and gives light to the eyes.
The fear of the Lord is clean and endures for ever;* the judgments of the Lord are
    true and righteous altogether.
More to be desired are they than gold, more than much fine gold,* sweeter far than
    honey, than honey in the comb.
By them also is your servant enlightened,* and in keeping them there is great
    reward.
Psalm 19:7–11

The Refrain
It is better to rely on the Lord* than to put any trust in flesh.
It is better to rely on the Lord* than to put any trust in rulers.

*The Gloria**

The Lord's Prayer

The Prayer Appointed for the Week

O God, the strength of all who put their trust in you: Mercifully accept my prayers; and because in my weakness I can do nothing good without you, give me the help of your grace, that in keeping your commandments I may please you in both will and deed; through Jesus Christ my Lord, who lives and reigns with you and the Holy Spirit, one God, for ever and ever. *Amen.* †

The Concluding Prayer of the Church

God of justice, God of mercy, bless all those who are surprised with pain this day from suffering caused by their own weakness or that of others. Let what we suffer teach us to be merciful; let our sins teach us to forgive. This I ask through the intercession of Jesus and all who died forgiving those who oppressed them. *Amen.* †

The Vespers Office   **To Be Observed on the Hour or Half Hour Between 5 and 8 p.m.**

The Call to Prayer

Let us give thanks to the LORD for his mercy* and the wonders he does for his children.

Psalm 107:8

The Request for Presence

You are good and you bring forth good;* instruct me in your statutes.

Psalm 119:68

The Greeting

You are the LORD, most high over all the earth;* you are exalted far above all gods.

Psalm 97:9

The Hymn

Creator Spirit, by whose aid
The world's foundations first were laid,
Come, visit every humble mind;
Come, pour your joys on human-kind;
From sin and sorrow set us free,
And make your temples fit for thee.

O Source of uncreated light,
The Father's promised Paraclete,
Thrice holy Fount, Thrice holy Fire,
Our hearts and heavenly love inspire;
Come and your sacred unction bring
To sanctify us while we sing.

Plenteous of grace, come from on high,
Rich in your seven-fold energy;
Make us eternal truth receive,

And practice all that we believe;
Give us yourself, that we may see
The Father and the Son by thee.

John Dryden

The Refrain for the Vespers Lessons
The LORD, the God of gods, has spoken;* he has called the earth from the rising of
the sun to its setting.

Psalm 50:1

The Vespers Psalm   *O Mighty LORD, Your Faithfulness Is All Around You*
Who is like you, LORD God of hosts?* O mighty LORD, your faithfulness is all
around you.
You rule the raging of the sea* and still the surging of its waves.
You have crushed Rahab of the deep with a deadly wound;* you have scattered
your enemies with your mighty arm.
Yours are the heavens; the earth also is yours;* you laid the foundations of the
world and all that is in it.
You have made the north and the south;* Tabor and Hermon rejoice in your Name.
You have a mighty arm;* strong is your hand and high is your right hand.
Righteousness and justice are the foundations of your throne;* love and truth go
before your face.

Psalm 89:8–14

The Refrain
The LORD, the God of gods, has spoken;* he has called the earth from the rising of
the sun to its setting.

The Gloria

The Lord's Prayer

The Prayer Appointed for the Week
O God, the strength of all who put their trust in you: Mercifully accept my
prayers; and because in my weakness I can do nothing good without you, give
me the help of your grace, that in keeping your commandments I may please
you in both will and deed; through Jesus Christ my Lord, who lives and reigns
with you and the Holy Spirit, one God, for ever and ever. *Amen.* †

The Concluding Prayer of the Church
God our Father in Heaven have mercy on us.
God the Son, Redeemer of the world have mercy on us.
God the Holy Spirit have mercy on us.
Holy Trinity, one God have mercy on us.

Traditional

The Morning Office **To Be Observed on the Hour or Half Hour**

Between 6 and 9 a.m.

The Call to Prayer
Come, let us sing to the LORD; . . . For the LORD is a great God,* and a great King
above all gods.

Psalm 95:1, 3

The Request for Presence
Gladden the soul of your servant,* for to you, O LORD, I lift up my soul.

Psalm 86:4

The Greeting
Exalt yourself above the heavens, O God,* and your glory over all the earth.

Psalm 57:6

The Refrain for the Morning Lessons
Let not those who hope in you be put to shame through me, Lord GOD of hosts;*
let not those who seek you be disgraced because of me.

Psalm 69:7

A Reading
Jesus taught the people, saying: "You have heard how it was said: *Eye for eye and
tooth for tooth.* But I say this to you: offer no resistance to the wicked. On the
contrary, if anyone hits you on the right cheek, offer him the other as well; if
someone wishes to go to law with you to get your tunic, let him have your
cloak as well."

Matthew 5:38–41

The Refrain
Let not those who hope in you be put to shame through me, Lord GOD of hosts;*
let not those who seek you be disgraced because of me.

The Morning Psalm *Your Throne, O God, Endures For Ever and Ever*

My heart is stirring with a noble song; let me recite what I have fashioned for the
king;* my tongue shall be the pen of a skilled writer.
You are the fairest of men;* grace flows from your lips, because God has blessed
you for ever.
Strap your sword upon your thigh, O mighty warrior,* in your pride and in your
majesty.
Ride out and conquer in the cause of truth* and for the sake of justice.
Your right hand will show you marvelous things;* your arrows are very sharp, O
mighty warrior.
The peoples are falling at your feet,* and the king's enemies are losing heart.
Your throne, O God, endures for ever and ever,* a scepter of righteousness is the
scepter of your kingdom; you love righteousness and hate iniquity.
Therefore God, your God, has anointed you* with the oil of gladness above your
fellows.

Psalm 45:1–8

The Refrain
Let not those who hope in you be put to shame through me, Lord GOD of hosts;*
   let not those who seek you be disgraced because of me.

The Gloria*

The Lord's Prayer

The Prayer Appointed for the Week
O God, the strength of all who put their trust in you: Mercifully accept my
   prayers; and because in my weakness I can do nothing good without you, give
   me the help of your grace, that in keeping your commandments I may please
   you in both will and deed; through Jesus Christ my Lord, who lives and reigns
   with you and the Holy Spirit, one God, for ever and ever. *Amen.* †

The Concluding Prayer of the Church
Lord God, almighty and everlasting Father, you have brought me in safety to this
   new day: Preserve me with your mighty power, that I may not fall into sin, nor
   be overcome by adversity; and in all I do direct me to the fulfilling of your purpose; through Jesus Christ my Lord. *Amen.* †

The Midday Office   **To Be Observed on the Hour or Half Hour**
                              Between 11 a.m. and 2 p.m.

The Call to Prayer
Be strong and let your heart take courage,* all you who wait for the LORD.
                              Psalm 31:24

The Request for Presence
Hear my cry, O God,* and listen to my prayer.
I call upon you from the ends of the earth.
                              Psalm 61:1–2

The Greeting
I love you, O LORD my strength,* O LORD my stronghold, my crag, and my haven.
                              Psalm 18:1

The Refrain for the Midday Lessons
Though my father and my mother forsake me,* the LORD will sustain me.
                              Psalm 27:14

A Reading
Again, do not listen to all that people say, then you will not hear your servant
   abusing you. For often, as you very well know, you have abused others.
                              Ecclesiastes 7:21–22

The Refrain
Though my father and my mother forsake me,* the LORD will sustain me.

The Midday Psalm   *The Righteous Will Be Kept in Everlasting Remembrance*
Light shines in the darkness for the upright;* the righteous are merciful and full of
   compassion.
It is good for them to be generous in lending* and to manage their affairs with
   justice.

For they will never be shaken;* the righteous will be kept in everlasting remembrance.

They will not be afraid of any evil rumors;* their heart is right; they put their trust in the Lord.

Their heart is established and will not shrink,* until they see their desire upon their enemies.

They have given freely to the poor,* and their righteousness stands fast for ever; they will hold up their head with honor.

The wicked will see it and be angry; they will gnash their teeth and pine away;* the desires of the wicked will perish.

Psalm 112:4–10

The Refrain

Though my father and my mother forsake me,* the LORD will sustain me.

The Cry of the Church

In the evening, in the morning, and at noonday, I will complain and lament,* and he will hear my voice.

Psalm 55:18

The Lord's Prayer

The Prayer Appointed for the Week

O God, the strength of all who put their trust in you: Mercifully accept my prayers; and because in my weakness I can do nothing good without you, give me the help of your grace, that in keeping your commandments I may please you in both will and deed; through Jesus Christ my Lord, who lives and reigns with you and the Holy Spirit, one God, for ever and ever. *Amen.* †

The Concluding Prayer of the Church

God of mercy,
this midday moment of rest
is your welcome gift.
Bless the work we have begun,
and make good its defects
and let us finish it in a way that pleases you.
Grant this through Christ our Lord.

THE LITURGY OF THE HOURS, VOL. III

The Vespers Office   **To Be Observed on the Hour or Half Hour Between 5 and 8 p.m.**

The Call to Prayer

Come, let us sing to the LORD;* let us shout for joy to the Rock of our salvation.

Let us come before his presence with thanksgiving* and raise a loud shout to him with psalms.

For the Lord is a great God,* and a great King above all gods.
In his hands are the caverns of the earth,* and the heights of the hills are his also.
The sea is his, for he made it,* and his hands have molded the dry land.

Psalm 95:1–5

The Request for Presence
To you I lift up my eyes,* to you enthroned in the heavens.

Psalm 123:1

The Greeting
I put my trust in your mercy;* my heart is joyful because of your saving help.

Psalm 13:5

The Hymn

O Holy Spirit, by whose breath;
Life rises vibrant out of death;
Come to create, renew, inspire;
Kindle in our hearts your fire.

You are the seeker's sure resource,
Of burning love the living source,
Protector in the midst of strife,
The giver and the Lord of life.

Flood our dull senses with your light;
In mutual love our hearts unite.
Your power the whole creation fills;
Confirm our weak, uncertain wills.

From inner strife grant us release;
Turn nations to the ways of peace.
To fuller life your people bring
That as one body we may sing:

Praise to the Father, Christ his Word,
And to the Spirit: God the Lord,
To whom all honor, glory be
Both now and for eternity.

Rabanus Maurus

The Refrain for the Vespers Lessons
For we are your people and the sheep of your pasture;* we will give you thanks
for ever and show forth your praise from age to age.

Psalm 79:13

The Vespers Psalm   *Those Who Sowed with Tears Will Reap with Songs of Joy*
When the Lord restored the fortunes of Zion,* then were we like those who
dream.
Then was our mouth filled with laughter,* and our tongue with shouts of joy.
Then they said among the nations,* "The Lord has done great things for them."
The Lord has done great things for us,* and we are glad indeed.
Restore our fortunes, O Lord,* like the watercourses of the Negev.
Those who sowed with tears* will reap with songs of joy.
Those who go out weeping, carrying the seed,* will come again with joy,
shouldering their sheaves.

Psalm 126:1–7

The Refrain
For we are your people and the sheep of your pasture;* we will give you thanks
for ever and show forth your praise from age to age.

The Cry of the Church
O God, come to my assistance! O Lord, make haste to help me!

The Lord's Prayer

The Prayer Appointed for the Week
O God, the strength of all who put their trust in you: Mercifully accept my
 prayers; and because in my weakness I can do nothing good without you, give
 me the help of your grace, that in keeping your commandments I may please
 you in both will and deed; through Jesus Christ my Lord, who lives and reigns
 with you and the Holy Spirit, one God, for ever and ever. *Amen.* †

The Concluding Prayer of the Church
May God, the Lord, bless us with heavenly benediction, and make us pure and
 holy in his sight.
May the riches of his glory abound in us.
May He instruct us with the word of truth, inform us with the Gospel of salvation,
 and enrich us with his love, Through Jesus Christ, our Lord.

Gelasian Sacramentary

The Morning Office   **To Be Observed on the Hour or Half Hour**
                                Between 6 and 9 a.m.

The Call to Prayer
I will call upon God,* and the LORD will deliver me.
God, who is enthroned of old, will hear me.

Psalm 55:17, 20

The Request for Presence
Our God will come and will not keep silence;* before him there is a consuming
 flame, and round about him a raging storm.

Psalm 50:3

The Greeting
For your Name's sake, O LORD,* forgive my sin, for it is great.

Psalm 25:10

The Refrain for the Morning Lessons
Help me, O LORD my God;* save me for your mercy's sake.

Psalm 109:25

A Reading
Jesus said: "If your right eye should be your downfall, tear it out and throw it
 away; for it will do you less harm to lose one part of yourself than to have your
 whole body thrown into hell. And if your right hand should be your downfall,
 cut it off and throw it away; for it will do you less harm to lose one part of
 yourself than to have your whole body thrown into hell."

Matthew 5:29–30

The Refrain
Help me, O Lord my God;* save me for your mercy's sake.

The Morning Psalm　　　　　　　　*Let Them Offer a Sacrifice of Thanksgiving*
He sent forth his word and healed them* and saved them from the grave.
Let them give thanks to the Lord for his mercy* and the wonders he does for his
　　children.
Let them offer a sacrifice of thanksgiving* and tell of his acts with shouts of joy.
Psalm 107:20–22

The Refrain
Help me, O Lord my God;* save me for your mercy's sake.

The Cry of the Church
O God, come to my assistance! O Lord, make haste to help me!

The Lord's Prayer

The Prayer Appointed for the Week
O God, the strength of all who put their trust in you: Mercifully accept my
　　prayers; and because in my weakness I can do nothing good without you, give
　　me the help of your grace, that in keeping your commandments I may please
　　you in both will and deed; through Jesus Christ my Lord, who lives and reigns
　　with you and the Holy Spirit, one God, for ever and ever. *Amen.* †

The Concluding Prayer of the Church
Lord God, almighty and everlasting Father, you have brought me in safety to this
　　new day: Preserve me with your mighty power, that I may not fall into sin, nor
　　be overcome by adversity; and in all I do direct me to the fulfilling of your pur-
　　pose; through Jesus Christ my Lord. *Amen.* †

The Midday Office　　　　　　**To Be Observed on the Hour or Half Hour**
　　　　　　　　　　　　　　　　　　　Between 11 a.m. and 2 p.m.

The Call to Prayer
Worship the Lord in the beauty of holiness;* let the whole earth tremble before him.
Psalm 96:9

The Request for Presence
Remember not our past sins; let your compassion be swift to meet us.
Psalm 79:8

The Greeting
There is forgiveness with you;* therefore you shall be feared.
Psalm 130:3

The Refrain for the Midday Lessons
The LORD has pleasure in those who fear him,* in those who await his gracious favor.

Psalm 147:12

A Reading
Children, our love must not be just words or mere talk, but something active and genuine. This will be the proof that we belong to the truth, and it will convince us in his presence, even if our own feelings condemn us, that God is greater than our feelings and knows all things.

I John 3:18–20

The Refrain
The LORD has pleasure in those who fear him,* in those who await his gracious favor.

The Midday Psalm   *Into Your Hands I Commend My Spirit*
In you, O LORD, have I taken refuge; let me never be put to shame;* deliver me in your righteousness.
Incline your ear to me;* make haste to deliver me.
Be my strong rock, a castle to keep me safe, for you are my crag and my stronghold;* for the sake of your Name, lead me and guide me.
Into your hands I commend my spirit,* for you have redeemed me, O LORD, O God of truth.

Psalm 31:1–3, 5

The Refrain
The LORD has pleasure in those who fear him,* in those who await his gracious favor.

The Small Verse
Create in me a clean heart, O God,* and renew a right spirit within me.
Cast me not away from your presence* and take not your holy Spirit from me.
Give me the joy of your saving help again* and sustain me with your bountiful spirit.

Psalm 51:11–13

The Lord's Prayer

The Prayer Appointed for the Week
O God, the strength of all who put their trust in you: Mercifully accept my prayers; and because in my weakness I can do nothing good without you, give me the help of your grace, that in keeping your commandments I may please you in both will and deed; through Jesus Christ my Lord, who lives and reigns with you and the Holy Spirit, one God, for ever and ever. *Amen.* †

The Concluding Prayer of the Church
Lord Jesus Christ, by your death you took away the sting of death: Grant me to so follow in faith where you have led the way, that I may at length fall asleep peacefully in you and wake in your likeness; for your tender mercies' sake. *Amen.* †

The Vespers Office   **To Be Observed on the Hour or Half Hour Between 5 and 8 p.m.**

The Call to Prayer
May these words of mine please him;* I will rejoice in the LORD.

Psalm 104:35

The Request for Presence
Remember not our past sins;* let your compassion be swift to meet us; . . .
Help us, O God our Savior, for the glory of your Name;* deliver us and forgive us
    our sins, for your Name's sake.

Psalm 79:8–9

The Greeting
You are to be praised, O God, in Zion . . .
To you that hear prayer shall all flesh come,* because of their transgressions.

Psalm 65:1–2

The Hymn   *God of Our Fathers*

God of our fathers, whose almighty hand
Leads forth in beauty all the starry band
Of shining worlds in splendor through the skies,
Our grateful songs before Your throne arise.

From war's alarms, from deadly pestilence,
Be Your strong arm our eternal defense;
Your true religion in our hearts increase,
Your bounteous goodness nourish us in peace.

Refresh Your people on their toilsome way,
Lead us from night to never ending day;
Fill all our lives with love and grace divine,
And glory, laud, and praise ever be Thine.

Daniel C. Roberts

The Refrain for the Vespers Lessons
Remember not the sins of my youth and my transgressions;* remember me
    according to your love and for the sake of your goodness, O LORD.

Psalm 25:6

The Vespers Psalm   *Cleanse Me from My Secret Faults*
Who can tell how often he offends?* cleanse me from my secret faults.
Above all, keep your servant from presumptuous sins; let them not get dominion
    over me;* then shall I be whole and sound, and innocent of a great offense.

Psalm 19:12–13

The Refrain
Remember not the sins of my youth and my transgressions;* remember me
    according to your love and for the sake of your goodness, O LORD.

The Cry of the Church
Lord, have mercy on us. Christ, have mercy on us. Lord, have mercy on us.

The Lord's Prayer

The Prayer Appointed for the Week

O God, the strength of all who put their trust in you: Mercifully accept my
prayers; and because in my weakness I can do nothing good without you, give
me the help of your grace, that in keeping your commandments I may please
you in both will and deed; through Jesus Christ my Lord, who lives and reigns
with you and the Holy Spirit, one God, for ever and ever. *Amen.* †

Concluding Prayers of the Church

Almighty God, who has promised to hear the petitions of those who ask in your
Son's Name: I beseech you mercifully to incline your ear to me who have made
my prayers and supplications to you; and grant that those things which I have
faithfully asked according to your will may effectually be obtained, to the relief
of my necessity, and to the setting forth of your glory; through Jesus Christ my
Lord. *Amen.* †

May the souls of the faithful departed, through the mercy of God, rest in eternal
peace. Amen.

The Morning Office   **To Be Observed on the Hour or Half Hour**
                            Between 6 and 9 a.m.

The Call to Prayer

Let us give thanks to the LORD for his mercy* and the wonders he does for his
children.
For he satisfies the thirsty* and fills the hungry with good things.

based on Psalm 107:8–9

The Request for Presence

Give ear to my words, O LORD;* consider my meditation.

Psalm 5:1

The Greeting

Out of the mouths of infants and children, O LORD,* your majesty is praised above
the heavens.

based on Psalm 8:2

The Refrain for the Morning Lessons

I am small and of little account* yet I do not forget your commandments.

Psalm 119:141

A Reading

As they traveled along they met a man on the road who said, 'I will follow you
wherever you go.' Jesus answered, 'Foxes have holes and the birds of the air
have nests, but the Son of man has nowhere to lay his head.' Another to whom
he said, 'Follow me,' replied, 'Let me go and bury my father first.' But he
answered, 'Leave the dead to bury their dead; your duty is to go and spread
the news of the kingdom of God.'

Luke 9:57–60

The Refrain
I am small and of little account* yet I do not forget your commandments.

The Morning Psalm   *Renew a Right Spirit Within Me*
Create in me a clean heart, O God,* and renew a right spirit within me.
Cast me not away from your presence* and take not your holy Spirit from me.
Give me the joy of your saving help again* and sustain me with your bountiful Spirit.
I shall teach your ways to the wicked,* and sinners shall return to you.

Psalm 51:11–14

The Refrain
I am small and of little account* yet I do not forget your commandments.

The Cry of the Church
O Lamb of God, that takes away the sins of the world, have mercy upon me.
O Lamb of God, that takes away the sins of the world, have mercy upon me.
O Lamb of God, that takes away the sins of the world, grant me your peace.

The Lord's Prayer

The Prayer Appointed for the Week
O God, the strength of all who put their trust in you: Mercifully accept my
prayers; and because in my weakness I can do nothing good without you, give
me the help of your grace, that in keeping your commandments I may please
you in both will and deed; through Jesus Christ my Lord, who lives and reigns
with you and the Holy Spirit, one God, for ever and ever. *Amen.* †

The Concluding Prayer of the Church
Lord God, almighty and everlasting Father, you have brought me in safety to this
new day: Preserve me with your mighty power, that I may not fall into sin, nor
be overcome by adversity; and in all I do direct me to the fulfilling of your purpose; through Jesus Christ my Lord. *Amen.* †

The Midday Office   **To Be Observed on the Hour or Half Hour**
Between 11 a.m. and 2 p.m.

The Call to Prayer
Let the righteous be glad and rejoice before God;

Psalm 68:3

The Request for Presence
You are the LORD; do not withhold your compassion from me;* let your love and
your faithfulness keep me safe forever,

Psalm 40:12

The Greeting
Therefore I will praise you upon the lyre for your faithfulness, O my God;* I will
sing to you with the harp, O Holy One of Israel.

Psalm 71:22

The Refrain for the Midday Lessons
For the LORD God is both sun and shield;* he will give grace and glory.

Psalm 84:10

A Reading
That day, the root of Jesse, standing as a signal for all the peoples, will be sought
out by the nations and its home will be glorious. When that day comes, the
Lord will raise his hand a second time to ransom the remnant of his people . . .

Isaiah 11:10–11

The Refrain
For the LORD God is both sun and shield;* he will give grace and glory.

The Midday Psalm   *Your Love, O LORD, For Ever Will I Sing*
Your love, O LORD, for ever will I sing;* from age to age my mouth will proclaim
your faithfulness.
For I am persuaded that your love is established for ever;* you have set your
faithfulness firmly in the heavens.

Psalm 89:1–2

The Refrain
For the LORD God is both sun and shield;* he will give grace and glory.

The Gloria*

The Lord's Prayer

The Prayer Appointed for the Week
O God, the strength of all who put their trust in you: Mercifully accept my
prayers; and because in my weakness I can do nothing good without you, give
me the help of your grace, that in keeping your commandments I may please
you in both will and deed; through Jesus Christ my Lord, who lives and reigns
with you and the Holy Spirit, one God, for ever and ever. *Amen.* †

The Concluding Prayer of the Church
Almighty God, who after the creation of the world rested from all works and sanctified a day of rest for all your creatures: Grant that I, putting away all earthly
anxieties, may be duly prepared for the service of public worship, and grant as
well that my Sabbath upon earth may be a preparation for the eternal rest
promised to your people in heaven; through Jesus Christ our Lord. *Amen.* †

The Vespers Office   **To Be Observed on the Hour or Half Hour**
Between 5 and 8 p.m.

The Call to Prayer
Great is the LORD and greatly to be praised;* there is no end to his greatness.

Psalm 145:3

The Request for Presence
"Hide not your face from your servant;* be swift and answer me, . . .
Draw near to me and redeem me; . . ."

Psalm 69:19–20

The Greeting
Blessed is the LORD!* for he has heard the voice of my prayer.

Psalm 28:7

The Hymn   Rejoice

Rejoice, the Lord is King!	His kingdom can not fail;
Your Lord and King adore!	He rules over earth and heaven;
Mortals, give thanks and sing,	The keys of death and hell
And triumph ever more.	To Christ the Lord are given.
Lift up your heart!	Lift up your heart!
Lift up your voice!	Lift up your voice!
Rejoice! Again I say, Rejoice!	Rejoice! Again I say, Rejoice!
The Lord the Savior reigns,	Rejoice in glorious hope!
The God of truth and love:	Our Lord the Judge shall come,
When he had purged our stains,	And take his servants up
He took his seat above.	To their eternal home.
Lift up your heart!	Lift up your heart!
Lift up your voice!	Lift up your voice!
Rejoice! Again I say, Rejoice!	Rejoice! Again I say, Rejoice!

Charles Wesley

The Refrain for the Vespers Lessons
Therefore I will praise you upon the lyre for your faithfulness, O my God;* I will
    sing to you with the harp, O Holy One of Israel.

Psalm 71:22

The Vespers Psalm   *That Which We Have Heard and Known*
That which we have heard and known, and what our forefathers have told us,* we
    will not hide from their children.
We will recount to generations to come the praiseworthy deeds and the power of
    the LORD,* and the wonderful works he has done.
He gave his decrees to Jacob and established a law for Israel,* which he com-
    manded them to teach their children;
That the generations to come might know, and the children yet unborn;* that they
    in their turn might tell it to their children;
So that they might put their trust in God,* and not forget the deeds of God, but
    keep his commandments;
And not be like their forefathers, a stubborn and rebellious generation,* a generation
    whose heart was not steadfast, and whose spirit was not faithful to God.

Psalm 78:3–8

The Refrain
Therefore I will praise you upon the lyre for your faithfulness, O my God;* I will sing to you with the harp, O Holy One of Israel.

*The Gloria**

The Lord's Prayer

The Prayer Appointed for the Week
O God, the strength of all who put their trust in you: Mercifully accept my prayers; and because in my weakness I can do nothing good without you, give me the help of your grace, that in keeping your commandments I may please you in both will and deed; through Jesus Christ my Lord, who lives and reigns with you and the Holy Spirit, one God, for ever and ever. *Amen.* †

The Concluding Prayer of the Church
O God, the source of eternal light: Shed forth your unending day upon all of us who watch for you, that our lips may praise you, our lives may bless you, and our worship may give you glory; through Jesus Christ our Lord. *Amen.* †

The Morning Office   **To Be Observed on the Hour or Half Hour**
                                                      Between 6 and 9 a.m.

The Call to Prayer
Enter his gates with thanksgiving; go into his courts with praise;* give thanks to him and call upon his Name.

Psalm 100:3

The Request for Presence
Satisfy us by your loving-kindness in the morning* so shall we rejoice and be glad all the days of our life.

Psalm 90:14

The Greeting
I will give thanks to you, O Lord, with my whole heart;* I will tell of all your marvelous works.
I will be glad and rejoice in you;* I will sing your Name, O Most High.

Psalm 9:1–2

The Refrain for the Morning Lessons
In God the Lord, whose word I praise, in God I trust and will not be afraid,* for what can mortals do to me?

Psalm 56:10

A Reading

Jesus said: "Can you not buy five sparrows for two pennies? And yet not one is forgotten in God's sight. Why, every hair on your head has been counted. There is no need to be afraid: you are worth more than many sparrows."

Luke 12:6–7

The Refrain

In God the LORD, whose word I praise, in God I trust and will not be afraid,* for what can mortals do to me?

The Morning Psalm   *The LORD Takes Pleasure in His People*

Sing to the LORD a new song;* sing his praise in the congregation of the faithful.

Let Israel rejoice in his Maker;* let the children of Zion be joyful in their King.

Let them praise his Name in the dance;* let them sing praise to him with timbrel and harp.

For the LORD takes pleasure in his people* and adorns the poor with victory.

Let the faithful rejoice in triumph;* let them be joyful on their beds.

Psalm 149:1–5

The Refrain

In God the LORD, whose word I praise, in God I trust and will not be afraid,* for what can mortals do to me?

*The Gloria**

The Lord's Prayer

The Prayer Appointed for the Week

O Lord, you have taught us that without love whatever we do is worth nothing: Send your Holy Spirit and pour into my heart your greatest gift, which is love, the true bond of peace and of all virtue, without which whoever lives is accounted dead before you. Grant this for the sake of your only Son Jesus Christ, who lives and reigns with you and the Holy Spirit, one God, now and for ever. *Amen.* †

The Concluding Prayer of the Church

Lord God, almighty and everlasting Father, you have brought me in safety to this new day: Preserve me with your mighty power, that I may not fall into sin, nor be overcome by adversity; and in all I do direct me to the fulfilling of your purpose; through Jesus Christ my Lord. *Amen.* †

The Midday Office   **To Be Observed on the Hour or Half Hour**
                                        Between 11 a.m. and 2 p.m.

The Call to Prayer

Sing to the LORD and bless his Name;* proclaim the good news of his salvation from day to day.

Declare his glory among the nations* and his wonders among all peoples.

Psalm 96:2–3

The Request for Presence
Let my cry come before you, O LORD;* give me understanding, according to your
word.

Psalm 119:169

The Greeting
Lord, you have been our refuge* from one generation to another.
Before the mountains were brought forth, or the land and the earth were born,*
from age to age you are God.

Psalm 90:1–2

The Refrain for the Midday Lessons
And now, you kings, be wise;* be warned, you rulers of the earth.
Submit to the LORD with fear,* and with trembling bow before him.

Psalm 2:10–11

A Reading
I, Nebuchadnezzar, raised my eyes to heaven . . . And I blessed the Most High,
praising and glorifying him who lives for ever, for his empire is an everlasting
empire, his kingship endures, age after age. All who dwell on earth count for
nothing; as he thinks fit, he disposes the army of heaven and those who dwell
on earth. No one can arrest his hand or ask him, "What have you done?" At
that moment my reason returned and, for the honor of my royal state, my glory
and splendor returned too. My counselors and noblemen acclaimed me; I was
restored to my throne, and to my past greatness even more was added. And
now I, Nebuchadnezzar, praise, extol and glorify the King of Heaven, all of
whose deeds are true, all of whose ways are right, and who can humble those
who walk in pride.

Daniel 5:31–34

The Refrain
And now, you kings, be wise;* be warned, you rulers of the earth.
Submit to the LORD with fear,* and with trembling bow before him.

The Midday Psalm   *He Declares His Word to Jacob*
Worship the LORD, O Jerusalem;* praise your God, O Zion;
For he has strengthened the bars of your gates;* he has blessed your children
within you.
He has established peace on your borders;* he satisfies you with the finest wheat.
He sends out his command to the earth,* and his word runs very swiftly.
He gives snow like wool;* he scatters hoarfrost like ashes.
He scatters his hail like bread crumbs;* who can stand against his cold?
He sends forth his word and melts them;* he blows with his wind, and the waters
flow.
He declares his word to Jacob,* his statutes and his judgments to Israel.
He has not done so to any other nation;* to them he has not revealed his judgments.

Psalm 147:13–21

The Refrain
And now, you kings, be wise;* be warned, you rulers of the earth.
Submit to the LORD with fear,* and with trembling bow before him.

The Small Verse
Let us bless the Lord. And all that is within me, forget not his benefits.

The Lord's Prayer

The Prayer Appointed for the Week
O Lord, you have taught us that without love whatever we do is worth nothing:
Send your Holy Spirit and pour into my heart your greatest gift, which is love,
the true bond of peace and of all virtue, without which whoever lives is
accounted dead before you. Grant this for the sake of your only Son Jesus
Christ, who lives and reigns with you and the Holy Spirit, one God, now and
for ever. *Amen.* †

The Concluding Prayer of the Church
O God, you make me glad with the weekly remembrance of the glorious resurrection of your Son my Lord: Give me this day such blessing through my worship
of you, that the week to come may be spent in your favor; through Jesus Christ
our Lord. *Amen.* †

The Vespers Office　　　　　　　　**To Be Observed on the Hour or Half Hour**
　　　　　　　　　　　　　　　　　　　　Between 5 and 8 p.m.

The Call to Prayer
Praise the Name of the LORD;* give praise, you servants of the LORD,
You who stand in the house of the LORD,* in the courts of the house of our God.
Praise the LORD, for the LORD is good;* sing praises to his Name, for it is lovely.
Psalm 135:1–3

The Request for Presence
Incline your ear to me;* make haste to deliver me.
Psalm 31:2

The Greeting
The Lord is in his holy temple; Let all the earth keep silence before him. *Amen.*

The Hymn　　　　　　　　　　　　　　*God the Father, Heavenly Light*
　O Trinity of blessed light,　　　　　To God the Father, heavenly Light,
　O Unity of princely might,　　　　　To Christ revealed in earthly night,
　The fiery sun now goes his way;　　　To God the Holy Ghost we raise
　Please shed within our hearts your ray　Our equal and unceasing praise.
　　　　　　　　　　　　　　　　　　　　Latin, 6th C.
　To you our morning song of praise,
　To you our evening prayer we raise;
　O grant us with your saints on high
　To praise you through eternity.

The Refrain for the Vespers Lessons
Give thanks to the LORD, for he is good,* and his mercy endures for ever.

Psalm 107:1

The Vespers Psalm   *My Soul Is Athirst for the Living God*
As the deer longs for the water-brooks,* so longs my soul for you, O God.
My soul is athirst for God, athirst for the living God;* when shall I come to appear
    before the presence of God?
My tears have been my food day and night, while all day long they say to me,*
    "Where now is your God?"
I pour out my soul when I think on these things:* how I went with the multitude
    and led them into the house of God,
With the voice of praise and thanksgiving,* among those who keep holy-day.
Why are you so full of heaviness, O my soul?* and why are you so disquieted
    within me?
Put your trust in God;* for I will yet give thanks to him, who is the help of my
    countenance, and my God.

Psalm 42:1–7

The Refrain
Give thanks to the LORD, for he is good,* and his mercy endures for ever.

*The Gloria**

The Lord's Prayer

The Prayer Appointed for the Week
O Lord, you have taught us that without love whatever we do is worth nothing:
    Send your Holy Spirit and pour into my heart your greatest gift, which is love,
    the true bond of peace and of all virtue, without which whoever lives is
    accounted dead before you. Grant this for the sake of your only Son Jesus
    Christ, who lives and reigns with you and the Holy Spirit, one God, now and
    for ever. *Amen.* †

The Concluding Prayer of the Church
Lord God, whose Son our Savior Jesus Christ, triumphed over the powers of death
    and prepares for us our place in the new Jerusalem: Grant that I, who have this
    day given thanks for the resurrection, may praise you in the City of which he is
    the light, and where he lives and reigns for ever and ever. *Amen.* †

The Morning Office   **To Be Observed on the Hour or Half Hour**
                                                      Between 6 and 9 a.m.

The Call to Prayer
Be strong and let your heart take courage,* all you who wait for the LORD.

Psalm 31:24

The Request for Presence
O Lord, watch over us* and save us from this generation for ever.

Psalm 12:7

The Greeting
Restore us, O God of hosts;* show the light of your countenance, and we shall be
saved.

Psalm 80:3

The Refrain for the Morning Lessons
You strengthen me more and more;* you enfold me and comfort me.

Psalm 71:21

A Reading
He sat down opposite the treasury and watched people putting money into the
treasury, and many of the rich put in a great deal. A poor widow came and put
in two small coins, the equivalent of a penny. Then he called his disciples and
said to them, 'In truth I tell you, this poor widow has put more in than all who
have contributed to the treasury; for they have all put in money they could
spare, but she in her poverty has put in everything she possessed, all she had to
live on.'

Mark 12:41–44

The Refrain
You strengthen me more and more;* you enfold me and comfort me.

The Morning Psalm *He Holds Our Souls in Life*
Bless our God, you peoples;* make the voice of his praise to be heard;
Who holds our souls in life,* and will not allow our feet to slip.
For you, O God, have proved us;* you have tried us just as silver is tried.
You brought us into the snare;* you laid heavy burdens upon our backs.
You let enemies ride over our heads; we went through fire and water;* but you
    brought us out into a place of refreshment.
I will enter your house with burnt-offerings and will pay you my vows,* which I
    promised with my lips and spoke with my mouth when I was in trouble.
If I had found evil in my heart,* the Lord would not have heard me;
But in truth God has heard me;* he has attended to the voice of my prayer.

Psalm 66:7–12, 16–17

The Refrain
You strengthen me more and more;* you enfold me and comfort me.

*The Gloria**

The Lord's Prayer

The Prayer Appointed for the Week
O Lord, you have taught us that without love whatever we do is worth nothing:
    Send your Holy Spirit and pour into my heart your greatest gift, which is love,
    the true bond of peace and of all virtue, without which whoever lives is

accounted dead before you. Grant this for the sake of your only Son Jesus Christ, who lives and reigns with you and the Holy Spirit, one God, now and for ever. *Amen.* †

Concluding Prayers of the Church
Heavenly Father, in you I live and have my being: I humbly pray you so to guide and govern me by your Holy Spirit, that in all the cares and occupations if my life I may not forget you, but may remember that I am ever walking in your sight; through Jesus Christ my Lord. *Amen.* †

Lord God, almighty and everlasting Father, you have brought me in safety to this new day: Preserve me with your mighty power, that I may not fall into sin, nor be overcome by adversity; and in all I do direct me to the fulfilling of your purpose; through Jesus Christ my Lord. Amen. †

The Midday Office **To Be Observed on the Hour or Half Hour Between 11 a.m. and 2 p.m.**

The Call to Prayer
Praise the Lord, O my soul!* I will praise the Lord as long as I live; I will sing praises to God while I have my being.

Psalm 146:1

The Request for Presence
Bow your heavens, O Lord, and come down;* touch the mountains, and they shall smoke.
Hurl the lightning and scatter them;* shoot out your arrows and rout them.
Stretch out your hand from on high;* rescue me and deliver me from the great waters, from the hand of foreign peoples,
Whose mouths speak deceitfully* and whose right hand is raised in falsehood.

Psalm 144:5–8

The Greeting
To you I lift up my eyes,* to you enthroned in the heavens.
As the eyes of the servants look to the hand of their masters,* and the eyes of a maid to the hand of her mistress,
So our eyes look to the Lord our God,* until he shows us his mercy.

Psalm 123:1–3

The Refrain for the Midday Lessons
Into your hands I commend my spirit,* for you have redeemed me, O Lord, O God of truth.

Psalm 31:5

A Reading
Children, do not let anyone lead you astray. Whoever acts uprightly is upright, just as He is upright.

I John 3:7

The Refrain
Into your hands I commend my spirit,* for you have redeemed me, O LORD, O
    God of truth.

The Midday Psalm   *I Will Walk in the Presence of the LORD*
Gracious is the LORD and righteous;* our God is full of compassion.
The LORD watches over the innocent;* I was brought very low, and he helped me.
Turn again to your rest, O my soul,* for the LORD has treated you well.
For you have rescued my life from death,* my eyes from tears, and my feet from
    stumbling.
I will walk in the presence of the LORD* in the land of the living.

                                                           Psalm 116:4–8

The Refrain
Into your hands I commend my spirit,* for you have redeemed me, O LORD, O
    God of truth.

The Cry of the Church
Lord, have mercy on us. Christ, have mercy on us. Lord, have mercy on us.

The Lord's Prayer

The Prayer Appointed for the Week
O Lord, you have taught us that without love whatever we do is worth nothing:
    Send your Holy Spirit and pour into my heart your greatest gift, which is love,
    the true bond of peace and of all virtue, without which whoever lives is
    accounted dead before you. Grant this for the sake of your only Son Jesus
    Christ, who lives and reigns with you and the Holy Spirit, one God, now and
    for ever. *Amen.* †

The Concluding Prayer of the Church
Almighty and eternal God, ruler of all things in heaven and earth: Mercifully
    accept my prayers, and strengthen me to do your will; through Jesus Christ our
    Lord. *Amen.* †

The Vespers Office   **To Be Observed on the Hour or Half Hour**
                                              Between 5 and 8 p.m.

The Call to Prayer
The righteous will be glad . . .
And they will say, "Surely, there is a reward for the righteous;* surely, there is a
    God who rules in the earth."

                                                           Psalm 58:10–11

The Request for Presence
Make me understand the way of your commandments,* that I may meditate on
    your marvelous works.

                                                           Psalm 119:27

The Greeting
You have made me glad by your acts, O Lord;* and I shout for joy because of the works of your hands.

Psalm 92:4

The Hymn   *Night Is Drawing Nigh*
Now the day is over, night is drawing nigh,
  Shadows of the evening steal across the sky.
Jesus, give the weary calm and sweet repose;
  With your tenderest blessing may our eyelids close.
Grant to little children visions bright of thee.
  Guard the sailors tossing on the sea.
Comfort every sufferer watching late in pain;
  Those who plan some evil from their sin restrain.
Through the long night watches may your angels spread
  Their wings above me, watching round my bed.
When the morning wakens then I may arise
  Pure and fresh and sinless in your holy eyes.

Sabine Baring-Gould

The Refrain for the Vespers Lessons
My mouth shall speak of wisdom,* and my heart shall meditate on understanding.

Psalm 49:2

The Vespers Psalm   *Your Wonders Are More Than I Can Count*
Great things are they that you have done, O Lord my God! how great your
 wonders and your plans for us!* there is none who can be compared with you.
Oh, that I could make them known and tell them!* but they are more than I can
 count.

Psalm 40:5–6

The Refrain
My mouth shall speak of wisdom,* and my heart shall meditate on understanding.

The Gloria*

The Lord's Prayer

The Prayer Appointed for the Week
O Lord, you have taught us that without love whatever we do is worth nothing:
 Send your Holy Spirit and pour into my heart your greatest gift, which is love,
 the true bond of peace and of all virtue, without which whoever lives is
 accounted dead before you. Grant this for the sake of your only Son Jesus
 Christ, who lives and reigns with you and the Holy Spirit, one God, now and
 for ever. *Amen.* †

The Concluding Prayer of the Church
O God, the King eternal, whose light divides the day from the night and turns the
 shadow of death into the morning: Drive far from me all wrong desires, incline

my heart to keep your law, and guide my feet into the way of peace; that, having done your will with cheerfulness during the day, I may, when night comes, rejoice to give you thanks; through Jesus Christ my Lord. *Amen.* †

The Morning Office   **To Be Observed on the Hour or Half Hour Between 6 and 9 a.m.**

The Call to Prayer
Be glad, you righteous, and rejoice in the Lord;* shout for joy, all who are true of heart.

Psalm 32:12

The Request for Presence
Open my eyes, that I may see* the wonders of your law.

Psalm 119:18

The Greeting
With my whole heart I seek you;* let me not stray from your commandments.

Psalm 119:10

The Refrain for the Morning Lessons
I hate those who have a divided heart,* but your law do I love.

Psalm 119:113

A Reading
Jesus said to the people: ". . . what king marching to war against another king would not first sit down and consider whether with ten thousand men he could stand up to the other who was advancing against him with twenty thousand? If not, then while the other king was still a long way off, he would send envoys to sue for peace. So in the same way, none of you can be my disciple without giving up all that he owns."

Luke 14:31–33

The Refrain
I hate those who have a divided heart,* but your law do I love.

The Morning Psalm   *He Brought Them to the Harbor They Were Bound for*
Some went down to the sea in ships* and plied their trade in deep waters;
They beheld the works of the Lord* and his wonder in the deep.
Then he spoke, and a stormy wind arose,* which tossed high the waves of the sea.
They mounted up to the heavens and fell back to the depths;* their hearts melted because of their peril.
They reeled and staggered like drunkards* and were at their wits' end.
Then they cried to the Lord in their trouble,* and he delivered them from their distress.
He stilled the storm to a whisper* and quieted the waves of the sea.
Then they were glad because of the calm,* and he brought them to the harbor they were bound for.

Let them give thanks to the LORD for his mercy* and the wonders he does for his children.
Let them exalt him in the congregation of the people* and praise him in the council of the elders.

Psalm 107:23–32

The Refrain
I hate those who have a divided heart,* but your law do I love.

The Small Verse
The Lord is my shepherd and nothing is wanting to me. In green pastures He has settled me.

THE SHORT BREVIARY

The Lord's Prayer

The Prayer Appointed for the Week
O Lord, you have taught us that without love whatever we do is worth nothing: Send your Holy Spirit and pour into my heart your greatest gift, which is love, the true bond of peace and of all virtue, without which whoever lives is accounted dead before you. Grant this for the sake of your only Son Jesus Christ, who lives and reigns with you and the Holy Spirit, one God, now and for ever. *Amen.* †

The Concluding Prayer of the Church
Lord God, almighty and everlasting Father, you have brought me in safety to this new day: Preserve me with your mighty power, that I may not fall into sin, nor be overcome by adversity; and in all I do direct me to the fulfilling of your purpose; through Jesus Christ my Lord. *Amen.* †

The Midday Office

To Be Observed on the Hour or Half Hour Between 11 a.m. and 2 p.m.

The Call to Prayer
Know this, The LORD himself is God;* he himself made us, and we are his; we are his people and the sheep of his pasture.

Psalm 100:2

The Request for Presence
Open my eyes, that I may see* the wonders of your law.

Psalm 119:18

The Greeting
I restrain my feet from every evil way,* that I may keep your word.

Psalm 119:101

The Refrain for the Midday Lessons
Blessed be God, who has not rejected my prayer,* nor withheld his love from me.

Psalm 66:18

A Reading

You have not seen him, yet you love him; and still without seeing him you believe in him and are already filled with a joy that is so glorious that it cannot be described; and you are sure of the goal of your faith, that is, the salvation of your souls.

1 Peter 1:8–9

The Refrain

Blessed be God, who has not rejected my prayer,* nor withheld his love from me.

The Midday Psalm   *We Flourish like a Flower of the Field*

Our days are like the grass;* we flourish like a flower of the field;
When the wind goes over it, it is gone,* and its place shall know it no more.
But the merciful goodness of the LORD endures for ever on those who fear him,*
    and his righteousness on children's children.

Psalm 103:15–17

The Refrain

Blessed be God, who has not rejected my prayer,* nor withheld his love from me.

The Small Verse

Create in me a clean heart, O God,* and renew a right spirit within me.
Cast me not away from your presence* and take not your holy Spirit from me.
Give me the joy of your saving help again* and sustain me with your bountiful spirit.

Psalm 51:11–13

The Lord's Prayer

The Prayer Appointed for the Week

O Lord, you have taught us that without love whatever we do is worth nothing: Send your Holy Spirit and pour into my heart your greatest gift, which is love, the true bond of peace and of all virtue, without which whoever lives is accounted dead before you. Grant this for the sake of your only Son Jesus Christ, who lives and reigns with you and the Holy Spirit, one God, now and for ever. *Amen.* †

The Concluding Prayer of the Church   *The Privilege Is Ours to Share in the Loving*

Almighty God, our heavenly Father, the privilege is ours to share in the loving, healing, reconciling mission of your Son Jesus Christ, our Lord, in this age and wherever we are. Since without you we can do no good thing:

    May your Spirit make us wise;
    May your Spirit guide us;
    May your Spirit renew us;
    May your Spirit strengthen us;

So that we will be:

    Strong in faith,
    Discerning in proclamation,
    Courageous in witness,
    Persistent in good deeds.

This we ask through the name of the Father.

Church of the Province of the West Indies

The Vespers Office   **To Be Observed on the Hour or Half Hour**
                                          Between 5 and 8 p.m.

The Call to Prayer
Blessed be the Lord, the God of Israel, from everlasting and to everlasting;* and
    let all people say, "Amen!"

                                                            Psalm 106:48

The Request for Presence
Be my strong rock, a castle to keep me safe;* you are my crag and my stronghold.

                                                            Psalm 71:3

The Greeting
Your way, O God, is holy;* who is as great as our God?

                                                            Psalm 77:13

The Hymn   *Jesus, Lover of My Soul*
    Jesus, lover of my soul, let me to your bosom fly,
    While the nearer waters roll, while the tempest still is high:
    Hide, O my Savior, hide, till the storm of life is passed;
    Safe into the haven guide; O receive my soul at last.

    Other refuge have I none; hangs my helpless soul on thee;
    Leave, O leave me not alone, still support and comfort me:
    All my trust on you is laid, all my help from you I bring;
    Cover my defenseless head with the shadow of your wing.

    Plenteous grace with you is found, grace to cover all my sin;
    Let the healing streams abound; make and keep me pure within.

                                                            Charles Wesley

The Refrain for the Vespers Lessons
Truth shall spring up from the earth,* and righteousness shall look down from
    heaven.

                                                            Psalm 85:11

The Vespers Psalm   *This Is the Lord's Doing*
Open for me the gates of righteousness;* I will enter them; I will offer thanks to the
    Lord.
"This is the gate of the Lord;* he who is righteous may enter."
I will give thanks to you, for you answered me* and have become my salvation.
The same stone which the builders rejected* has become the chief cornerstone.
This is the Lord's doing,* and it is marvelous in our eyes.
On this day the Lord has acted;* we will rejoice and be glad in it.

                                                            Psalm 118:19–24

The Refrain
Truth shall spring up from the earth,* and righteousness shall look down from
    heaven.

The Cry of the Church
In the evening, in the morning, and at noonday, I will complain and lament,* and
he will hear my voice.

Psalm 55:18

The Lord's Prayer

The Prayer Appointed for the Week
O Lord, you have taught us that without love whatever we do is worth nothing:
Send your Holy Spirit and pour into my heart your greatest gift, which is love,
the true bond of peace and of all virtue, without which whoever lives is
accounted dead before you. Grant this for the sake of your only Son Jesus
Christ, who lives and reigns with you and the Holy Spirit, one God, now and
for ever. *Amen.* †

The Concluding Prayer of the Church
Lord Jesus, stay with me, for evening is at hand and the day is past; be my companion in the way, kindle my heart, and awaken hope, that I may know you as
you are revealed in Scripture and in the breaking of bread. Grant this for the
sake of your love toward me. *Amen.* †

The Morning Office　　　　　**To Be Observed on the Hour or Half Hour
Between 6 and 9 a.m.**

The Call to Prayer
Wake up, my spirit; awake lute and harp;* I myself will waken the dawn.

Psalm 57:8

The Request for Presence
O God of hosts,* show the light of your countenance, and we shall be saved.

Psalm 80:7

The Greeting
My lips will sing with joy when I play to you,* and so will my soul, which you
have redeemed.

Psalm 71:23

The Refrain for the Morning Lessons
Send forth your strength, O God;* establish, O God, what you have wrought for us.

Psalm 68:28

A Reading
Jesus said: "In all truth I tell you, everyone who commits sin is a slave. Now a
slave has no permanent standing in the household, but a son belongs to it forever. So if the Son sets you free, you will indeed be free."

John 8:34–36

The Refrain
Send forth your strength, O God;* establish, O God, what you have wrought for us.

The Morning Psalm   *Happy Are the People of Whom This Is So*
Rescue me from the hurtful sword* and deliver me from the hand of foreign
    peoples,
Whose mouths speak deceitfully* and whose right hand is raised in falsehood.
May our sons be like plants well nurtured from their youth,* and our daughters
    like sculptured corners of a palace.
May our barns be filled to overflowing with all manner of crops;* may the flocks
    in our pastures increase by thousands and tens of thousands; may our cattle be
    fat and sleek.
May there be no breaching of the walls, no going into exile,* no wailing in the
    public squares.
Happy are the people of whom this is so!* happy are the people whose God is the
    LORD!

Psalm 144:11–16

The Refrain
Send forth your strength, O God;* establish, O God, what you have wrought for us.

*The Gloria**

The Lord's Prayer

The Prayer Appointed for the Week
O Lord, you have taught us that without love whatever we do is worth nothing:
    Send your Holy Spirit and pour into my heart your greatest gift, which is love,
    the true bond of peace and of all virtue, without which whoever lives is
    accounted dead before you. Grant this for the sake of your only Son Jesus
    Christ, who lives and reigns with you and the Holy Spirit, one God, now and
    for ever. *Amen.* †

The Concluding Prayer of the Church
Lord God, almighty and everlasting Father, you have brought me in safety to this
    new day: Preserve me with your mighty power, that I may not fall into sin, nor
    be overcome by adversity; and in all I do direct me to the fulfilling of your pur-
    pose; through Jesus Christ my Lord. *Amen.* †

The Midday Office   **To Be Observed on the Hour or Half Hour**
                                         Between 11 a.m. and 2 p.m.

The Call to Prayer
Sing praise to the LORD who dwells in Zion;* proclaim to the peoples the things he
    has done.

Psalm 9:11

The Request for Presence
Send out your light and your truth, that they may lead me,* and bring me to your
    holy hill and to your dwelling.

Psalm 43:3

The Greeting
How glorious you are!* more splendid than the everlasting mountains!

Psalm 76:4

The Refrain for the Midday Lessons
Away from me, you wicked!* I will keep the commandments of my God.

Psalm 119:115

A Reading
At the signal given by the voice of the Archangel and the trumpet of God, the Lord himself will come down from heaven; those who have died in Christ will be the first to rise, and only after that shall we who remain alive be taken up into the clouds, together with them, to meet the Lord in the air. This is the way we shall be with the Lord for ever. With such thoughts as these, then, you should encourage one another.

I Thessalonians 4:16–18

The Refrain
Away from me, you wicked!* I will keep the commandments of my God.

The Midday Psalm   *Give Praise, You Servants of the LORD*
Give praise, you servants of the LORD;* praise the Name of the LORD.
Let the Name of the LORD be blessed,* from this time forth for evermore.
From the rising of the sun to its going down* let the Name of the LORD be praised.
The LORD is high above all nations,* and his glory above the heavens.
Who is like the LORD our God, who sits enthroned on high* but stoops to behold the heavens and the earth?
He takes up the weak out of the dust* and lifts up the poor from the ashes.
He sets them with the princes,* with the princes of his people.
He makes the woman of a childless house* to be a joyful mother of children.

Psalm 113

The Refrain
Away from me, you wicked!* I will keep the commandments of my God.

*The Gloria**

The Lord's Prayer

The Prayer Appointed for the Week
O Lord, you have taught us that without love whatever we do is worth nothing: Send your Holy Spirit and pour into my heart your greatest gift, which is love, the true bond of peace and of all virtue, without which whoever lives is accounted dead before you. Grant this for the sake of your only Son Jesus Christ, who lives and reigns with you and the Holy Spirit, one God, now and for ever. *Amen.* †

The Concluding Prayer of the Church
O Almighty God, who pours out on all who desire it the spirit of grace and of supplication: Deliver me, when I draw near to you, from coldness of heart and

wanderings of mind, that with steadfast thoughts and kindled affections we may worship you in spirit and in truth; through Jesus Christ our Lord. *Amen.* †

The Vespers Office   **To Be Observed on the Hour or Half Hour**
                                           Between 5 and 8 p.m.

The Call to Prayer

Know that the LORD does wonders for the faithful;* when I call upon the LORD, he
   will hear me.
Tremble, then, and do not sin;* speak to your heart in silence upon your bed.
Offer the appointed sacrifices* and put your trust in the LORD.

Psalm 4:3–5

The Request for Presence

O LORD, do not forsake me;* be not far from me, O my God.
Make haste to help me,* O Lord of my salvation.

Psalm 38:21–22

The Greeting

As the deer longs for the water-brooks,* so longs my soul for you, O God.

Psalm 42:1

The Hymn   *From Psalm 136*

Let us with a gladsome mind praise the Lord, for He is kind:
For His mercies shall endure, ever faithful, ever sure.

Let us sound His Name abroad, for of gods He is the God:
For His mercies shall endure, ever faithful, ever sure.

He, with all commanding might, filled the new-made world with light:
For His mercies shall endure, ever faithful, ever sure.

All things living He does feed; His full hand supplies their need:
For His mercies shall endure, ever faithful, ever sure.

Let us then with gladsome minds praise the Lord for He is kind:
For His mercies shall endure, ever faithful, ever sure.

John Milton

The Refrain for the Vespers Lessons

Turn again to your rest, O my soul,* for the LORD has treated you well.
For you have rescued my life from death,* my eyes from tears, and my feet from
   stumbling.

Psalm 116:6–7

The Vespers Psalm   *One Thing I Seek*

One thing have I asked of the LORD; one thing I seek;* that I may dwell in the
   house of the LORD all the days of my life;
To behold the fair beauty of the LORD* and to seek him in his temple.

Psalm 27:5–6

The Refrain
Turn again to your rest, O my soul,* for the LORD has treated you well.
For you have rescued my life from death,* my eyes from tears, and my feet from
stumbling.

The Small Verse
Lord, let your way be known upon the earth; Your saving health among all
nations.
Let not the needy, O Lord, be forgotten; Nor the hope of the poor be taken away.
Create in me a clean heart, O God; And sustain me in your Holy Spirit.

The Lord's Prayer

The Prayer Appointed for the Week
O Lord, you have taught us that without love whatever we do is worth nothing:
Send your Holy Spirit and pour into my heart your greatest gift, which is love,
the true bond of peace and of all virtue, without which whoever lives is
accounted dead before you. Grant this for the sake of your only Son Jesus
Christ, who lives and reigns with you and the Holy Spirit, one God, now and
for ever. *Amen.* †

The Concluding Prayer of the Church
Lord Jesus, stay with me, for evening is at hand and the day is past; be my companion in the way, kindle my heart, and awaken hope, that I may know you as
you are revealed in Scripture and the breaking of bread. Grant this for the sake
of your love. *Amen.* †

The Morning Office   **To Be Observed on the Hour or Half Hour**
                                        Between 6 and 9 a.m.

The Call to Prayer
Let us bless the LORD* from this time forth for evermore.
                                        adapted from Psalm 115:18

The Request for Presence
Turn to me and have mercy upon me;* . . . and save the child of your handmaid.
                                        Psalm 86:16

The Greeting
You are my hiding-place . . . * you surround me with shouts of deliverance.
                                        Psalm 32:8

The Refrain for the Morning Lessons
Behold, God is my helper;* it is the Lord who sustains my life.
                                        Psalm 54:4

A Reading
In the beginning was the Word: the Word was with God and the Word was God.
He was with God in the beginning. Through him all things came into being,

not one thing came into being except through him. What has come into being in him was life, life that was the light of men; and light shines in the darkness, and darkness could not overpower it.

John 1:1–5

The Refrain
Behold, God is my helper;* it is the Lord who sustains my life.

The Morning Psalm   *Show the Light of Your Countenance, and We Shall Be Saved*
Hear, O Shepherd of Israel, leading Joseph like a flock;* shine forth, you that are enthroned upon the cherubim.
In the presence of Ephraim, Benjamin, and Manasseh,* stir up your strength and come to help us.
Restore us, O God of hosts;* show the light of your countenance, and we shall be saved.

Psalm 80:1–3

The Refrain
Behold, God is my helper;* it is the Lord who sustains my life.

*The Gloria**

The Lord's Prayer

The Prayer Appointed for the Week
O Lord, you have taught us that without love whatever we do is worth nothing: Send your Holy Spirit and pour into my heart your greatest gift, which is love, the true bond of peace and of all virtue, without which whoever lives is accounted dead before you. Grant this for the sake of your only Son Jesus Christ, who lives and reigns with you and the Holy Spirit, one God, now and for ever. *Amen.* †

The Concluding Prayer of the Church
Lord God, almighty and everlasting Father, you have brought me in safety to this new day: Preserve me with your mighty power, that I may not fall into sin, nor be overcome by adversity; and in all I do direct me to the fulfilling of your purpose; through Jesus Christ my Lord. *Amen.* †

The Midday Office   **To Be Observed on the Hour or Half Hour**
Between 11 a.m. and 2 p.m.

The Call to Prayer
Come, let us sing to the Lord;* let us shout for joy to the Rock of our salvation.

Psalm 95:1

The Request for Presence
May God be merciful to us and bless us,* show us the light of his countenance and come to us.

Psalm 67:1

The Greeting

Splendor and honor and kingly power are yours by right, O Lord our God, For
    you created everything that is, and by your will they were created and have
    their being.

Revelation 4:11

The Refrain for the Midday Lessons

I have been young and now I am old,* but never have I seen the righteous
    forsaken, or their children begging bread.

Psalm 37:26

A Reading

In the abundance of his glory may he, through the Spirit, enable you to grow firm
    in power with regard to your inner self, so that Christ may live in your hearts
    through faith, and then, planted in love and built on love, with all God's holy
    people you will have the strength to grasp the breadth and the length, the
    height and the depth; so that, knowing the love of Christ, which is beyond
    knowledge, you may be filled with the utter fullness of God.

Ephesians 3:16–19

The Refrain

I have been young and now I am old,* but never have I seen the righteous
    forsaken, or their children begging bread.

The Midday Psalm   *Happy Are They Who Consider the Poor and Needy*

Happy are they who consider the poor and needy!* the LORD will deliver them in
    the time of trouble.
The LORD preserves them and keeps them alive, so that they may be happy in the
    land;* he does not hand them over to the will of their enemies.
The LORD sustains them on their sickbed* and ministers to them in their illness.

Psalm 41:1–3

The Refrain

I have been young and now I am old,* but never have I seen the righteous
    forsaken, or their children begging bread.

The Gloria*

The Lord's Prayer

The Prayer Appointed for the Week

O Lord, you have taught us that without love whatever we do is worth nothing:
    Send your Holy Spirit and pour into my heart your greatest gift, which is love,
    the true bond of peace and of all virtue, without which whoever lives is
    accounted dead before you. Grant this for the sake of your only Son Jesus
    Christ, who lives and reigns with you and the Holy Spirit, one God, now and
    for ever. *Amen.* †

The Concluding Prayer of the Church
You gather us together in faith, O God, as a loving mother and a gentle father.
Help us to remember that your dwelling place is built upon love and peace,
and that to bring about your reign on earth we must follow your way of peace.
We pray for all governments and legislatures that they may be mindful of the
rights of all peoples of this world to live in peace and dignity. Grant this in the
name of Jesus. *Amen.*

The New Companion to the Breviary

The Vespers Office   **To Be Observed on the Hour or Half Hour**
Between 5 and 8 p.m.

The Call to Prayer
Bless our God, you peoples;* make the voice of his praise to be heard;
Who holds our souls in life,* and will not allow our feet to slip.

Psalm 66:7–8

The Request for Presence
Show me the light of your countenance, O God, and come to me.

adapted from Psalm 67:1

The Greeting
Whom have I in heaven but you?* and having you I desire nothing upon earth.

Psalm 73:25

The Refrain for the Vespers Lessons
I have been sustained by you ever since I was born; from my mother's womb you
have been my strength;* my praise shall be always of you.

Psalm 71:6

The Hymn

On the night before he suffered,
Seated with his chosen band,
Jesus when they all had feasted,
Faithful to the Law's command,
Far more precious food provided:
Gave himself with his own hand.

Word made flesh, true bread of heaven,
By his word made flesh to be,
From the wine his blood is taken,
Though our senses can not see,
Faith alone which is unshaken
Shows pure hearts the mystery.

Therefore we, before him falling,
This great sacrament revere;
Ancient forms are now departed,
For new acts of grace are here,
Faith our feeble senses aiding,
Makes the Savior's presence clear.

St. Thomas Aquinas

The Refrain for the Vespers Lessons
I have been sustained by you ever since I was born; from my mother's womb you
have been my strength;* my praise shall be always of you.

The Vespers Psalm *How Shall We Sing the* Lord'*s Song Upon an Alien Soil*
By the waters of Babylon we sat down and wept,* when we remembered you, O
    Zion.
As for our harps, we hung them up* on the trees in the midst of that land.
For those who led us away captive asked us for a song, and our oppressors called
    for mirth:* "Sing us one of the songs of Zion."
How shall we sing the Lord's song* upon an alien soil.
If I forget you, O Jerusalem,* let my right hand forget its skill.
Let my tongue cleave to the roof of my mouth if I do not remember you,* if I do
    not set Jerusalem above my highest joy.

Psalm 137:1–6

The Refrain
I have been sustained by you ever since I was born; from my mother's womb you
    have been my strength;* my praise shall be always of you.

The Cry of the Church
O God, come to my assistance! O Lord, make haste to help me!

The Lord's Prayer

The Prayer Appointed for the Week
O Lord, you have taught us that without love whatever we do is worth nothing: Send
    your Holy Spirit and pour into my heart your greatest gift, which is love, the true
    bond of peace and of all virtue, without which whoever lives is accounted dead
    before you. Grant this for the sake of your only Son Jesus Christ, who lives and
    reigns with you and the Holy Spirit, one God, now and for ever. *Amen.* †

The Concluding Prayer of the Church
Almighty Father, you have given us strength to work throughout this day. Receive
    our evening sacrifice of praise in thanksgiving for your countless gifts. We ask
    this through our Lord Jesus Christ, your Son, who lives and reigns with you
    and the Holy Spirit, one God, for ever and ever. *Amen.*

The Liturgy of the Hours, Vol. III

The Morning Office **To Be Observed on the Hour or Half Hour**
Between 6 and 9 a.m.

The Call to Prayer
Bless our God, you peoples;* make the voice of his praise to be heard;
Who holds our souls in life,* and will not allow our feet to slip.

Psalm 66:7–8

The Request for Presence
I call with my whole heart;* answer me, O Lord, that I may keep your statutes.
Hear my voice, O Lord, according to your loving-kindness;* according to your
    judgments, give me life.

Psalm 119:145ff

The Greeting

I am bound by the vow I made to you, O God;* I will present to you thank-offerings;
For you have rescued my soul from death and my feet from stumbling,* that I may
walk before God in the light of the living.

Psalm 56:11–12

The Refrain for the Morning Lessons

Keep watch over my life, for I am faithful;* save your servant whose trust is in you.

adapted from Psalm 86:2

A Reading

Jesus taught us, saying: "It is someone who is forgiven little who shows little love."

Luke 7:47

The Refrain

Keep watch over my life, for I am faithful;* save your servant whose trust is in you.

The Morning Psalm   *Happy Are the People Whose Strength Is in You*

Happy are they who dwell in your house!* they will always be praising you.
Happy are the people whose strength is in you!* whose hearts are set on the
pilgrims' way.
Those who go through the desolate valley will find it a place of springs,* for the
early rains have covered it with pools of water.
They will climb from height to height,* and the God of gods will reveal himself in
Zion.
LORD God of hosts, hear my prayer;* hearken, O God of Jacob.
Behold our defender, O God;* and look upon the face of your Anointed.
For one day in your courts is better than a thousand in my own room,* and to stand
at the threshold of the house of my God than to dwell in the tents of the wicked.

Psalm 84:3–9

The Refrain

Keep watch over my life, for I am faithful;* save your servant whose trust is in you.

The Cry of the Church

Lord, have mercy on us. Christ, have mercy on us. Lord, have mercy on us.

The Lord's Prayer

The Prayer Appointed for the Week

O Lord, you have taught us that without love whatever we do is worth nothing:
Send your Holy Spirit and pour into my heart your greatest gift, which is love,
the true bond of peace and of all virtue, without which whoever lives is
accounted dead before you. Grant this for the sake of your only Son Jesus
Christ, who lives and reigns with you and the Holy Spirit, one God, now and
for ever. *Amen.* †

The Concluding Prayer of the Church

Lord God, almighty and everlasting Father, you have brought me in safety to this
new day: Preserve me with your mighty power, that I may not fall into sin, nor

be overcome by adversity; and in all I do direct me to the fulfilling of your purpose; through Jesus Christ my Lord. *Amen.* †

The Midday Office   **To Be Observed on the Hour or Half Hour**
Between 11 a.m. and 2 p.m.

The Call to Prayer
"Come now, let us reason together," says the Lord.

Isaiah 1:18, KJV

The Request for Presence
O God, be not far from me;* come quickly to help me, O my God.

Psalm 71:12

The Greeting
"You are my God, and I will thank you;* you are my God and I will exalt you."

Psalm 118:28

The Refrain for the Midday Lessons
The same stone that the builders rejected* has become the chief cornerstone.
This is the LORD's doing,* and it is marvelous in our eyes.

Psalm 118:22–23

A Reading
He was marked out before the world was made, and was revealed at the final
    point of time for your sake.

I Peter 1:20

The Refrain
The same stone that the builders rejected* has become the chief cornerstone.
This is the LORD's doing,* and it is marvelous in our eyes.

The Midday Psalm   *We Are His*
Be joyful in the LORD, all you lands;* serve the LORD with gladness and come
    before his presence with a song.
Know this: The LORD himself is God;* he himself has made us, and we are his; we
    are his people and the sheep of his pasture.
Enter his gates with thanksgiving; go into his courts with praise;* give thanks to
    him and call upon his Name.
For the LORD is good; his mercy is everlasting;* and his faithfulness endures from
    age to age.

Psalm 100:1–4

The Refrain
The same stone that the builders rejected* has become the chief cornerstone.
This is the LORD's doing,* and it is marvelous in our eyes.

The Cry of the Church
Lord, have mercy on us. Christ, have mercy on us. Lord, have mercy on us.

The Lord's Prayer

The Prayer Appointed for the Week

O Lord, you have taught us that without love whatever we do is worth nothing:
Send your Holy Spirit and pour into my heart your greatest gift, which is love,
the true bond of peace and of all virtue, without which whoever lives is
accounted dead before you. Grant this for the sake of your only Son Jesus
Christ, who lives and reigns with you and the Holy Spirit, one God, now and
for ever. *Amen.* †

The Concluding Prayer of the Church

Lord Jesus Christ, by your death you took away the sting of death: Grant me to so
follow in faith where you have led the way, that I may at length fall asleep
peacefully in you and wake in your likeness; for your tender mercies sake.
Amen. †

The Vespers Office

**To Be Observed on the Hour or Half Hour
Between 5 and 8 p.m.**

The Call to Prayer

O tarry and await the LORD's pleasure; be strong, and he shall comfort your heart;*
wait patiently for the LORD.

Psalm 27:18

The Request for Presence

Out of the depths have I called to you, O LORD; LORD, hear my voice;* let your ears
consider well the voice of my supplication.

Psalm 130:1

The Greeting

For your Name's sake, O LORD,* forgive my sin, for it is great.

Psalm 25:10

The Hymn

O sacred Head, now wounded, with grief and shame weighed down,
Now scornfully surrounded with thorns, your only crown:
How pale you are with anguish, with sore abuse and scorn!
How does that visage languish which once was bright as morn!

What you, O Lord, have suffered was all for sinner's gain;
Mine, mine was the transgression, but yours the deadly pain.
Lo, here I fall, my Savior! 'Tis I deserve your place;
Look on me with your favor, vouchsafe to me your grace.

What language shall I borrow to thank you, dearest friend,
For this your dying sorrow, your pity without end?
O make me yours forever; and should I fainting be,
Lord, let me never, never outlive my love for thee.

Bernard of Clairvaux

The Refrain for the Vespers Lessons
Let not those who hope in you be put to shame through me, Lord GOD of Hosts;*
    let not those who seek you be disgraced because of me, O God of Israel.

Psalm 69:7

The Vespers Psalm   *This God Is Our God For Ever and Ever*
We have waited in silence on your loving-kindness, O God,* in the midst of your
    temple.
Your praise, like your Name, O God, reaches to the world's end;* your right hand
    is full of justice.
Let Mount Zion be glad and the cities of Judah rejoice,* because of your
    judgments.
Make the circuit of Zion; walk round about her;* count the number of her
    towers.
Consider well her bulwarks; examine her strongholds;* that you may tell those
    who come after.
This God is our God for ever and ever;* he shall be our guide for evermore.

Psalm 48:8–13

The Refrain
Let not those who hope in you be put to shame through me, Lord GOD of Hosts;*
    let not those who seek you be disgraced because of me, O God of Israel.

The Cry of the Church
Lord, have mercy on us. Christ, have mercy on us. Lord, have mercy on us.

The Lord's Prayer

The Prayer Appointed for the Week
O Lord, you have taught us that without love whatever we do is worth nothing:
    Send your Holy Spirit and pour into my heart your greatest gift, which is love,
    the true bond of peace and of all virtue, without which whoever lives is
    accounted dead before you. Grant this for the sake of your only Son Jesus
    Christ, who lives and reigns with you and the Holy Spirit, one God, now and
    for ever. *Amen.* †

Concluding Prayers of the Church
Almighty God, who has promised to hear the petitions of those who ask in your
    Son's Name: I beseech you mercifully to incline your ear to me who have made
    my prayers and supplications to you; and grant that those things which I have
    faithfully asked according to your will, may effectually be obtained, to the
    relief of my necessity, and to the setting forth of your glory; through Jesus
    Christ my Lord. *Amen.* †

May the souls of the faithful departed, through the mercy of God, rest in eternal
    peace. *Amen.*

The Morning Office   **To Be Observed on the Hour or Half Hour**
                                          Between 6 and 9 a.m.

The Call to Prayer
Let us come before his presence with thanksgiving* and raise a loud shout to him
    with psalms.

Psalm 95:2

The Request for Presence
LORD God of hosts, hear my prayer;* hearken, O God of Jacob.

Psalm 84:7

The Greeting
My heart is firmly fixed, O God, my heart is fixed;* I will sing and make melody.
Wake up, my spirit; awake, lute and harp;* I myself will awaken the dawn.
I will confess you among the peoples, O LORD;* I will sing praise to you among the
    nations.
For your loving-kindness is greater than the heavens,* and your faithfulness
    reaches to the clouds.
Exalt yourself above the heavens, O God,* and your glory over all the earth.

Psalm 57:7–11

The Refrain for the Morning Lessons
"I will appoint a time," says God;* "I will judge with equity . . ."

Psalm 75:2

A Reading
Jesus taught the disciples, saying: "In truth I tell you, when everything is made
    new again and the Son of man is seated on his throne of glory, you yourselves
    will sit on twelve thrones to judge the twelve tribes of Israel. And everyone
    who had left houses, brothers, sisters, father, mother, children or land for the
    sake of my name will receive a hundred times as much, and also inherit eternal
    life. Many who are first will be last, and the last, first."

Matthew 19:28–30

The Refrain
"I will appoint a time," says God;* "I will judge with equity . . ."

The Morning Psalm   *The LORD Awoke*
Then the LORD woke as though from sleep,* like a warrior refreshed with wine.
He chose instead the tribe of Judah* and Mount Zion, which he loved.
He built his sanctuary like the heights of heaven,* like the earth which he founded
    for ever.
He chose David his servant,* and took him away from the sheepfolds.
He brought him from following the ewes,* to be a shepherd over Jacob his people
    and over Israel his inheritance.
So he shepherded them with a faithful and true heart* and guided them with the
    skillfulness of his hands.

Psalm 78:65, 68–72

The Refrain
"I will appoint a time," says God;* "I will judge with equity . . ."

The Small Verse
The LORD is a great God,* and a great King above all gods.
In his hand are the caverns of the earth,* and the heights of the hills are his also.
The sea is his, for he made it,* and his hands have molded the dry land.

Psalm 95:3–5

The Lord's Prayer

The Prayer Appointed for the Week
O Lord, you have taught us that without love whatever we do is worth nothing:
Send your Holy Spirit and pour into my heart your greatest gift, which is love,
the true bond of peace and of all virtue, without which whoever lives is
accounted dead before you. Grant this for the sake of your only Son Jesus
Christ, who lives and reigns with you and the Holy Spirit, one God, now and
for ever. *Amen.* †

The Concluding Prayer of the Church
Lord God, almighty and everlasting Father, you have brought me in safety to this
new day: Preserve me with your mighty power, that I may not fall into sin, nor
be overcome by adversity; and in all I do direct me to the fulfilling of your purpose; through Jesus Christ my Lord. *Amen.* †

The Midday Office **To Be Observed on the Hour or Half Hour**
Between 11 a.m. and 2 p.m.

The Call to Prayer
Ascribe to the LORD, you families of the peoples;* ascribe to the LORD honor and
power.
Ascribe to the LORD the honor due his Name;* bring offerings and come into his
courts.
Worship the LORD in the beauty of holiness;* let the whole earth tremble before
him.
Tell it out among the nations: "The LORD is King!"* he has made the world so firm
that it cannot be moved; he will judge the peoples with equity."

Psalm 96:7–10

The Request for Presence
Hear, O Shepherd of Israel, leading Joseph like a flock;* shine forth, you that are
enthroned upon the cherubim.
In the presence of Ephraim, Benjamin, and Manasseh,* stir up your strength and
come to help us.
Restore us, O God of hosts;* show the light of your countenance, and we shall be
saved.

Psalm 80:1–3

The Greeting

Into your hands I commend my spirit,* for you have redeemed me, O Lord, O
God of truth.

Psalm 31:5

The Refrain for the Midday Lessons

Let all the earth fear the Lord;* let all who dwell in the world stand in awe of him.

Psalm 33:8

A Reading

This alone is my conclusion: God has created man straightforward, and human
artifices are human inventions.

Ecclesiastes 7:29

The Refrain

Let all the earth fear the Lord;* let all who dwell in the world stand in awe of him.

The Midday Psalm   Come and Listen

Come and listen, all you who fear God,* and I will tell you what he has done
for me.

I called out to him with my mouth,* and his praise was on my tongue.

If I had found evil in my heart,* the Lord would not have heard me;

But in truth God has heard me;* he has attended to the voice of my prayer.

Blessed be God, who has not rejected my prayer,* nor withheld his love from me.

Psalm 66:14–18

The Refrain

Let all the earth fear the Lord;* let all who dwell in the world stand in awe of him.

The Gloria*

The Lord's Prayer

The Prayer Appointed for the Week

O Lord, you have taught us that without love whatever we do is worth nothing:
Send your Holy Spirit and pour into my heart your greatest gift, which is love,
the true bond of peace and of all virtue, without which whoever lives is
accounted dead before you. Grant this for the sake of your only Son Jesus
Christ, who lives and reigns with you and the Holy Spirit, one God, now and
for ever. *Amen.* †

The Concluding Prayer of the Church

Almighty God, who after the creation of the world rested from all your works
and sanctified a day of rest for all your creatures: Grant that I, putting away
all earthly anxieties, may be duly prepared for the service of public worship,
and grant as well that my Sabbath upon earth may be a preparation for the
eternal rest promised to your people in heaven; through Jesus Christ our
Lord. *Amen.*

The Vespers Office   **To Be Observed on the Hour or Half Hour**
                                      Between 5 and 8 p.m.

The Call to Prayer
Sing with joy to God our strength* and raise a loud shout to the God of Jacob.
Raise a song and sound the timbrel,* the merry harp and the lyre.
Blow the ram's-horn at the new moon,* and at the full moon, the day of our feast.
Psalm 81:1–3

The Request for Presence
O God, do not be silent;* do not keep still nor hold your peace, O God.
Psalm 83:1

The Greeting
I will sing of mercy and justice;* to you, O Lord, will I sing praises.
Psalm 101:1

The Hymn   *O God of Truth*
O God of truth, O Lord of might,   Grant this, O Father ever one
Disposing time and change aright,   With Jesus Christ your only Son
Who clothes the splendid morning ray   And Holy Ghost, whom all adore,
And gives the heat at noon of day: Reigning and blessed for evermore.
                                        adapted from The Short Breviary
Extinguish every sinful fire,
And banish every ill desire;
And while you keep the body whole
Shed forth your peace upon the soul.

The Refrain for the Vespers Lessons
I will give you thanks for what you have done* and declare the goodness of your
    Name in the presence of the godly.
Psalm 52:9

The Vespers Psalm   *This Is Glory for All His Faithful People*
Let them praise his Name in the dance;* let them sing praise to him with timbrel
    and harp.
For the Lord takes pleasure in his people* and adorns the poor with victory.
Let the praises of God be in their throat* . . . this is glory for all his faithful people.
Psalm 149:4–6a, 9b

The Refrain
I will give you thanks for what you have done* and declare the goodness of your
    Name in the presence of the godly.

The Small Verse
The Lord is my shepherd and nothing is wanting to me. In green pastures He hath
    settled me.
The Short Breviary

The Lord's Prayer

The Prayer Appointed for the Week

O Lord, you have taught us that without love whatever we do is worth nothing: Send your Holy Spirit and pour into my heart your greatest gift, which is love, the true bond of peace and of all virtue, without which whoever lives is accounted dead before you. Grant this for the sake of your only Son Jesus Christ, who lives and reigns with you and the Holy Spirit, one God, now and for ever. *Amen.* †

The Concluding Prayer of the Church

Grant I pray, O Lord God, to me Your servant that I may evermore enjoy health of mind and body, and by the glorious intercession of the Blessed Mary ever Virgin be delivered from present sorrow and attain everlasting happiness. Through our Lord Jesus Christ, Your Son, who lives and reigns with You in the unity of the Holy Ghost, God, world without end. *Amen.*

adapted from The Short Breviary

The Morning Office   **To Be Observed on the Hour or Half Hour**
                                          Between 6 and 9 a.m.

The Call to Prayer

Sing to the Lord, you servants of his;* give thanks for the remembrance of his holiness.

For his wrath endures but the twinkling of an eye,* his favor for a lifetime.

Psalm 30:4–5

The Request for Presence

I cry out to you, O Lord;* I say, "You are my refuge, my portion in the land of the living."

Psalm 142:5

The Greeting

Glory to God in the highest,
        and peace to his people on earth.
Lord God, heavenly King,
almighty God and Father,
        we worship you, we give you thanks,
        we praise you for your glory.
Lord Jesus Christ, only Son of the Father,
Lord God, Lamb of God,
you take away the sins of the world:
        have mercy on us;

you are seated at the right hand of the Father:
>receive our prayer.
For you alone are the Holy One,
you alone are the Lord,
you alone are the Most High,
>Jesus Christ,
>with the Holy Spirit,
>in the glory of God the Father. *Amen.*

>>>*Gloria in Excelsis*

The Refrain for the Morning Lessons
On this day the Lord has acted;* we will rejoice and be glad in it.

>>>*Psalm 118:24*

A Reading
Jesus said: "I have come to bring fire to the earth, and how I wish it were blazing already! There is a baptism I must still receive, and what constraint I am under until it is completed!"

>>>*Luke 12:49–50*

The Refrain
On this day the Lord has acted;* we will rejoice and be glad in it.

The Morning Psalm   *So That a People Yet Unborn May Praise the Lord*
Let this be written for a future generation,* so that a people yet unborn may praise the Lord.
For the Lord looked down from his holy place on high;* from the heavens he beheld the earth;
That he might hear the groan of the captive* and set free those condemned to die;
That they may declare in Zion the Name of the Lord,* and his praise in Jerusalem;
When the peoples are gathered together,* and the kingdoms also, to serve the Lord.

>>>*Psalm 102:18–22*

The Refrain
On this day the Lord has acted;* we will rejoice and be glad in it.

The Cry of the Church
O God, come to my assistance! O Lord, make haste to help me!

The Lord's Prayer

The Prayer Appointed for the Week
Most loving Father, whose will it is for us to give thanks for all things, to fear nothing but the loss of you, and to cast all our care on you who cares for us: Preserve me from faithless fears and worldly anxieties, that no clouds of this mortal life may hide from me the light of that love which is immortal, and which you have manifested to us in your Son Jesus Christ our Lord; who lives and reigns with you, in the unity of the Holy Spirit, one God, now and for ever. *Amen.* †

The Concluding Prayer of the Church
Lord God, almighty and everlasting Father, you have brought me in safety to this
new day: Preserve me with your mighty power, that I may not fall into sin, nor
be overcome by adversity; and in all I do direct me to the fulfilling of your purpose; through Jesus Christ my Lord. *Amen.* †

The Midday Office   **To Be Observed on the Hour or Half Hour**
                                                  Between 11 a.m. and 2 p.m.

The Call to Prayer
Open my lips, O Lord,* and my mouth shall proclaim your praise.
Had you desired it, I would have offered sacrifice,* but you take no delight in
burnt-offerings.
The sacrifice of God is a troubled spirit;* and a broken and contrite heart, O God,
you will not despise.

Psalm 51:16–18

The Request for Presence
Show us the light of your countenance, O God,* and come to us.

based on Psalm 67:1

The Greeting
You, O LORD, are my lamp;* my God, you make my darkness bright.
With you I will break down an enclosure;* with the help of my God I will scale any
wall.

Psalm 18:29–30

The Refrain for the Midday Lessons
Happy are those who trust in the LORD!* they do not resort to evil spirits or turn to
false gods.

Psalm 40:4

A Reading
"For me it will be as in the days of Noah when I swore that Noah's waters should
never flood the world again. So now I swear never to be angry with you and
never to rebuke you again. For the mountains may go away and the hills may
totter, but my faithful love will never leave you, my covenant of peace will
never totter," says YAHWEH who takes pity on you.

Isaiah 54:9–10

The Refrain
Happy are those who trust in the LORD!* they do not resort to evil spirits or turn to
false gods.

The Midday Psalm   *May They Prosper Who Love You*
I was glad when they said to me,* "Let us go to the house of the LORD."
Now our feet are standing* within your gates, O Jerusalem.
Jerusalem is built as a city* that is at unity with itself;

To which the tribes go up, the tribes of the LORD,* the assembly of Israel, to praise the Name of the LORD.

For there are the thrones of judgment,* the thrones of the house of David.

Pray for the peace of Jerusalem:* "May they prosper who love you.

Peace be within your walls* and quietness within your towers.

For my brethren and companions' sake,* I pray for your prosperity.

Because of the house of the LORD our God,* I will seek to do you good."

Psalm 122

The Refrain
Happy are those who trust in the LORD!* they do not resort to evil spirits or turn to false gods.

The Cry of the Church
Even so, come Lord Jesus!

The Lord's Prayer

The Prayer Appointed for the Week
Most loving Father, whose will it is for us to give thanks for all things, to fear nothing but the loss of you, and to cast all our care on you who cares for us: Preserve me from faithless fears and worldly anxieties, that no clouds of this mortal life may hide from me the light of that love which is immortal, and which you have manifested to us in your Son Jesus Christ our Lord; who lives and reigns with you, in the unity of the Holy Spirit, one God, now and for ever. *Amen.* †

The Concluding Prayer of the Church
O God, you make me glad with the weekly remembrance of the glorious resurrection of your Son my Lord: Give me this day such blessing through my worship of you, that the week to come may be spent in your favor; through Jesus Christ our Lord. *Amen.* †

The Vespers Office   **To Be Observed on the Hour or Half Hour Between 5 and 8 p.m.**

The Call to Prayer
Bless the LORD, O my soul,* and all that is within me, bless his holy Name.

Bless the LORD, O my soul,* and forget not all his benefits.

Psalm 103:1–2

The Request for Presence
The LORD will hear the desire of the humble;* you will strengthen their heart and your ears shall hear.

Psalm 10:18

The Greeting
O gracious Light,
pure brightness of the everlasting Father in heaven,
O Jesus Christ, holy and blessed!

Now as we come to the setting of the sun,
and our eyes behold the vesper light,
we sing your praises O God: Father, Son and Holy Spirit.

You are worthy at all times to be praised by happy voices,
O Son of God, O giver of life,
and to be glorified through all the worlds.

Phos Hilaron

The Hymn   *Come, Pure Hearts*
Come, pure hearts, in joyful measure
sing of those who spread the treasure
          in the truth of God enshrined;
blessed tidings of salvation,
peace on earth their proclamation,
          love from God to lost mankind.

See the rivers four that gladden,
with their streams, the better Eden
          planted by our Lord most dear;
Christ the fountain, these the waters;
drink, O Zion's son and daughters,
          drink, and find salvation here.

O that we, your truth confessing,
and your holy word possessing,
          Jesus may your love adore;
unto you our voices raising,
you with all your ransomed praising,
          ever and for evermore.

Latin, 12th C.

The Refrain for the Vespers Lessons
The LORD has heard my supplication;* the LORD accepts my prayer.

Psalm 6:9

The Vespers Psalm   *I Am with Him in Trouble*
Because he is bound to me in love, therefore will I deliver him;* I will protect him,
    because he knows my Name.
He shall call upon me, and I will answer him;* I am with him in trouble; I will
    rescue him and bring him to honor.
With long life will I satisfy him,* and show him my salvation.

Psalm 91:14–16

The Refrain
The LORD has heard my supplication;* the LORD accepts my prayer.

The Small Verse
The Lord is my shepherd and nothing is wanting to me.* In green pastures He has
settled me.

A SHORT BREVIARY

The Lord's Prayer

The Prayer Appointed for the Week
Most loving Father, whose will it is for us to give thanks for all things, to fear nothing
but the loss of you, and to cast all our care on you who cares for us: Preserve me
from faithless fears and worldly anxieties, that no clouds of this mortal life may
hide from me the light of that love which is immortal, and which you have manifested to us in your Son Jesus Christ our Lord; who lives and reigns with you, in
the unity of the Holy Spirit, one God, now and for ever. *Amen.* †

The Concluding Prayer of the Church
Heavenly Father, Shepherd of your people, thank you for your servant Matthias,
who was faithful in the care and nurture of your flock; and I pray that, following his example, and the teaching of his holy life, I may by your grace grow
into the stature of the fullness of our Lord and Savior Jesus Christ; who lives
and reigns with you and the Holy Spirit, one God, for ever and ever. *Amen.* †

The Morning Office   **To Be Observed on the Hour or Half Hour
Between 6 and 9 a.m.**

The Call to Prayer
Bless the LORD, you angels of his, you mighty ones who do his bidding,* and
hearken to the voice of his word.
Bless the LORD, all you his hosts,* you ministers of his who do his will.
Bless the LORD, all you works of his, in all places of his dominion;* bless the LORD,
O my soul.

Psalm 103:20–22

The Request for Presence
Let those who seek you rejoice and be glad in you;* let those who love your
salvation say forever, "Great is the LORD!"

Psalm 70:4

The Greeting
Therefore my heart sings to you without ceasing;* O LORD my God, I will give you
thanks for ever.

Psalm 30:13

The Refrain for the Morning Lessons
May you be blessed by the LORD,* the maker of heaven and earth.

A Reading

One day Peter stood up to speak to the brothers—there were about a hundred and twenty people in the congregation. 'Brothers,' he said, 'the passage of scripture had to be fulfilled in which the Holy Spirit, speaking through David, foretells the fate of Judas, who acted as a guide to the men who arrested Jesus—after being one of our number and sharing our ministry . . . Now in the Book of Psalms it says: *Reduce his encampment to ruin and leave his tent unoccupied.* And again: *Let someone else take over his office.* Out of the men who have been with us the whole time that the Lord Jesus was living with us, from the time when John was baptizing until the day when he was taken up from us— one must be appointed to serve with us as a witness to his resurrection.' Having nominated two candidates, Joseph known as Barsabbas, whose surname was Justus, and Matthias, they prayed, 'Lord, you can read everyone's heart: show us therefore which of these two you have chosen to take over this ministry and apostolate, which Judas abandoned to go to his proper place.' They then drew lots for them, and as the lot fell to Matthias, he was listed as one of the twelve apostles.

Acts 1:15–17, 20–26

The Refrain
May you be blessed by the LORD,* the maker of heaven and earth.

The Morning Psalm   *The Fear of the LORD Is the Beginning of Wisdom*
I will give thanks to the LORD with my whole heart,* in the assembly of the
      upright, in the congregation.
Great are the deeds of the LORD!* they are studied by all who delight in them.
His work is full of majesty and splendor,* and his righteousness endures for ever.
He makes his marvelous works to be remembered;* the LORD is gracious and full
      of compassion.
The works of his hands are faithfulness and justice;* all his commandments are sure.
They stand fast for ever and ever,* because they are done in truth and equity.
He sent redemption to his people; he commanded his covenant for ever,* holy and
      awesome is his Name.

Psalm 111:1–4, 7–9

The Refrain
May you be blessed by the LORD,* the maker of heaven and earth.

The Small Verse
Open, Lord, my eyes that I may see.
Open, Lord, my ears that I may hear.
Open, Lord, my heart and my mind that I may understand.
So shall I turn to you and be healed.

Traditional

The Lord's Prayer

The Prayer Appointed for the Week
Most loving Father, whose will it is for us to give thanks for all things, to fear
nothing but the loss of you, and to cast all our care on you who cares for us:
Preserve me from faithless fears and worldly anxieties, that no clouds of this
mortal life may hide from me the light of that love which is immortal, and
which you have manifested to us in your Son Jesus Christ our Lord; who lives
and reigns with you, in the unity of the Holy Spirit, one God, now and for ever.
Amen. †

Concluding Prayers of the Church
Almighty God, who in the place of Judas chose your faithful servant Matthias to
be numbered among the Twelve: Grant that your Church, being delivered from
false apostles, may always be guided and governed by faithful and true pas-
tors; through Jesus Christ our Lord, who lives and reigns with you, in the unity
of the Holy Spirit, now and for ever. *Amen.* †

Lord God, almighty and everlasting Father, you have brought me in safety to this
new day: Preserve me with your mighty power, that I may not fall into sin, nor
be overcome by adversity; and in all I do direct me to the fulfilling of your purpose; through Jesus Christ my Lord. *Amen.*

The Midday Office　　　　**To Be Observed on the Hour or Half Hour
Between 11 a.m. and 2 p.m.**

The Call to Prayer
The righteous will rejoice in the LORD and put their trust in him,* and all who are
true of heart will glory.

Psalm 64:10

The Request for Presence
Show us the light of your countenance, O God,* and come to us.

based on Psalm 67:1

The Greeting
Happy are the people whose strength is in you!* whose hearts are set on the
pilgrims' way.

Psalm 84:4

The Refrain for the Midday Lessons
Happy are they who fear the LORD,* and who follow in his ways!

Psalm 128:1

A Reading
Our homeland is in heaven and it is from there that we are expecting a Savior, the
Lord Jesus Christ.

Philippians 3:20

The Refrain
Happy are they who fear the LORD,* and who follow in his ways!

The Midday Psalm   *Blessed Be God Who Has Never Withheld His Love*
Come and listen, all you who fear God,* and I will tell you what he has done for me.
I called out to him with my mouth,* and his praise was on my tongue.
If I had found evil in my heart,* the Lord would not have heard me;
But in truth God has heard me;* he has attended to the voice of my prayer.
Blessed be God, who has not rejected my prayer,* nor withheld his love from me.

Psalm 66:14–18

The Refrain
Happy are they who fear the LORD,* and who follow in his ways!

The Small Verse
Blessed be the Name of the Lord and blessed be the people who are called by it.

The Lord's Prayer

The Prayer Appointed for the Week
Most loving Father, whose will it is for us to give thanks for all things, to fear
    nothing but the loss of you, and to cast all our care on you who cares for us:
    Preserve me from faithless fears and worldly anxieties, that no clouds of this
    mortal life may hide from me the light of that love which is immortal, and
    which you have manifested to us in your Son Jesus Christ our Lord; who lives
    and reigns with you, in the unity of the Holy Spirit, one God, now and for ever.
    Amen. †

The Concluding Prayer of the Church
O God, by whose grace your servant Matthias, kindled with the flame of your
    love, became a burning and a shining light in your Church: Grant that I also
    may be aflame with the spirit of love and discipline, and walk before you as a
    child of light; through Jesus Christ our Lord, who lives and reigns with you in
    the unity of the Holy Spirit, one God, now and forever. *Amen.* †

The Vespers Office   **To Be Observed on the Hour or Half Hour**
                                          Between 5 and 8 p.m.

The Call to Prayer
It is a good thing to give thanks to the LORD* and to sing praises to your Name, O
    Most High;
To tell of your loving-kindness early in the morning* and of your faithfulness in
    the night season.

Psalm 92:1–2

The Request for Presence
Hear my prayer, O God;* give ear to the words of my mouth.

Psalm 54:2

The Greeting
I will thank you, O LORD my God, with all my heart,* and glorify your Name for
   evermore.

Psalm 86:12

The Hymn
   Now let the earth with joy resound
   And heaven the chant re-echo round;
   Nor heaven nor earth too high can raise
   The great Apostles'—glorious praise!

   Sickness and health your voice obey,
   At your command they go or stay;
   From sin's disease my soul restore,
   In good confirm me more and more.

   So when the world is at its end
   And Christ to judgment shall descend,
   May I be called those joys to see
   Prepared from all eternity.

   Praise to the Father, with the Son
   And Paraclete for ever one:
   To You, O holy Trinity
   Be praise for all eternity.
adapted from THE SHORT BREVIARY

The Refrain for the Vespers Lessons
I will bless the LORD who gives me counsel;* my heart teaches me, night after night.

Psalm 16:7

The Vespers Psalm   **Show Me the Road That I Must Walk**
My spirit faints within me;* my heart within me is desolate.
I remember the time past; I muse upon all your deeds;* I consider the works of
   your hands.
I spread out my hands to you;* my soul gasps to you like a thirsty land.
O LORD, make haste to answer me; my spirit fails me;* do not hide your face from
   me or I shall be like those who go down to the Pit.
Let me hear of your loving-kindness in the morning, for I put my trust in you;*
   show me the road that I must walk, for I lift up my soul to you.

Psalm 143:4–8

The Refrain
I will bless the LORD who gives me counsel;* my heart teaches me, night after night.

The Small Verse
Happy are the people whose strength is in you!* whose hearts are set on the
   pilgrim's way,

For one day in your courts is better than a thousand in my own room,* and to stand at the threshold of the house of my God than to dwell in the tents of the wicked.

Psalm 84:4, 9

The Lord's Prayer

The Prayer Appointed for the Week

Most loving Father, whose will it is for us to give thanks for all things, to fear nothing but the loss of you, and to cast all our care on you who cares for us: Preserve me from faithless fears and worldly anxieties, that no clouds of this mortal life may hide from me the light of that love which is immortal, and which you have manifested to us in your Son Jesus Christ our Lord; who lives and reigns with you, in the unity of the Holy Spirit, one God, now and for ever. *Amen.* †

Concluding Prayers of the Church

Almighty God, by your Holy Spirit you have made us one with your saints in heaven and on earth: grant that in my earthly pilgrimage I may always be supported by this fellowship of love and prayer, and know myself to be surrounded by their witness to your power and mercy. I ask this for the sake of Jesus Christ, in whom all my intercessions are acceptable through the Spirit, and who lives and reigns for ever and ever. *Amen.* †

Save me, O Lord, while I am awake, And keep me while I sleep. That I may wake in Christ and rest in peace.

adapted from The Short Breviary

The Morning Office　　　　**To Be Observed on the Hour or Half Hour Between 6 and 9 a.m.**

The Call to Prayer

Search for the LORD and his strength;* continually seek his face.

Psalm 105:4

The Request for Presence

Show your goodness, O LORD, to those who are good* and to those who are true of heart.

Psalm 125:4

The Greeting

You have set up a banner for those who fear you* . . .
Save us by your right hand and answer us.*

Psalm 60:4–5

The Refrain for the Morning Lessons

Our days are like the grass;* we flourish like a flower of the field;
When the wind goes over it, it is gone,* and its place shall know it no more.

Psalm 103:15–16

A Reading

John's disciples and the Pharisees were keeping a fast, when some people came to
him and said to him, 'Why is it that John's disciples and the disciples of the
Pharisees fast, but your disciples do not?' Jesus replied, 'Surely the bridegroom's attendants cannot fast while the bridegroom is still with them? As long
as they have the bridegroom they cannot fast,. But the time will come when the
bridegroom is taken away from them, and then, on that day, they will fast.'

Mark 2:18–20

The Refrain

Our days are like the grass;* we flourish like a flower of the field;
When the wind goes over it, it is gone,* and its place shall know it no more.

The Morning Psalm   *Whoever Does These Things Shall Never Be Overthrown*

Lord, who may dwell in your tabernacle?* who may abide upon your holy hill?
Whoever leads a blameless life and does what is right,* who speaks the truth from
his heart.
There is no guile upon his tongue; he does no evil to his friend;* he does not heap
contempt upon his neighbor.
In his sight the wicked is rejected,* but he honors those who fear the Lord.
He has sworn to do no wrong* and does not take back his word.
He does not give his money in hope of gain,* nor does he take a bribe against the
innocent.
Whoever does these things* shall never be overthrown.

Psalm 15

The Refrain

Our days are like the grass;* we flourish like a flower of the field;
When the wind goes over it, it is gone,* and its place shall know it no more.

The Small Verse

Lord, have mercy; Christ, have mercy; Lord, have mercy.

The Lord's Prayer

The Prayer Appointed for the Week

Most loving Father, whose will it is for us to give thanks for all things, to fear
nothing but the loss of you, and to cast all our care on you who cares for us:
Preserve me from faithless fears and worldly anxieties, that no clouds of this
mortal life may hide from me the light of that love which is immortal, and
which you have manifested to us in your Son Jesus Christ our Lord; who lives
and reigns with you, in the unity of the Holy Spirit, one God, now and for ever.
Amen. †

The Concluding Prayer of the Church

Lord God, almighty and everlasting Father, you have brought me in safety to this
new day: Preserve me with your mighty power, that I may not fall into sin, nor
be overcome by adversity; and in all I do direct me to the fulfilling of your purpose; through Jesus Christ my Lord. *Amen.* †

The Midday Office   **To Be Observed on the Hour or Half Hour**
Between 11 a.m. and 2 p.m.

The Call to Prayer
Sing to the LORD and bless his Name;* proclaim the good news of his salvation
    from day to day.
Declare his glory among the nations* and his wonders among all peoples.
For great is the LORD and greatly to be praised;* he is more to be feared than
    all gods.

Psalm 96:2–4

The Request for Presence
I have gone astray like a sheep that is lost;* search for your servant, for I do not
    forget your commandments.

Psalm 119:176

The Greeting
When your word goes forth it gives light;* it gives understanding to the simple.

Psalm 119:130

The Refrain for the Midday Lessons
He will not let your foot be moved* and he who watches over you will not
    fall asleep.

Psalm 121:3

A Reading
Make sure that no one captivates you with the empty lure of a 'philosophy' of the
    kind that human beings hand on, based on the principles of this world and not
    on Christ.

Colossians 2:8

The Refrain
He will not let your foot be moved* and he who watches over you will not
    fall asleep.

The Midday Psalm   *The LORD Will Not Abandon His People*
He that planted the ear, does he not hear?* he that formed the eye, does he not see?
He who admonishes the nations, will he not punish?* he who teaches all the
    world, has he no knowledge?
The LORD knows our human thoughts;* how like a puff of wind they are.
Happy are they whom you instruct, O Lord!* whom you teach out of your law;
To give them rest in evil days,* until a pit is dug for the wicked.
For the LORD will not abandon his people,* nor will he forsake his own.
For judgment will again be just,* and all the true of heart will follow it.

Psalm 94:9–15

The Refrain
He will not let your foot be moved* and he who watches over you will not
    fall asleep.

The Cry of the Church
O Lord, hear my prayer and let my cry come to you. Thanks be to God.
The Short Breviary

The Lord's Prayer

The Prayer Appointed for the Week
Most loving Father, whose will it is for us to give thanks for all things, to fear
nothing but the loss of you, and to cast all our care on you who cares for us:
Preserve me from faithless fears and worldly anxieties, that no clouds of this
mortal life may hide from me the light of that love which is immortal, and
which you have manifested to us in your Son Jesus Christ our Lord; who lives
and reigns with you, in the unity of the Holy Spirit, one God, now and for ever.
Amen. †

The Concluding Prayer of the Church
God of mystery, God of love, send your Spirit into our hearts with gifts of wisdom
and peace, fortitude and charity. We long to love and serve you. Faithful God,
make us faithful. This we ask through the intercession of all your saints. *Amen.*
The New Companion to the Breviary

The Vespers Office **To Be Observed on the Hour or Half Hour**
Between 5 and 8 p.m.

The Call to Prayer
Worship the LORD in the beauty of holiness;* let the whole earth tremble before
him.
Psalm 31:3

The Request for Presence
Your word is a lantern to my feet* and a light upon my path.
Accept, O LORD, the willing tribute of my lips,* and teach me your judgments.
Psalm 119:105ff

The Greeting
You, O LORD, are my lamp;* my God, you make my darkness bright.
Psalm 18:29

The Hymn
O brightness of the immortal Father's face,
most holy, heavenly, blessed,
Lord Jesus Christ, in whom truth and grace
are visibly expressed:
The sun is sinking now, and one by one
the lamps of evening shine;
We hymn the Father eternal, and the Son,
and Holy Ghost Divine.

You are worthy at all times to receive
  our hallowed praises, Lord.
O Son of God, be you, in whom we live,
  through all the world adored.
Greek, 3rd C.

The Refrain for the Vespers Lessons
Your love, O Lord, for ever will I sing;* from age to age my mouth will proclaim
  your faithfulness.

Psalm 89:1

The Vespers Psalm *A Broken and Contrite Heart, O God, You Will Not Despise*
Open my lips, O Lord,* and my mouth shall proclaim your praise.
Had you desired it, I would have offered sacrifice,* but you take no delight in
  burnt-offerings.
The sacrifice of God is a troubled spirit;* a broken and contrite heart, O God, you
  will not despise.

Psalm 51:16–18

The Refrain
Your love, O Lord, for ever will I sing;* from age to age my mouth will proclaim
  your faithfulness.

The Cry of the Church
Lord, have mercy on us. Christ, have mercy on us. Lord, have mercy on us.

The Lord's Prayer

The Prayer Appointed for the Week
Most loving Father, whose will it is for us to give thanks for all things, to fear
  nothing but the loss of you, and to cast all our care on you who cares for us:
  Preserve me from faithless fears and worldly anxieties, that no clouds of this
  mortal life may hide from me the light of that love which is immortal, and
  which you have manifested to us in your Son Jesus Christ our Lord; who lives
  and reigns with you, in the unity of the Holy Spirit, one God, now and for ever.
  Amen. †

The Concluding Prayer of the Church
Protect me, Lord, as I stay awake; watch over me as I sleep, that awake I may
  watch with Christ, and asleep, rest in his peace. *Amen.*

The Morning Office   **To Be Observed on the Hour or Half Hour
Between 6 and 9 a.m.**

The Call to Prayer
Love the Lord, all you who worship him;* the Lord protects the faithful, but
  repays to the full those who act haughtily.

Psalm 31:23

The Request for Presence
O LORD, I call to you; my Rock, do not be deaf to my cry;* lest, if you do not hear
me, I become like those who go down to the Pit.

Psalm 28:1

The Greeting
Your way, O God, is holy;* who is as great as our God?

Psalm 77:13

The Refrain for the Morning Lessons
Protect my life and deliver me;* let me not be put to shame, for I have trusted in
you.

Psalm 25:19

A Reading
. . . They made their way through Galilee; and he did not want anyone to know,
because he was instructing his disciples; he was telling them, 'The Son of man
will be delivered into the power of men; they will put him to death; and three
days after he has been put to death he will rise again.' But they did not understand what he said and were afraid to ask him.

Mark 9:30–32

The Refrain
Protect my life and deliver me;* let me not be put to shame, for I have trusted in
you.

The Morning Psalm   *In the Shadow of Your Wings Will I Take Refuge*
Be merciful to me, O God, be merciful, for I have taken refuge in you;* in the
shadow of your wings will I take refuge until this time of trouble has gone by.
I will call upon the Most High God,* the God who maintains my cause.
He will send from heaven and save me; he will confound those who trample upon
me;* God will send forth his love and his faithfulness.

Psalm 57:1–3

The Refrain
Protect my life and deliver me;* let me not be put to shame, for I have trusted in
you.

The Cry of the Church
In the evening, in the morning, and at noonday, I will complain and lament, and
he will hear my voice.

Psalm 55:18

The Lord's Prayer

The Prayer Appointed for the Week
Most loving Father, whose will it is for us to give thanks for all things, to fear
nothing but the loss of you, and to cast all our care on you who cares for us:
Preserve me from faithless fears and worldly anxieties, that no clouds of this
mortal life may hide from me the light of that love which is immortal, and

which you have manifested to us in your Son Jesus Christ our Lord; who lives and reigns with you, in the unity of the Holy Spirit, one God, now and for ever. *Amen.* †

The Concluding Prayer of the Church
Lord God, almighty and everlasting Father, you have brought me in safety to this new day: Preserve me with your mighty power, that I may not fall into sin, nor be overcome by adversity; and in all I do direct me to the fulfilling of your purpose; through Jesus Christ my Lord. *Amen.* †

The Midday Office   **To Be Observed on the Hour or Half Hour**
Between 11 a.m. and 2 p.m.

The Call to Prayer
Sing to the LORD with thanksgiving;* make music to our God upon the harp.
Psalm 147:7

The Request for Presence
Hear the voice of my prayer when I cry out to you,* when I lift up my hands to your holy of holies.
Psalm 28:2

The Greeting
You are the LORD, most high over all the earth;* you are exalted far above all gods.
Psalm 97:9

The Refrain for the Midday Lessons
Tell it out among all the nations: "The LORD is King!* he has made the world so firm that it cannot be moved; he will judge all the peoples with equity."
Psalm 96:10

A Reading
With you is Wisdom, she who knows your works, she who was present when you made the world; she understands what is pleasing in your eyes and what agrees with your commandments. Dispatch her from the holy heavens, send her forth from your throne of glory to help me and to toil with me and teach me what is pleasing to you; since she knows and understands everything, she will guide me prudently in my actions and will protect me with her glory. Then all I do will be acceptable . . .
Wisdom 9:9–12

The Refrain
Tell it out among all the nations: "The LORD is King!* he has made the world so firm that it cannot be moved; he will judge all the peoples with equity."

The Midday Psalm   ***Righteousness and Justice Are the Foundations of His Throne***
The LORD is King; let the earth rejoice;* let the multitude of the isles be glad.
Clouds and darkness are round about him,* righteousness and justice are the foundations of his throne.

A fire goes before him* and burns up his enemies on every side.
His lightnings light up the world;* the earth sees it and is afraid.
The mountains melt like wax at the presence of the LORD,* at the presence of the
Lord of the whole earth.
The heavens declare his righteousness,* and all the peoples see his glory.

Psalm 97:1–6

The Refrain
Tell it out among all the nations: "The LORD is King!* he has made the world so
firm that it cannot be moved; he will judge all the peoples with equity."

The Small Verse
Happy are the people whose strength is in you!* whose hearts are set on the
pilgrims' way,
For one day in your courts is better than a thousand in my own room,* and to
stand at the threshold of the house of my God than to dwell in the tents of the
wicked.

Psalm 84:4, 9

The Lord's Prayer

The Prayer Appointed for the Week
Most loving Father, whose will it is for us to give thanks for all things, to fear
nothing but the loss of you, and to cast all our care on you who cares for us:
Preserve me from faithless fears and worldly anxieties, that no clouds of this
mortal life may hide from me the light of that love which is immortal, and
which you have manifested to us in your Son Jesus Christ our Lord; who lives
and reigns with you, in the unity of the Holy Spirit, one God, now and for ever.
Amen. †

The Concluding Prayer of the Church
Let us bless the Lord God living and true! Let us always render him praise, glory,
honor, blessing, and all good things! Amen. Amen. So be it! So be it!

St. Francis of Assisi

The Vespers Office　　　　**To Be Observed on the Hour or Half Hour
Between 5 and 8 p.m.**

The Call to Prayer
Sing to God, O kingdoms of the earth;* sing praises to the Lord.
He rides in the heavens, the ancient heavens;* he sends forth his voice, his mighty
voice.

Psalm 68:33–34

The Request for Presence
Protect me, O God, for I take refuge in you;* I have said to the LORD, "You are my
Lord, my good above all other."

Psalm 16:1

The Greeting
Praise God from whom all blessings flow; Praise Him all creatures here below;
Praise Him above, you heavenly hosts; Praise Father, Son, and Holy Ghost.

Doxology

The Hymn
Eternal Ruler of the ceaseless round
    of circling planets singing on their way,
Guide of the nations from the night profound
    into the glory of the perfect day;
Rule in our hearts, that we may ever be
    guided and strengthened and upheld by thee.

We would be one in hatred of all wrong,
    one in the love of all things sweet and fair,
One with the joy that breaks into song,
    and with the grief that trembles into prayer;
One in the power that makes your children free
    to follow truth, and thus to follow thee.

John Chadwick

The Refrain for the Vespers Lessons
I will bear witness that the LORD is righteous;* I will praise the Name of the LORD
Most High.

Psalm 7:18

The Vespers Psalm   *Turn Again to Your Rest, O My Soul*
The LORD watches over the innocent;* I was brought very low, and he helped me.
Turn again to your rest, O my soul,* for the LORD has treated you well.
For you have rescued my life from death,* my eyes from tears, and my feet from
    stumbling.
I will walk in the presence of the LORD* in the land of the living.

Psalm 116:5–8

The Refrain
I will bear witness that the LORD is righteous;* I will praise the Name of the LORD
Most High.

The Cry of the Church
Even so, come Lord Jesus!

The Lord's Prayer

The Prayer Appointed for the Week
Most loving Father, whose will it is for us to give thanks for all things, to fear
    nothing but the loss of you, and to cast all our care on you who cares for us:
    Preserve me from faithless fears and worldly anxieties, that no clouds of this
    mortal life may hide from me the light of that love which is immortal, and
    which you have manifested to us in your Son Jesus Christ our Lord; who lives

and reigns with you, in the unity of the Holy Spirit, one God, now and for ever.
Amen. †

The Concluding Prayer of the Church
Spirit of God, promise of Jesus, come to our help at the close of this day. Come
with forgiveness and healing love. Come with life and hope. Come with all
that we need to continue in the way of your truth. So may we praise you in the
Trinity forever. *Amen.*

The New Companion to the Breviary

The Morning Office   **To Be Observed on the Hour or Half Hour Between 6 and 9 a.m.**

The Call to Prayer
Wake up, my spirit; awake lute and harp;* I myself will waken the dawn.

Psalm 57:8

The Request for Presence
You are the Lord; do not withhold your compassion from me;* let your love and
your faithfulness keep me safe for ever.

Psalm 40:12

The Greeting
My heart is firmly fixed, O God, my heart is fixed;* I will sing and make melody.

Psalm 57:7

The Refrain for the Morning Lessons
Cast your burden upon the Lord, and he will sustain you;* he will never let the
righteous stumble.

Psalm 55:24

A Reading
Jesus said: "Now the hour has come for the Son of man to be glorified. In all truth I
tell you, unless a wheat grain falls on earth and dies, it remains only a single
grain; but if it dies, it yields a rich harvest."

John 12:23–24

The Refrain
Cast your burden upon the Lord, and he will sustain you;* he will never let the
righteous stumble.

The Morning Psalm   *May the Lord Strengthen You Out of Zion*
May the Lord answer you in the day of trouble,* the Name of the God of Jacob
defend you;
Send you help from his holy place* and strengthen you out of Zion;
Remember all your offerings* and accept your burnt sacrifice;
Grant you your heart's desire* and prosper all your plans.

We will shout for joy at your victory and triumph in the Name of our God;* may the LORD grant all your requests.

Psalm 20:1–5

The Refrain
Cast your burden upon the LORD, and he will sustain you;* he will never let the righteous stumble.

The Small Verse
My soul thirsts for the strong, living God and all that is within me cries out to him.

The Lord's Prayer

The Prayer Appointed for the Week
Most loving Father, whose will it is for us to give thanks for all things, to fear nothing but the loss of you, and to cast all our care on you who cares for us: Preserve me from faithless fears and worldly anxieties, that no clouds of this mortal life may hide from me the light of that love which is immortal, and which you have manifested to us in your Son Jesus Christ our Lord; who lives and reigns with you, in the unity of the Holy Spirit, one God, now and for ever. *Amen.* †

The Concluding Prayer of the Church
Lord God, almighty and everlasting Father, you have brought me in safety to this new day: Preserve me with your mighty power, that I may not fall into sin, nor be overcome by adversity; and in all I do direct me to the fulfilling of your purpose; through Jesus Christ my Lord. *Amen.* †

The Midday Office   **To Be Observed on the Hour or Half Hour**
Between 11 a.m. and 2 p.m.

The Call to Prayer
"Come now, let us reason together," says the LORD.

Isaiah 1:18, KJV

The Request for Presence
Awake, O my God, decree justice;* let the assembly of peoples gather around you. Let the malice of the wicked come to an end, but establish the righteous;* for you test the mind and heart, O righteous God.

Psalm 7:7, 10

The Greeting
Deliver me, O LORD, by your hand* from those whose portion in life is this world.

Psalm 17:14

The Refrain for the Midday Lessons
Righteousness shall go before him,* and peace shall be a pathway for his feet.

Psalm 85:13

A Reading
His commandment is this, that we should believe in the name of his Son Jesus
   Christ and that we should love each other as he commanded us. Whoever
   keeps his commandments remains in God, and God in him. And this is the
   proof that he remains in us: the Spirit that he has given us.

I John 3:23–24

The Refrain
Righteousness shall go before him,* and peace shall be a pathway for his feet.

The Midday Psalm   *You Lengthen My Stride Beneath Me*
It is God who girds me about with strength* and makes my way secure.
He makes me sure-footed like a deer* and lets me stand firm on the heights.
He trains my hands for battle* and my arms for bending even a bow of bronze.
You have given me your shield of victory;* your right hand also sustains me; your
   loving care makes me great.
.You lengthen my stride beneath me,* and my ankles do not give way.

Psalm 18:33–37

The Refrain
Righteousness shall go before him,* and peace shall be a pathway for his feet.

The Cry of the Church
Lord, have mercy on us. Christ, have mercy on us. Lord, have mercy on us.

The Lord's Prayer

The Prayer Appointed for the Week
Most loving Father, whose will it is for us to give thanks for all things, to fear
   nothing but the loss of you, and to cast all our care on you who cares for us:
   Preserve me from faithless fears and worldly anxieties, that no clouds of this
   mortal life may hide from me the light of that love which is immortal, and
   which you have manifested to us in your Son Jesus Christ our Lord; who lives
   and reigns with you, in the unity of the Holy Spirit, one God, now and for ever.
   Amen. †

The Concluding Prayer of the Church
Renew in my heart, O God, the gift of your Holy Spirit, so that I may love you
   fully in all that I do and love all others as Christ loves me. May all that I do proclaim the good news that you are God with us. *Amen.* †

The Vespers Office   **To Be Observed on the Hour or Half Hour**
                                          Between 5 and 8 p.m.

The Call to Prayer
O tarry and await the LORD's pleasure; be strong, and he shall comfort your heart;*
   wait patiently for the LORD.

Psalm 27:18

The Request for Presence
Open my eyes, that I may see* the wonders of your law.
Psalm 119:18

The Greeting
Your statutes have been like songs to me* wherever I have lived as a stranger.
I remember your Name in the night, O LORD,* and dwell upon your law.
This is how it has been with me,* because I have kept your commandments.
Psalm 119:54–56

The Hymn   ***Jubilate! Amen!***
Now on land and sea descending,
Brings the night its peace profound;
Let our vesper hymn be blending
With holy calm around.
      Jubilate! Jubilate!
      Jubilate! Amen!
Let our vesper hymn be blending
With holy calm around.

Soon as dies the sunset glory,
Stars of heaven shine out above,
Telling still the ancient story,
Their Creator's changeless love.
      Jubilate! Jubilate!
      Jubilate! Amen!
Telling still the ancient story,
Their Creator's changeless love.

Now, our wants and burdens leaving
To God's care who cares for all,
Cease we fearing, cease we grieving;
Touched by God our burdens fall.
      Jubilate! Jubilate!
      Jubilate! Amen!
Cease we fearing, cease we grieving;
Touched by God our burdens fall.

As the darkness deepens o'er us,
Lo! Eternal stars arise;
Hope and faith and love rise glorious,
Shining in the Spirit's skies.
      Jubilate! Jubilate!
      Jubilate! Amen!
Hope and faith and love rise glorious,
Shining in the Spirit's skies.
Samuel Longfellow

The Refrain for the Vespers Lessons
'I am the Alpha and the Omega,' says the Lord God, who is, who was, and who is
to come, the Almighty.

Revelation 1:8

The Vespers Psalm   *The LORD Is My Shepherd*
The LORD is my shepherd;* I shall not be in want.
He makes me lie down in green pastures* and leads me beside still waters.
He revives my soul* and guides me along right pathways for his Name's sake.
Though I walk through the valley of the shadow of death, I shall fear no evil;* for
    you are with me; your rod and your staff, they comfort me.
You spread a table before me in the presence of those who trouble me;* you have
    anointed my head with oil, and my cup is running over.
Surely your goodness and mercy shall follow me all the days of my life,* and I will
    dwell in the house of the LORD for ever.

Psalm 23

The Refrain
'I am the Alpha and the Omega,' says the Lord God, who is, who was, and who is
to come, the Almighty.

The Cry of the Church
Be, Lord, my helper and forsake me not. Do not despise me, O God, my savior.

THE SHORT BREVIARY

The Lord's Prayer

The Prayer Appointed for the Week
Most loving Father, whose will it is for us to give thanks for all things, to fear nothing
    but the loss of you, and to cast all our care on you who cares for us: Preserve me
    from faithless fears and worldly anxieties, that no clouds of this mortal life may
    hide from me the light of that love which is immortal, and which you have mani-
    fested to us in your Son Jesus Christ our Lord; who lives and reigns with you, in
    the unity of the Holy Spirit, one God, now and for ever. *Amen.* †

The Concluding Prayer of the Church
Lord Jesus Christ, you said to your apostles, "Peace I give to you; my own peace I
    leave with you." Regard not my sins, but my faith, and give to me a place in the
    peace and unity of that heavenly City, where with the Father and the Holy
    Spirit you live and reign, now and forever. *Amen.* †

The Morning Office   **To Be Observed on the Hour or Half Hour**
Between 6 and 9 a.m.

The Call to Prayer
Come now and see the works of God,* how wonderful he is in his doing toward
    all people.

Psalm 66:4

The Request for Presence
Satisfy us by your loving-kindness in the morning;* so shall we rejoice and be glad
all the days of our life.

Psalm 90:14

The Greeting
Save us, O LORD our God, and gather us from among the nations,* that we may
give thanks to your holy Name and glory in your praise.

Psalm 106:47

The Refrain for the Morning Lessons
Mercy and truth have met together;* righteousness and peace have kissed
each other.

Psalm 85:10

A Reading
Then Jesus said to his disciples, 'If anyone wants to be a follower of mine, let him
renounce himself and take up his cross and follow me. Anyone who wants to
save his life will lose it; but anyone who loses his life for my sake will find it.'

Matthew 16:24–25

The Refrain
Mercy and truth have met together;* righteousness and peace have kissed
each other.

The Morning Psalm   *We Walk, O LORD, in the Light of Your Presence*
Righteousness and justice are the foundations of your throne;* love and truth go
before your face.
Happy are the people who know the festal shout!* they walk, O LORD, in the light
of your presence.
They rejoice daily in your Name;* they are jubilant in your righteousness.
For you are the glory of their strength,* and by your favor our might is exalted.
Truly, the LORD is our ruler;* the Holy One of Israel is our King.

Psalm 89:14–18

The Refrain
Mercy and truth have met together;* righteousness and peace have kissed
each other.

The Cry of the Church
Lord, have mercy on us. Christ, have mercy on us. Lord, have mercy on us.

The Lord's Prayer

The Prayer Appointed for the Week
Most loving Father, whose will it is for us to give thanks for all things, to fear
nothing but the loss of you, and to cast all our care on you who cares for us:
Preserve me from faithless fears and worldly anxieties, that no clouds of this

mortal life may hide from me the light of that love which is immortal, and which you have manifested to us in your Son Jesus Christ our Lord; who lives and reigns with you, in the unity of the Holy Spirit, one God, now and for ever. *Amen.* †

The Concluding Prayer of the Church

Lord God, almighty and everlasting Father, you have brought me in safety to this new day: Preserve me with your mighty power, that I may not fall into sin, nor be overcome by adversity; and in all I do direct me to the fulfilling of your purpose; through Jesus Christ my Lord. *Amen.* †

The Midday Office   **To Be Observed on the Hour or Half Hour Between 11 a.m. and 2 p.m.**

The Call to Prayer

God is the LORD; he has shined upon us;* form a procession with branches up to the horns of the altar.

Psalm 118:27

The Request for Presence

Set watch before my mouth, O LORD, and guard the door of my lips.

Psalm 141:3

The Greeting

Remember your word to your servant,* because you have given me hope.
This is my comfort in my trouble,* that your promise gives me life.

Psalm 119:49–50

The Refrain for the Midday Lessons

For God alone my soul in silence waits;* from him comes my salvation.

Psalm 62:1

A Reading

. . . Teach each other, and advise each other, in all wisdom. With gratitude in your hearts sing psalms and hymns and inspired songs to God; and whatever you say or do, let it be in the name of the Lord Jesus, in thanksgiving to God the Father through him.

Colossians 3:16–17

The Refrain

For God alone my soul in silence waits;* from him comes my salvation.

The Midday Psalm   *With You Is the Well of Life*

Your love, O LORD, reaches to the heavens,* and your faithfulness to the clouds.
Your righteousness is like the strong mountains, your justice like the great deep;* you save both man and beast, O LORD.
How priceless is your love, O God!* your people take refuge under the shadow of your wings.

Continue your loving-kindness to those who know you,* and your favor to those who are true of heart.

Psalm 36:5–7, 10

The Refrain
For God alone my soul in silence waits;* from him comes my salvation.

The Cry of the Church
In the evening, in the morning and at noonday, I will complain and lament,* and he will hear my voice.

Psalm 55:18

The Lord's Prayer

The Prayer Appointed for the Week
Most loving Father, whose will it is for us to give thanks for all things, to fear nothing but the loss of you, and to cast all our care on you who cares for us: Preserve me from faithless fears and worldly anxieties, that no clouds of this mortal life may hide from me the light of that love which is immortal, and which you have manifested to us in your Son Jesus Christ our Lord; who lives and reigns with you, in the unity of the Holy Spirit, one God, now and for ever. *Amen.* †

The Concluding Prayer of the Church
Almighty God, whose most dear Son went not up to the joy before he first suffered pain, and did not enter into glory before he was crucified: Mercifully grant that I, walking in the way of the cross, may find it to be none other than the way of life and peace; through Jesus Christ your Son my Lord. *Amen.* †

The Vespers Office   **To Be Observed on the Hour or Half Hour Between 5 and 8 p.m.**

The Call to Prayer
Praise the Lord, all you nations;* laud him, all you peoples.
For his loving-kindness toward us is great,* and the faithfulness of the Lord endures for ever.

Psalm 117:1–2

The Request for Presence
Help us, O God our Savior, for the glory of your Name;* deliver us and forgive us our sins, for your Name's sake.

Psalm 79:9

The Greeting
You are to be praised, O God, in Zion . . . To you that hear prayer shall all flesh come,* because of their transgressions.

Psalm 65:1–2

The Hymn

The day is past and over; all thanks, O Lord, to thee!
I ask that offenseless now the hours of dark may be,
O Jesus, keep me in your sight, and guard me through the coming night.

The joys of day are over; I lift my heart to thee,
and ask you that sinless now the hours of dark may be.
O Jesus, make their darkness light, and guard me through the coming night.

The toils of day are over; I raise my hymn to thee,
and ask that free from terrors now the hours of dark may be.
O Jesus, keep me in your sight, and guard me through the coming night.

Please be my soul's preserver, O God, for you do know
how many are the perils through which I have to go.
Lord Jesus Christ, O hear my call, save and guard me from them all.

Greek, 6th C.

The Refrain for the Vespers Lesson

Your love, O Lord, reaches to the heavens,* and your faithfulness to the clouds.

Psalm 36:5

The Vespers Psalm   The Lord Shall Preserve You

I lift up my eyes to the hills;* from where is my help to come?
My help comes from the Lord,* the maker of heaven and earth.
He will not let your foot be moved* and he who watches over you will not
    fall asleep.
Behold, he who keeps watch over Israel* shall neither slumber nor sleep;
The Lord himself watches over you;* the Lord is your shade at your right hand,
So that the sun shall not strike you by day,* nor the moon by night.
The Lord shall preserve you from all evil;* it is he who shall keep you safe.
The Lord shall watch over your going out and your coming in,* from this time
    forth for evermore.

Psalm 121

The Refrain

Your love, O Lord, reaches to the heavens,* and your faithfulness to the clouds.

The Small Verse

The people that walked in darkness have seen a great light; on the inhabitants of a
    country in shadow dark as death light has blazed forth.

Isaiah 9:1

The Lord's Prayer

The Prayer Appointed for the Week

Most loving Father, whose will it is for us to give thanks for all things, to fear nothing
    but the loss of you, and to cast all our care on you who cares for us: Preserve me
    from faithless fears and worldly anxieties, that no clouds of this mortal life may

hide from me the light of that love which is immortal, and which you have manifested to us in your Son Jesus Christ our Lord; who lives and reigns with you, in the unity of the Holy Spirit, one God, now and for ever. *Amen.* †

Concluding Prayers of the Church
Lord Jesus Christ, by your death you took away the sting of death: Grant me so to follow in faith where you have led the way, that I may at length fall asleep peacefully in you and wake up in your likeness; for your tender mercies' sake. *Amen.* †

May the souls of the faithful departed, through the mercy of God, rest in eternal peace. *Amen.*

The Morning Office   **To Be Observed on the Hour or Half Hour Between 6 and 9 a.m.**

The Call to Prayer
I will call upon God, and the LORD will deliver me.
In the evening, in the morning, and at the noonday, he will hear my voice.
He will bring me safely back . . . God who is enthroned of old, will hear me. †

The Request for Presence
Show us your mercy, O LORD,* and grant us your salvation.
Psalm 85:7

The Greeting
Happy are those whom you choose and draw to your courts to dwell there!* they will be satisfied by the beauty of your house, by the holiness of your temple.
Psalm 65:4

The Refrain for the Morning Lessons
Happy are the people whose strength is in you!* whose hearts are set on the pilgrims' way.
Psalm 84:4

A Reading
Filled with the Holy Spirit, Jesus left the Jordan and was led by the Spirit into the desert, for forty days being put to the test by the devil. During that time he ate nothing and at the end he was hungry. Then the devil said to him, 'If you are the Son of God, tell this stone to turn into a loaf.' But Jesus replied, 'Scripture says: *Human beings live not on bread alone.*' Then leading him to a height, the devil showed him in a moment of time all the kingdoms of the world and said to him, 'I will give you all this power and their splendor, for it has been handed over to me, for me to give to anyone I choose. Do homage, then, to me and it shall all be yours.' But Jesus answered him, 'Scripture says: *You must do homage to the Lord your God, him alone you must serve.*' Then he led him to Jerusalem and set him on the parapet of the Temple. 'If you are Son of God,' he said to him, 'throw yourself down from here, for scripture says: *He has given his angels orders*

about you, to guard you and again: *They will carry you in their arms in case you trip over a stone.'* But Jesus answered him, 'Scripture says: *Do not put the Lord your God to the test.'* Having exhausted every way of putting him to the test, the devil left him, until the opportune moment.

Luke 4:1–13

The Refrain
Happy are the people whose strength is in you!* whose hearts are set on the pilgrims' way.

The Morning Psalm   To You, O My Strength, Will I Sing
For my part, I will sing of your strength;* I will celebrate your love in the morning;
For you have become my stronghold,* a refuge in the day of my trouble.
To you, O my Strength, will I sing;* for you, O God, are my stronghold and my merciful God.

Psalm 59:18–20

The Refrain
Happy are the people whose strength is in you!* whose hearts are set on the pilgrims' way.

The Small Verse
My soul has a desire and longing for the courts of the LORD;* my heart and my flesh rejoice in the living God.

Psalm 84:1

The Lord's Prayer

The Prayer Appointed for the Week
Most loving Father, whose will it is for us to give thanks for all things, to fear nothing but the loss of you, and to cast all our care on you who cares for us: Preserve me from faithless fears and worldly anxieties, that no clouds of this mortal life may hide from me the light of that love which is immortal, and which you have manifested to us in your Son Jesus Christ our Lord; who lives and reigns with you, in the unity of the Holy Spirit, one God, now and for ever. *Amen.* †

The Concluding Prayer of the Church
Lord God, almighty and everlasting Father, you have brought me in safety to this new day: Preserve me with your mighty power, that I may not fall into sin, nor be overcome by adversity; and in all I do direct me to the fulfilling of your purpose; through Jesus Christ my Lord. *Amen.* †

The Midday Office   To Be Observed on the Hour or Half Hour
Between 11 a.m. and 2 p.m.

The Call to Prayer
How good it is to sing praises to our God!* how pleasant it is to honor him with praise!

Psalm 147:1

The Request for Presence
Remember me, O Lord, with the favor you have for your people,* and visit me
　　with your saving help;
That I may see the prosperity of your elect and be glad with the gladness of your
　　people,* that I may glory with your inheritance.

Psalm 106:4–5

The Greeting
In you, O Lord, have I taken refuge;* let me never be ashamed.

Psalm 71:1

The Refrain for the Midday Lessons
Your statutes have been like songs to me* wherever I have lived like a stranger.

Psalm 119:54

A Reading
I am coming to put you on trial and I shall be a ready witness against sorcerers,
　　adulterers, perjurers, and against those who oppress the wage-earner, the
　　widow and the orphan, and who rob the foreigner of his rights and do not
　　respect me, says Yahweh Sabaoth.

Malachi 3:5

The Refrain
Your statutes have been like songs to me* wherever I have lived like a stranger.

The Midday Psalm
The Lord loveth His foundation upon the holy mountains,* the gates of Sion more
　　than all the tents of Jacob.
Glorious things are said of thee,* O city of God!
I will number Rahab and Babylon* among those avowing Me;
Behold the Philistines and Tyre and the people of Ethiopia* are gathered there.
Shall it not be said on Sion: "This man and that is born therein,* and the Most High
　　Himself hath founded her?"
In His book the Lord recordeth nations and princes* who hail from there.
This is the joyous cry of all: "My dwelling is in thee!"

Psalm 86, The Short Breviary

The Refrain
Your statutes have been like songs to me* wherever I have lived like a stranger.

The Cry of the Church
Lord, have mercy on us. Christ, have mercy on us. Lord, have mercy on us.

The Lord's Prayer

The Prayer Appointed for the Week
Most loving Father, whose will it is for us to give thanks for all things, to fear nothing
　　but the loss of you, and to cast all our care on you who cares for us: Preserve me

from faithless fears and worldly anxieties, that no clouds of this mortal life may hide from me the light of that love which is immortal, and which you have manifested to us in your Son Jesus Christ our Lord; who lives and reigns with you, in the unity of the Holy Spirit, one God, now and for ever. *Amen.* †

The Concluding Prayer of the Church
Almighty God, who after the creation of the world rested from all your works and sanctified a day of rest for all your creatures: Grant that I, putting away all earthly anxieties, may be duly prepared for the service of public worship, and grant as well that my Sabbath upon earth may be a preparation for the eternal rest promised to your people in heaven; through Jesus Christ our Lord. *Amen.* †

The Vespers Office   **To Be Observed on the Hour or Half Hour Between 5 and 8 p.m.**

The Call to Prayer
Let the Name of the LORD be blessed,* from this time forth for evermore.
From the rising of the sun to its going down* let the Name of the LORD be praised.
Psalm 113:2–3

The Request for Presence
Let my cry come before you, O LORD;* give me understanding, according to
    your word.
Let my supplication come before you;* deliver me, according to your promise.
Psalm 119:169–170

The Greeting
The Lord is in his holy temple; Let all the earth keep silence before him. *Amen.*

The Hymn   *A Story to Tell the Nations*
We've a story to tell to the nations,
That shall turn their hearts to right,
A story of truth and mercy,
A story of peace and light.
For the darkness shall turn to dawning,
And the dawning to noonday bright;
And Christ's great kingdom shall come to earth,
The kingdom of love and light.

We've a song to be sung to the nations,
That shall lift their hearts to the Lord,
A song that shall conquer evil
And shatter spear and sword.
For the darkness shall turn to dawning,
And the dawning to noonday bright;
And Christ's great kingdom shall come to earth,
The kingdom of love and light.

We've a Savior to show the nations,
Who the path of sorrow has trod,
That all of the world's peoples
Might come to the truth of God.
For the darkness shall turn to dawning,
And the dawning to noonday bright;
And Christ's great kingdom shall come to earth,
The kingdom of love and light.

H. Ernest Nichol

The Refrain for the Vespers Lessons
Turn again to your rest, O my soul,* for the LORD has treated you well.

Psalm 116:6

The Vespers Psalm   *You Will Arise and Have Compassion on Zion*
You will arise and have compassion on Zion, for it is time to have mercy upon
    her;* indeed, the appointed time has come.
For your servants love her very rubble,* and are moved to pity even for her dust.
The nations shall fear your Name, O LORD,* and all the kings of the earth your
    glory.
For the LORD will build up Zion,* and his glory will appear.
He will look with favor on the prayer of the homeless;* he will not despise their
    plea.

Psalm 102:13–17

The Refrain
Turn again to your rest, O my soul,* for the LORD has treated you well.

The Small Verse
Keep me, Lord, as the apple of your eye and carry me under the shadow of your
    wings.

The Lord's Prayer

The Prayer Appointed for the Week
Most loving Father, whose will it is for us to give thanks for all things, to fear nothing
    but the loss of you, and to cast all our care on you who cares for us: Preserve me
    from faithless fears and worldly anxieties, that no clouds of this mortal life may
    hide from me the light of that love which is immortal, and which you have mani-
    fested to us in your Son Jesus Christ our Lord; who lives and reigns with you, in
    the unity of the Holy Spirit, one God, now and for ever. *Amen.* †

The Concluding Prayer of the Church
Almighty God, who after the creation of the world rested from all your works and
    sanctified a day of rest for all your creatures: Grant that I, putting away all
    earthly anxieties, may be duly prepared for the service of public worship, and
    grant as well that my Sabbath upon the earth may be a preparation for the eternal
    rest promised to your people in heaven; through Jesus Christ our Lord. *Amen.* †

The Morning Office   **To Be Observed on the Hour or Half Hour**
                                          Between 6 and 9 a.m.

The Call to Prayer
Ascribe to the Lord, you families of the peoples;* ascribe to the Lord honor and
    power.
Ascribe to the Lord the honor due his Name;* bring offerings and come into his
    courts.
Worship the Lord in the beauty of holiness;* let the whole world tremble before
    him.
                                                                Psalm 96:7–9

The Request for Presence
Send out your light and your truth, that they may lead me,* and bring me to your
    holy hill and to your dwelling;
That I may go to the altar of God, to the God of my joy and gladness;* and on the
    harp I will give thanks to you, O God my God.
                                                                Psalm 43:3–4

The Greeting
As the deer longs for the water-brooks,* so longs my soul for you, O God.
My soul is athirst for God, athirst for the living God.
                                                                Psalm 42:1–2

The Refrain for the Morning Lessons
For who is God, but the Lord?* who is the Rock except our God?
                                                                Psalm 18:32

A Reading
Jesus taught us, saying: "Be careful not to parade your uprightness in public to
    attract attention; otherwise you will lose all reward from your Father in
    heaven."
                                                                Matthew 6:1

The Refrain
For who is God, but the Lord?* who is the Rock except our God?

The Morning Psalm   *I Will Offer the Sacrifice of Thanksgiving*
O Lord, I am your servant;* I am your servant and the child of your handmaid;
    you have freed me from my bonds.
I will offer you the sacrifice of thanksgiving* and call upon the Name of the
    Lord.
I will fulfill my vows to the Lord* in the presence of all his people,
In the courts of the Lord's house,* in the midst of you, O Jerusalem. Hallelujah!
                                                                Psalm 116:14–17

The Refrain
For who is God, but the Lord?* who is the Rock except our God?

The Cry of the Church
Lord, have mercy on us. Christ, have mercy on us. Lord, have mercy on us.

The Lord's Prayer

The Prayer Appointed for the Week
O God, who before the passion of your only-begotten Son revealed his glory upon
the holy mountain: Grant that I, beholding by faith the light of his countenance, may be strengthened to bear my cross, and be changed into his likeness
from glory to glory; through Jesus Christ my Lord, who lives and reigns with
you and the Holy Spirit, one God, for ever and ever. *Amen.* †

The Concluding Prayer of the Church
Lord God, almighty and everlasting Father, you have brought me in safety to this
new day: Preserve me with your mighty power, that I may not fall into sin, nor
be overcome by adversity; and in all I do direct me to the fulfilling of your purpose; through Jesus Christ my Lord. *Amen.* †

The Midday Office   **To Be Observed on the Hour or Half Hour
Between 11 a.m. and 2 p.m.**

The Call to Prayer
Let all those whom the LORD has redeemed proclaim* that he redeemed them
from the hand of the foe.
He gathered them out of the lands;* from the east and from the west, from the
north and from the south.
He put their feet on a straight path* to go to a city where they might dwell.
Let them give thanks to the LORD for his mercy* and the wonders he does for his
children.

Psalm 107:2–3, 7–8

The Request for Presence
Let all who seek you rejoice in you and be glad;* let those who love your
salvation continually say, "Great is the LORD!"
Though I am poor and afflicted,* the LORD will have regard for me.
You are my helper and my deliverer;* do not tarry, O my God.

Psalm 40:17ff

The Greeting
I love you, O LORD my strength,* O LORD my stronghold, my crag, and my haven.
My God, my rock in whom I put my trust,* my shield, the horn of my salvation,
and my refuge; you are worthy of praise.

Psalm 18:1–2

The Refrain for the Midday Lessons
I will fulfill my vows to the LORD* in the presence of all his people.

Psalm 116:16

A Reading

Let us keep our eyes fixed on Jesus, who leads us in our faith and brings it to perfection: for the sake of the joy which lay ahead of him, he endured the cross, disregarding the shame of it, and *has taken his seat at the right* of God's throne. Think of the way he persevered against such opposition from sinners and then you will not lose heart and come to grief. In the fight against sin, you have not yet had to keep fighting to the point of bloodshed.

Hebrews 12:2–4

The Refrain

I will fulfill my vows to the Lord* in the presence of all his people.

The Midday Psalm   *The Fool Has Said, "There Is No God"*

The fool has said in his heart, "There is no God."* All are corrupt and commit abominable acts; there is none who does any good.

God looks down from heaven upon us all,* to see if there is any who is wise, if there is one who seeks after God.

Every one has proved faithless; all alike have turned bad;* there is none who does good; no, not one.

Have they no knowledge, those evildoers* who eat up my people like bread and do not call upon God?

See how greatly they tremble, such trembling as never was;* for God has scattered the bones of the enemy; they are put to shame, because God has rejected them.

Oh, that Israel's deliverance would come out of Zion!* when God restores the fortunes of his people Jacob will rejoice and Israel be glad.

Psalm 53

The Refrain

I will fulfill my vows to the Lord* in the presence of all his people.

The Cry of the Church

O God, come to my assistance! O Lord, make haste to help me!

The Lord's Prayer

The Prayer Appointed for the Week

O God, who before the passion of your only-begotten Son revealed his glory upon the holy mountain: Grant that I, beholding by faith the light of his countenance, may be strengthened to bear my cross, and be changed into his likeness from glory to glory; through Jesus Christ my Lord, who lives and reigns with you and the Holy Spirit, one God, for ever and ever. *Amen.* †

The Concluding Prayer of the Church

O God, you make me and your whole church glad with the weekly remembrance of the glorious resurrection of your Son our Lord: Give me this day such blessing through my worship of you, that the week to come may be spent in your favor; through Jesus Christ our Lord. *Amen.* †

The Vespers Office   To Be Observed on the Hour or Half Hour
                                            Between 5 and 8 p.m.

The Call to Prayer
Behold now, bless the LORD, all you servants of the LORD,* you that stand by
    night in the house of the LORD.

Psalm 134:1

The Request for Presence
For God alone my soul in silence waits;* truly, my hope is in him.

Psalm 62:6

The Greeting
I remember your Name in the night, O LORD,* and dwell upon your law.

Psalm 119:55

The Hymn   *Heal Us, Emmanuel*
    Heal us, Emmanuel, Hear our prayer; we wait to feel your touch;
    deep wounded souls to you repair, and Savior, we are such.

    Our faith is feeble, we confess we faintly trust your word;
    but will you pity us the less? Be that far from you, Lord!

    Remember him who once applied with trembling for relief;
    "Lord, I believe," with tears he cried; "O help my unbelief!"

    She, too who touched you in the press and healing virtue stole,
    was answered, "Daughter, go in peace: your faith has made you whole."

    Like her, with hopes and fears we come to touch you if we may;
    O send us not despairing home; send none unhealed away.

William Cowper

The Refrain for the Vespers Lessons
Behold, he who keeps watch over Israel* shall neither slumber nor sleep.

Psalm 121:4

The Vespers Psalm   *The Just Shall See His Face*
The LORD is in his holy temple;* the LORD's throne is in heaven.
His eyes behold the inhabited world;* his piercing eye weighs our worth.
The LORD weighs the righteous as well as the wicked,* but those who delight in
    violence he abhors.
Upon the wicked he shall rain coals of fire and burning sulfur;* a scorching wind
    shall be their lot.
For the LORD is righteous; he delights in righteous deeds;* and the just shall see
    his face.

Psalm 11:4–8

The Refrain
Behold, he who keeps watch over Israel* shall neither slumber nor sleep.

The Small Verse
Keep me, Lord, as the apple of your eye
And carry me under the shadow of your wings.

The Lord's Prayer

The Prayer Appointed for the Week
O God, who before the passion of your only-begotten Son revealed his glory upon
the holy mountain: Grant that I, beholding by faith the light of his countenance, may be strengthened to bear my cross, and be changed into his likeness
from glory to glory; through Jesus Christ my Lord, who lives and reigns with
you and the Holy Spirit, one God, for ever and ever. *Amen.* †

The Concluding Prayer of the Church
Protect me, Lord, as I stay awake; watch over me as I sleep, that awake I may
watch with Christ, and asleep, rest in peace. *Amen.*

The Morning Office **To Be Observed on the Hour or Half Hour**
Between 6 and 9 a.m.

The Call to Prayer
Let my mouth be full of your praise* and your glory all the day long.
Do not cast me off in my old age;* forsake me not when my strength fails.

Psalm 71:8–9

The Request for Presence
O LORD, my God, my Savior,* by day and night I cry to you.
Let my prayer enter into your presence.

Psalm 88:1–2

The Greeting
Show me your ways, O LORD,* and teach me your paths.
Lead me in your truth and teach me,* for you are the God of my salvation; in you
have I trusted all the day long.

Psalm 25:3–4

The Refrain for the Morning Lessons
Deliverance belongs to the LORD.* Your blessing be upon your people!

Psalm 3:8

A Reading
Now it happened that he was praying alone, and his disciples came to him and he
put this question to them, 'Who do the crowds say I am?' And they answered,
'Some say John the Baptist; others Elijah; others again one of the ancient
prophets come back to life.' 'But you,' he said to them, 'who do you say I am?'
It was Peter who spoke up. 'The Christ of God,' he said. But he gave them strict
orders and charged them not to say this to anyone. He said, 'The Son of man is
destined to suffer grievously, to be rejected by the elders and chief priests and
scribes and to be put to death, and to be raised up on the third day.'

Luke 9:18–22

The Refrain
Deliverance belongs to the LORD.* Your blessing be upon your people!

The Morning Psalm   *The LORD Knows the Way of the Righteous*
Happy are they who have not walked in the counsel of the wicked,* nor lingered
    in the way of sinners, nor sat in the seats of the scornful!
Their delight is in the law of the LORD,* and they meditate on his law day
    and night.
They are like trees planted by streams of water, bearing fruit in due season, with
    leaves that do not wither;* everything they do shall prosper.
It is not so with the wicked;* they are like chaff which the wind blows away.
Therefore the wicked shall not stand upright when judgment comes,* nor the
    sinner in the council of the righteous.
For the LORD knows the way of the righteous,* but the way of the wicked is
    doomed.

Psalm 1

The Refrain
Deliverance belongs to the LORD.* Your blessing be upon your people!

The Cry of the Church
O Lamb of God, that takes away the sins of the world, have mercy on me.
O Lamb of God, that takes away the sins of the world, have mercy on me.
O Lamb of God, that takes away the sins of the world, grant me your peace.

The Lord's Prayer

The Prayer Appointed for the Week
O God, who before the passion of your only-begotten Son revealed his glory upon
    the holy mountain: Grant that I, beholding by faith the light of his counte-
    nance, may be strengthened to bear my cross, and be changed into his likeness
    from glory to glory; through Jesus Christ my Lord, who lives and reigns with
    you and the Holy Spirit, one God, for ever and ever. *Amen.* †

The Concluding Prayer of the Church
Lord God, almighty and everlasting Father, you have brought me in safety to this
    new day: Preserve me with your mighty power, that I may not fall into sin, nor
    be overcome by adversity; and in all I do direct me to the fulfilling of your pur-
    pose; through Jesus Christ my Lord. *Amen.* †

The Midday Office   **To Be Observed on the Hour or Half Hour**
                                     Between 11 a.m. and 2 p.m.

The Call to Prayer
All who take refuge in you will be glad;* they will sing out their joy forever.
You will shelter them,* so that those who love your Name may exult in you.

For you, O LORD, will bless the righteous;* you will defend them with your favor as with a shield.

Psalm 5:13–15

The Request for Presence
You are the LORD; do not withhold your compassion from me;* let your love and your faithfulness keep me safe for ever.

Psalm 40:12

The Greeting
O LORD, what are we that you should care for us?* mere mortals that you should think of us?
We are like a puff of wind;* our days are passing like a shadow.

Psalm 144:3–4

The Refrain for the Midday Lessons
Protect my life and deliver me;* let me not be put to shame, for I have trusted in you.
Let integrity and uprightness preserve me,* for my hope is in you.

Psalm 25:19–20

A Reading
All who are guided by the Spirit of God are sons of God; for what you received was not the spirit of slavery to bring you back into fear; you received the spirit of adoption, enabling us to cry out, 'Abba, Father!' And if we are children, then we are heirs, heirs of God and joint-heirs with Christ, provided that we share his suffering, so as to share his glory.

Romans 8:14–15, 17

The Refrain
Protect my life and deliver me;* let me not be put to shame, for I have trusted in you.
Let integrity and uprightness preserve me,* for my hope is in you.

The Midday Psalm   *Behold, I Did Not Restrain My Lips*
I proclaimed righteousness in the great congregation;* behold, I did not restrain my lips; and that, O LORD, you know.
Your righteousness have I not hidden in my heart; I have spoken of your faithfulness and your deliverance;* I have not concealed your love and faithfulness from the great congregation.

Psalm 40:10–11

The Refrain
Protect my life and deliver me;* let me not be put to shame, for I have trusted in you.
Let integrity and uprightness preserve me,* for my hope is in you.

The Cry of the Church
O God, come to my assistance! O Lord, make haste to help me!

The Lord's Prayer

The Prayer Appointed for the Week
O God, who before the passion of your only-begotten Son revealed his glory upon
the holy mountain: Grant that I, beholding by faith the light of his countenance, may be strengthened to bear my cross, and be changed into his likeness
from glory to glory; through Jesus Christ my Lord, who lives and reigns with
you and the Holy Spirit, one God, for ever and ever. *Amen.* †

The Concluding Prayer of the Church
O God, whose blessed Son became poor that we through his poverty might be
rich: Deliver me from the inordinate love of this world, that I may serve you
with singleness of heart, and attain to the riches of the age to come; through
Jesus Christ my Lord, who lives and reigns with you and the Holy Spirit, one
God, now and for ever. *Amen.* †

The Vespers Office   **To Be Observed on the Hour or Half Hour**
Between 5 and 8 p.m.

The Call to Prayer
Love the LORD, all you who worship him;* the LORD protects the faithful, but
repays to the full those who act haughtily.

Psalm 31:23

The Request for Presence
Teach me your way, O LORD, and I will walk in your truth;* knit my heart to you
that I may fear your Name.

Psalm 86:11

The Greeting
Whom have I in heaven but you?* And having you I desire nothing upon earth.

Psalm 73:25

The Hymn   *Lenten Hymn*
Lord, who throughout these forty days for us did fast and pray,
Teach us with you to mourn our sins, and close by you to stay.

As You with Satan did contend and did the victory win,
O give us strength in you to fight, in you to conquer sin.

As you bore hunger and your thirst, so teach us, gracious Lord,
To die to self, and chiefly live by your most holy Word.

And through the days of penitence, and through your Passion-tide,
Yes, evermore, in life and death, Jesus! With us abide.

Abide with us, that so, this life of suffering over-past,
An Easter of unending joy we may attain at last!

Claudia Hernaman

The Refrain for the Vespers Lessons
Let Israel rejoice in his Maker;* let the children of Zion be joyful in their King.

Psalm 149:5

The Vespers Psalm   *You Yourself Created My Inmost Parts*
If I say, "Surely the darkness will cover me,* and the light around me turn to
   night,"
Darkness is not dark to you; the night is as bright as the day;* darkness and light
   to you are both alike.
For you yourself created my inmost parts;* you knit me together in my mother's
   womb.

Psalm 139:10–12

The Refrain
Let Israel rejoice in his Maker;* let the children of Zion be joyful in their King.

*The Gloria**

The Lord's Prayer

The Prayer Appointed for the Week
O God, who before the passion of your only-begotten Son revealed his glory upon
   the holy mountain: Grant that I, beholding by faith the light of his countenance, may be strengthened to bear my cross, and be changed into his likeness
   from glory to glory; through Jesus Christ my Lord, who lives and reigns with
   you and the Holy Spirit, one God, for ever and ever. *Amen.* †

The Concluding Prayer of the Church
   God be in my head
       and in my understanding.
   God be in mine eyes
       and in my looking.
   God be in my mouth
       and in my speaking.
   God be in my heart
       and in my thinking.
   God be at mine end
       and my departing.
Sarum Primer, 1527

The Morning Office   **To Be Observed on the Hour or Half Hour**
Between 6 and 9 a.m.

The Call to Prayer
Clap your hands, all you peoples;* shout to God with a cry of joy.
For the Lord Most High is to be feared;* he is the great King over all the earth.

He subdues the peoples under us,* and the nations under our feet.
He chooses our inheritance for us,* the pride of Jacob whom he loves.

Psalm 47:1–4

The Request for Presence
Early in the morning I cry out to you,* for in your word is my trust.

Psalm 119:147

The Greeting
Not to us, O Lord, not to us, but to your Name give glory;* because of your love
and because of your faithfulness.

Psalm 115:1

The Refrain for the Morning Lessons
Those who are planted in the house of the Lord* shall flourish in the courts of
our God.

Psalm 92:12

A Reading
Then some Sadduces—who deny the Resurrection—came to him . . . Jesus said to
them, 'Surely the reason why you are wrong is that you understand neither the
scriptures nor the power of God. Now about the dead rising again, have you
ever read the book of Moses, in the passage about the bush, how God spoke to
him and said: *I am the God of Abraham, the God of Isaac and the God of Jacob?* He is
God, not of the dead, but of the living. You are very much mistaken.'

Mark 12:18a, 24, 26–27

The Refrain
Those who are planted in the house of the Lord* shall flourish in the courts of our
God.

The Morning Psalm   *We Flourish Like a Flower of the Field*
Our days are like the grass;* we flourish like a flower of the field;
When the wind goes over it, it is gone,* and its place shall know it no more.
But the merciful goodness of the Lord endures for ever on those who fear him,*
and his righteousness on children's children;
On those who keep his covenant* and remember his commandments and
do them.

Psalm 103:15–18

The Refrain
Those who are planted in the house of the Lord* shall flourish in the courts of our
God.

The Short Verse
'I am the Alpha and the Omega,' says the Lord God, 'who is, who was, and who is
to come, the Almighty.'

Revelation 1:8

The Lord's Prayer

The Prayer Appointed for the Week
O God, who before the passion of your only-begotten Son revealed his glory upon the holy mountain: Grant that I, beholding by faith the light of his countenance, may be strengthened to bear my cross, and be changed into his likeness from glory to glory; through Jesus Christ my Lord, who lives and reigns with you and the Holy Spirit, one God, for ever and ever. *Amen.* †

The Concluding Prayer of the Church
Lord God, almighty and everlasting Father, you have brought me in safety to this new day: Preserve me with your mighty power, that I may not fall into sin, nor be overcome by adversity; and in all I do direct me to the fulfilling of your purpose; through Jesus Christ my Lord. *Amen.* †

The Midday Office   **To Be Observed on the Hour or Half Hour**
Between 11 a.m. and 2 p.m.

The Call to Prayer
God has gone up with a shout,* the LORD with the sound of the ram's-horn.
Psalm 47:5

The Request for Presence
Accept, O LORD, the willing tribute of my lips,* and teach me your judgments.
Psalm 119:108

The Greeting
I will offer you the sacrifice of thanksgiving* and call upon the Name of the LORD.
Psalm 116:15

The Refrain for the Midday Lessons
He shall say to the LORD, "You are my refuge and my stronghold,* my God in whom I put my trust."
Psalm 91:2

A Reading
'But now'—declares YAHWEH—'come back to me with all your heart, fasting, weeping, mourning.' Tear your hearts and not your clothes, and come back to YAHWEH your God, for he is gracious and compassionate, slow to anger, rich in faithful love . . .
Joel 2:12–13

The Refrain
He shall say to the LORD, "You are my refuge and my stronghold,* my God in whom I put my trust."

The Midday Psalm   *He Guides the Humble in Doing Right*

Gracious and upright is the LORD;* therefore he teaches sinners in his way.

He guides the humble in doing right* and teaches his way to the lowly.

All the paths of the LORD are love and faithfulness* to those who keep his
covenant and his testimonies.

Psalm 25:7–9

The Refrain

He shall say to the LORD, "You are my refuge and my stronghold,* my God in
whom I put my trust."

The Cry of the Church

Lord, have mercy on us. Christ, have mercy on us. Lord, have mercy on us.

The Lord's Prayer

The Prayer Appointed for the Week

O God, who before the passion of your only-begotten Son revealed his glory upon
the holy mountain: Grant that I, beholding by faith the light of his countenance, may be strengthened to bear my cross, and be changed into his likeness
from glory to glory; through Jesus Christ my Lord, who lives and reigns with
you and the Holy Spirit, one God, for ever and ever. *Amen.* †

The Concluding Prayer of the Church

Almighty and everlasting God, by whose Spirit the whole body of your faithful
people is governed and sanctified: Receive my supplications and prayers
which I offer before you for all members of your holy Church, that in our voca-
tion and ministry we all may truly and godly serve you, through our Lord and
Savior Jesus Christ. *Amen.*

The Vespers Office   **To Be Observed on the Hour or Half Hour**
Between 5 and 8 p.m.

The Call to Prayer

Come, let us bow down, and bend the knee,* and kneel before the LORD our
Maker.

For he is our God,* and we are the people of his pasture and the sheep of his hand.

Psalm 95:6–7

The Request for Presence

To you I lift up my eyes,* to you enthroned in the heavens.

Psalm 123:1

The Greeting

How priceless is your love, O God!* your people take refuge under the shadow of
your wings.

For with you is the well of life,* and in your light we see light.

Psalm 36:7, 9

The Hymn   *Dear Lord and Father of Mankind*

Dear Lord and Father of mankind,
Forgive our foolish ways;
Reclothe us in our rightful mind;
In purer lives Your service find,
In deeper reverence praise.

Drop Your still dews of quietness,
Till all our strivings cease;
Take from our souls the strain and stress,
And let our ordered lives confess
The beauty of Your peace.

Breathe through the heats of our desire
Your coolness and Your balm;
Let sense be dumb, let flesh retire;
Speak through the earthquake, wind and fire,
O still small voice of calm!

In simple trust like theirs who heard,
Beside the Syrian sea,
The gracious calling of the Lord,
Let us, like them, without a word,
Rise up and follow Thee.

                                        John G. Whittier

The Refrain for the Vespers Lessons
Come and listen, all you who fear God,* and I will tell you what he has done
    for me.

                                        Psalm 66:14

The Vespers Psalm   *He Strengthens Those in Whose Way He Delights*
Our steps are directed by the LORD;* he strengthens those in whose way he
    delights.
If they stumble, they shall not fall headlong,* for the LORD holds them by the hand.
I have been young and now I am old,* but never have I seen the righteous forsaken,
    or their children begging bread.

                                        Psalm 37:24–26

The Refrain
Come and listen, all you who fear God,* and I will tell you what he has done for
    me.

The Small Verse
Have mercy on me, Lord, have mercy.
Lord, show me your love and mercy; For I put my trust in you.
In you, Lord, is my hope; And I shall never hope in vain.

The Lord's Prayer

The Prayer Appointed for the Week
O God, who before the passion of your only-begotten Son revealed his glory upon
the holy mountain: Grant that I, beholding by faith the light of his countenance, may be strengthened to bear my cross, and be changed into his likeness
from glory to glory; through Jesus Christ my Lord, who lives and reigns with
you and the Holy Spirit, one God, for ever and ever. *Amen.* †

The Concluding Prayer of the Church
Blessed be God, who has not rejected my prayer,* nor withheld his love from me.

Psalm 66:18

The Morning Office

**To Be Observed on the Hour or Half Hour
Between 6 and 9 a.m.**

The Call to Prayer
Sing to the LORD a new song,* for he has done marvelous things.
With his right hand and his holy arm* has he won for himself the victory.
The LORD has made known his victory;* his righteousness has he openly shown in
the sight of the nations.

Psalm 98:1–3

The Request for Presence
Our soul waits for the LORD;* he is our help and our shield.
Indeed, our heart rejoices in him,* for in his holy Name we put our trust.
Let your loving-kindness, O LORD, be upon us,* as we have put our trust in you.

Psalm 33:20–22

The Greeting
How deep I find your thoughts, O God!* how great is the sum of them!
If I were to count them, they would be more in number than the sand;* to count
them all, my life span would need to be like yours.

Psalm 139:16–17

The Refrain for the Morning Lessons
I will confess you among the peoples, O LORD;* I will sing praises to you among
the nations.

Psalm 108:3

A Reading
Though they had been present when he gave so many signs, they did not believe
in him; this was to fulfill the words of the prophet Isaiah: *Lord, who has given
credence to what they have heard from us, and who has seen in it a revelation of the
Lord's arm?* Indeed, they were unable to believe because, as Isaiah says again:
*He has blinded their eyes, he has hardened their heart, to prevent them from using their
eyes to see, using their heart to understand, changing their ways and being healed by
me.* Isaiah said this because he saw his glory, and his words referred to Jesus.
And yet there were many who did believe in him, even among the leading

men, but they did not admit it, because of the Pharisees and for fear of being banned from the synagogue: they put human glory before God's glory.

John 12:27–43

The Refrain
I will confess you among the peoples, O LORD;* I will sing praises to you among the nations.

The Morning Psalm   *Those Who Act Deceitfully Shall Not Dwell in My House*
My eyes are upon the faithful in the land, that they may dwell with me,* and only those who lead a blameless life shall be my servants.
Those who act deceitfully shall not dwell in my house,* and those who tell lies shall not continue in my sight.
I will soon destroy all the wicked in the land,* that I may root out all evildoers from the city of the LORD.

Psalm 101:6–8

The Refrain
I will confess you among the peoples, O LORD;* I will sing praises to you among the nations.

The Small Verse
Today if you shall hear His voice, harden not your heart.

The Lord's Prayer

The Prayer Appointed for the Week
O God, who before the passion of your only-begotten Son revealed his glory upon the holy mountain: Grant that I, beholding by faith the light of his countenance, may be strengthened to bear my cross, and be changed into his likeness from glory to glory; through Jesus Christ my Lord, who lives and reigns with you and the Holy Spirit, one God, for ever and ever. *Amen.* †

The Concluding Prayer of the Church
Lord God, almighty and everlasting Father, you have brought me in safety to this new day: Preserve me with your mighty power, that I may not fall into sin, nor be overcome by adversity; and in all I do direct me to the fulfilling of your purpose; through Jesus Christ my Lord. *Amen.* †

The Midday Office   To Be Observed on the Hour or Half Hour
Between 11 a.m. and 2 p.m.

The Call to Prayer
Search for the LORD and his strength;* continually seek his face.
Remember the marvels he has done,* his wonders and the judgments of his mouth.

Psalm 105:4–5

The Request for Presence
Teach me your way, O LORD, and I will walk in your truth;* knit my heart to you
that I may fear your Name.

Psalm 86:11

The Greeting
My mouth shall recount your mighty acts and saving deeds all the day long;*
though I can not know the number of them.

Psalm 71:15

The Refrain for the Midday Lessons
The LORD has sworn an oath to David;* in truth, he will not break it:
"A son, the fruit of your body* will I set upon your throne."

Psalm 132:11–12

A Reading
Since he did not spare his own Son, but gave him up for the sake of all of us, then
can we not expect that with him he will freely give us all his gifts? Who can
bring any accusation against those that God has chosen? *When God grants saving justice who can condemn?* Are we not sure that it is Christ Jesus, who died—
yes and more, who was raised from the dead and is at God's right hand—and
who is adding his plea for us?

Romans 8:32–34

The Refrain
The LORD has sworn an oath to David;* in truth, he will not break it:
"A son, the fruit of your body* will I set upon your throne."

The Midday Psalm   *A Song of the Messiah*
O God, give to the king Your judgment,* and to the son of the king Your justice,
To judge Your people with justice,* and Your poor with judgment.
Let the mountains bring peace to the people* and the hills bring righteousness.

Psalm 72:1–7 adapted from THE SHORT BREVIARY

The Refrain
The LORD has sworn an oath to David;* in truth, he will not break it:
"A son, the fruit of your body* will I set upon your throne."

The Small Verse
The Lord is my shepherd and nothing is wanting to me.* In green pastures He has
settled me.

THE SHORT BREVIARY

The Lord's Prayer

The Prayer Appointed for the Week
O God, who before the passion of your only-begotten Son revealed his glory upon
the holy mountain: Grant that I, beholding by faith the light of his countenance, may be strengthened to bear my cross, and be changed into his likeness

from glory to glory; through Jesus Christ my Lord, who lives and reigns with you and the Holy Spirit, one God, for ever and ever. *Amen.* †

The Concluding Prayer of the Church

O Lord my God, to you and your service I devote myself, body, soul, and spirit. Fill my memory with the record of your mighty works; enlighten my understanding with the light of your Holy Spirit; and may all the desires of my heart and will center in what you would have me do. Make me an instrument of your salvation for the people entrusted to my care, and let me by my life and speaking set forth your true and living Word. Be always with me in carrying out the duties of my salvation; in praises heighten my love and gratitude; in speaking of You give me readiness of thought and expression; and grant that, by the clearness and bright-ness of your holy Word, all the world may be drawn to your blessed kingdom. All this I ask for the sake of your Son my Savior Jesus Christ. *Amen.* †

The Vespers Office **To Be Observed on the Hour or Half Hour Between 5 and 8 p.m.**

The Call to Prayer

Give thanks to the LORD, for he is good;* his mercy endures for ever.

Psalm 118:29

The Request for Presence

As the eyes of servants look to the hand of their masters,* and the eyes of a maid to the hand of her mistress,
So my eyes look to you, O Lord my God.

adapted from Psalm 123:2–3

The Greeting

You have turned my wailing into dancing;* you have put off my sack-cloth and clothed me with joy.
My heart sings to you without ceasing;* O LORD my God, I will give you thanks for ever.

Psalm 30:12–13

The Hymn   *O Love, How Deep*

O love, how deep, how broad, how high,
It fills the heart with ecstasy,
That God, the Son of God, should take
Our mortal form for mortals' sake!

For us baptized, for us he bore
His holy fast and hungered sore,
For us temptation sharp he knew;
For us the tempter overthrew.

For us he prayed; for us he taught;
For us his daily works he wrought;
By words and signs and actions thus
Still seeking not himself, but us.

For us to evil power betrayed,
Scourged, mocked, in purple robe arrayed,
He bore the shameful cross and death,
For us gave up his dying breath.

For us he rose from death again,
For us he went on high to reign;
For us he sent his Spirit here,
To guide, to strengthen, and to cheer.

All glory to our Lord and God
For love so deep, so high, so broad;
The Trinity whom we adore,
For ever and for evermore.

Latin, 15th C.

The Refrain for the Vespers Lessons

But you, O Lord, are gracious and full of compassion,* slow to anger, and full of
kindness and truth.

Psalm 86:15

The Vespers Psalm   *I Tell of Your Wonderful Works*

But I shall always wait in patience,* and shall praise you more and more.
My mouth shall recount your mighty acts and saving deeds all day long;* though I
cannot know the number of them.
I will begin with the mighty works of the Lord God;* I will recall your
righteousness, yours alone.
O God, you have taught me since I was young,* and to this day I tell of your
wonderful works.

Psalm 71:14–17

The Refrain

But you, O Lord, are gracious and full of compassion,* slow to anger, and full of
kindness and truth.

The Cry of the Church

In the evening, in the morning, and at noonday, I will complain and lament,* and
he will hear my voice.

Psalm 55:18

The Lord's Prayer

The Prayer Appointed for the Week

O God, who before the passion of your only-begotten Son revealed his glory upon
the holy mountain: Grant that I, beholding by faith the light of his counte-

nance, may be strengthened to bear my cross, and be changed into his likeness from glory to glory; through Jesus Christ my Lord, who lives and reigns with you and the Holy Spirit, one God, for ever and ever. *Amen.* †

The Concluding Prayer of the Church

I thank you, my God, for your care and protection this day, keeping me from physical harm and spiritual ignorance. I now place the work of the day into Your
hands, trusting that You will redeem my mistakes, and transform my accom-
plishments into works of praise.

And now I ask that You will work within me while I sleep, using the hours of my
rest to create in me a new mind and heart and soul.

May my mind, which during the day was directed to my work and activities,
through the night be directed wholly to You.

Jacob Boehme

The Morning Office

**To Be Observed on the Hour or Half Hour
Between 6 and 9 a.m.**

The Call to Prayer

Wake up, my spirit; awake lute and harp;* I myself will waken the dawn.

Psalm 57:8

The Request for Presence

O God of hosts,* show the light of your countenance, and we shall be saved.

Psalm 80:7

The Greeting

My lips will sing with joy when I play to you,* and so will my soul, which you
have redeemed.

Psalm 71:23

The Refrain for the Morning Lessons

Send forth your strength, O God;* establish, O God, what you have wrought
for us.

Psalm 68:28

A Reading

He said to his disciples, 'A time will come when you will long to see one of the
days of the Son of Man and will not see it. They will say to you, "Look, it is
there!" or, "Look, it is here!" Make no move; do not set off in pursuit; for as the
lightning flashing from one part of heaven lights up the other, so will be the
Son of man when his Day comes. But first he is destined to suffer grievously
and be rejected by this generation.'

Luke 17:22–25

The Refrain

Send forth your strength, O God;* establish, O God, what you have wrought
for us.

The Morning Psalm   *What Are We That You Should Care for Us*

O LORD, what are we that you should care for us?* mere mortals that you should
  think of us?
We are like a puff of wind;* our days are like a passing shadow.
Bow your heavens, O LORD, and come down;* touch the mountains, and they shall
  smoke.
Hurl the lightning and scatter them;* shoot out your arrows and rout them.
Stretch out your hand from on high;* rescue me and deliver me from the great
  waters, from the hand of foreign peoples,
Whose mouths speak deceitfully* and whose right hand is raised in falsehood.

Psalm 144:3–8

The Refrain

Send forth your strength, O God;* establish, O God, what you have wrought for us.

The Cry of the Church

In the evening, in the morning, and at noonday, I will complain and lament,* and
  he will hear my voice.

Psalm 55:18

The Lord's Prayer

The Prayer Appointed for the Week

O God, who before the passion of your only-begotten Son revealed his glory upon
  the holy mountain: Grant that I, beholding by faith the light of his countenance, may be strengthened to bear my cross, and be changed into his likeness
  from glory to glory; through Jesus Christ my Lord, who lives and reigns with
  you and the Holy Spirit, one God, for ever and ever. *Amen.* †

The Concluding Prayer of the Church

Lord God, almighty and everlasting Father, you have brought me in safety to this
  new day: Preserve me with your mighty power, that I may not fall into sin, nor
  be overcome by adversity; and in all I do direct me to the fulfilling of your purpose; through Jesus Christ my Lord. *Amen.* †

The Midday Office   **To Be Observed on the Hour or Half Hour**
                                         Between 11 a.m. and 2 p.m.

The Call to Prayer

"Come now, let us reason together," says the LORD.

Isaiah 1:18, KJV

The Request for Presence

Awake, O my God, decree justice;* let the assembly of peoples gather around you.
Let the malice of the wicked come to an end, but establish the righteous;* for you
  test the mind and heart, O righteous God.

Psalm 7:7, 10

The Greeting
Deliver me, O Lord, by your hand* from those whose portion in life is this
world; . . .

Psalm 17:14

The Refrain for the Midday Lessons
Righteousness shall go before him,* and peace shall be a pathway for his feet.

Psalm 85:13

A Reading
Seek out Yahweh while he is still to be found, call to him while he is still near. Let
the wicked abandon his way and the evil one his thoughts. Let him turn back
to Yahweh who will take pity on him, to our God, for he is rich in forgiveness;
for my thoughts are not your thoughts and your ways are not my ways,
declares Yahweh. For the heavens are as high above the earth as my ways are
above your ways, my thoughts above your thoughts.

Isaiah 55:6–9

The Refrain
Righteousness shall go before him,* and peace shall be a pathway for his feet.

The Midday Psalm   *You Will Save a Lowly People*
With the faithful you show yourself faithful, O God;* with the forthright you show
yourself forthright.
With the pure you show yourself pure,* but with the crooked you are wily.
You will save a lowly people,* but you will humble the haughty eyes.
You, O Lord, are my lamp;* my God, you make my darkness bright.
With you I will break down an enclosure;* with the help of my God I will scale any
wall.
As for God, his ways are perfect; the words of the Lord are tried in the fire;* he is a
shield to all who trust in him.
For who is God, but the Lord?* who is the Rock, except our God?

Psalm 18:26–32

The Refrain
Righteousness shall go before him,* and peace shall be a pathway for his feet.

The Cry of the Church
Lord, have mercy on us. Christ, have mercy on us. Lord, have mercy on us.

The Lord's Prayer

The Prayer Appointed for the Week
O God, who before the passion of your only-begotten Son revealed his glory upon
the holy mountain: Grant that I, beholding by faith the light of his countenance, may be strengthened to bear my cross, and be changed into his likeness
from glory to glory; through Jesus Christ my Lord, who lives and reigns with
you and the Holy Spirit, one God, for ever and ever. *Amen.* †

The Concluding Prayer of the Church
Renew in my heart, O God, the gift of your Holy Spirit, so that I may love you fully in all that I do and love all others as Christ loves me. May all that I do proclaim the good news that you are God with us. *Amen.* †

The Vespers Office **To Be Observed on the Hour or Half Hour Between 5 and 8 p.m.**

The Call to Prayer
O tarry and await the LORD's pleasure; be strong, and he shall comfort your heart;* wait patiently for the LORD.

Psalm 27:18

The Request for Presence
Open my eyes, that I may see* the wonders of your law.

Psalm 119:18

The Greeting
I remember your Name in the night, O LORD,* and dwell upon your law.
This is how it has been with me,* because I have kept your commandments.

Psalm 119:55–56

The Hymn

You ask what great thing I know,
That delights and stirs me so?
What high reward I'll win?
Whose the name I glory in?
Jesus Christ, the crucified.

This is the great thing I know;
This delights and stirs me so:
Faith in him who died to save,
Him who triumphed o'er the grave:
Jesus Christ, the crucified.

Johann Schwedler

Who is life in life to me?
Who the death of death will be?
Who will place me on his right,
With the countless hosts of light?
Jesus Christ, the crucified.

The Refrain for the Vespers Lessons
'I am the Alpha and the Omega,' says the Lord God, 'who is, who was, and who is to come, the Almighty.'

Revelation 1:8

The Vespers Psalm *The LORD Is My Shepherd*
The LORD is my shepherd;* I shall not be in want.
He makes me lie down in green pastures* and leads me beside still waters.
He revives my soul* and guides me along right pathways for his Name's sake.
Though I walk through the valley of the shadow of death, I shall fear no evil;* for you are with me; your rod and your staff, they comfort me.

You spread a table before me in the presence of those who trouble me;* you have anointed my head with oil, and my cup is running over.
Surely your goodness and mercy shall follow me all the days of my life,* and I will dwell in the house of the LORD for ever.

Psalm 23

The Refrain
'I am the Alpha and the Omega,' says the Lord God, 'who is, who was, and who is to come, the Almighty.'

The Cry of the Church
O Lord, hear my prayer and let my cry come to you. Thanks be to God.

THE SHORT BREVIARY

The Lord's Prayer

The Prayer Appointed for the Week
O God, who before the passion of your only-begotten Son revealed his glory upon the holy mountain: Grant that I, beholding by faith the light of his countenance, may be strengthened to bear my cross, and be changed into his likeness from glory to glory; through Jesus Christ my Lord, who lives and reigns with you and the Holy Spirit, one God, for ever and ever. *Amen.* †

The Concluding Prayer of the Church
Lord Jesus Christ, you said to your apostles, "Peace I give to you; my own peace I leave with you:" Regard not my sins, but my faith, and give to me a place in the peace and unity of that heavenly City, where with the Father and the Holy Spirit you live and reign, now and forever. *Amen.* †

The Morning Office

To Be Observed on the Hour or Half Hour Between 6 and 9 a.m.

The Call to Prayer
Sing to the LORD a new song,* for he has done marvelous things.
With his right hand and his holy arm* has he won for himself the victory.

Psalm 98:1–2

The Request for Presence
Let your loving-kindness be my comfort,* as you have promised to your servant.
Let your compassion come to me, that I may live,* for your law is my delight.

Psalm 119:76–77

The Greeting
I will confess you among the peoples, O LORD;* I will sing praises to you among the nations.
For your loving-kindness is greater than the heavens,* and your faithfulness reaches to the clouds.

Psalm 108:3–4

The Refrain for the Morning Lessons
So teach us to number our days* that we may apply our hearts to wisdom.

Psalm 90:12

A Reading
Jesus said: "Do not imagine that I have come to abolish the Law or the Prophets. I have come not to abolish but to complete them. In truth I tell you, till heaven and earth disappear, not one dot, not one little stroke, is to disappear from the Law until all its purpose is achieved."

Matthew 5:17–18

The Refrain
So teach us to number our days* that we may apply our hearts to wisdom.

The Morning Psalm   *The LORD Does Not Forsake His Faithful Ones*
Turn from evil, and do good,* and dwell in the land for ever.
For the LORD loves justice;* he does not forsake his faithful ones.
They shall be kept safe for ever,* but the offspring of the wicked shall be destroyed.
The righteous shall possess the land* and dwell in it for ever.
The mouth of the righteous utters wisdom,* and their tongue speaks what is right.
The law of their God is in their heart,* and their footsteps shall not falter.

Psalm 37:28–33

The Refrain
So teach us to number our days* that we may apply our hearts to wisdom.

The Small Verse
Let me seek the Lord while he may still be found.
I will call upon his name; while he is near.

Traditional

The Lord's Prayer

The Prayer Appointed for the Week
O God, who before the passion of your only-begotten Son revealed his glory upon the holy mountain: Grant that I, beholding by faith the light of his countenance, may be strengthened to bear my cross, and be changed into his likeness from glory to glory; through Jesus Christ my Lord, who lives and reigns with you and the Holy Spirit, one God, for ever and ever. *Amen.* †

The Concluding Prayer of the Church
Lord God, almighty and everlasting Father, you have brought me in safety to this new day: Preserve me with your mighty power, that I may not fall into sin, nor be overcome by adversity; and in all I do direct me to the fulfilling of your purpose; through Jesus Christ my Lord. *Amen.* †

The Midday Office   **To Be Observed on the Hour or Half Hour**
                                    Between 11 a.m. and 2 p.m.

The Call to Prayer
Sing to God, O kingdoms of the earth;* sing praises to the Lord.
He rides in the heavens, the ancient heavens;* he sends forth his voice, his mighty
     voice.

Psalm 68:33–34

The Request for Presence
May God be merciful to us and bless us,* show us the light of his countenance and
     come to us.
Let your ways be known upon the earth,* your saving health among all nations.

Psalm 67:1–2

The Greeting
Exalt yourself above the heavens, O God,* and your glory all over the earth.
So that those who are dear to you may be delivered,* save with your right hand
     and answer me.

Psalm 108:5–6

The Refrain for the Midday Lessons
Righteousness and justice are the foundations of your throne;* love and truth go
     before your face.

Psalm 89:14

A Reading
Fasting like yours today will never make your voice heard on high. Is that the sort
     of fast that pleases me, a day when a person inflicts pain on himself? Hanging
     your head like a reed, spreading out sackcloth and ashes? Is that what you call
     fasting, a day acceptable to YAHWEH? Is not this the sort of fast that pleases me:
     to break unjust fetters, to undo the thongs of the yoke. To let the oppressed go
     free, and to break all yokes? Is it not sharing your food with the hungry or shel-
     tering the homeless poor; if you see someone lacking in clothes, to clothe him,
     and not to turn away from your own kin? Then your light will blaze out like
     the dawn and your wound will be quickly healed over.

Isaiah 58:4–8

The Refrain
Righteousness and justice are the foundations of your throne;* love and truth go
     before your face.

The Midday Psalm   *The LORD Will Have Regard for Me*
You are the LORD; do not withhold your compassion from me;* let your love and
     your faithfulness keep me safe for ever,
For innumerable troubles have crowded upon me; my sins have overtaken me,
     and I cannot see;* they are more in number than the hairs of my head, and my
     heart fails me.

Be pleased, O LORD, to deliver me;* O LORD, make haste to help me.

Let them be ashamed and altogether dismayed who seek after my life to destroy it;* let them draw back and be disgraced who take pleasure in my misfortune.

Let those who say "Aha!" and gloat over me be confounded* because they are ashamed.

Let all who seek you rejoice in you and be glad;* let those who love your salvation continually say, "Great is the LORD!"

Though I am poor and afflicted,* the LORD will have regard for me.

You are my helper and my deliverer;* do not tarry, O my God.

Psalm 40:12–19

The Refrain
Righteousness and justice are the foundations of your throne;* love and truth go before your face.

The Small Verse
The Son of man shall be delivered over to the Gentiles to be mocked and scourged and crucified.

The Lord's Prayer

The Prayer Appointed for the Week
O God, who before the passion of your only-begotten Son revealed his glory upon the holy mountain: Grant that I, beholding by faith the light of his countenance, may be strengthened to bear my cross, and be changed into his likeness from glory to glory; through Jesus Christ my Lord, who lives and reigns with you and the Holy Spirit, one God, for ever and ever. *Amen.* †

The Concluding Prayer of the Church
Almighty God, whose most dear Son went not up to joy before he first suffered pain, and did not enter into glory before he was crucified: Mercifully grant that I, walking in the way of the cross, may find it to be none other than the way of life and peace; through Jesus Christ your son my Lord. *Amen.* †

The Vespers Office   **To Be Observed on the Hour or Half Hour Between 5 and 8 p.m.**

The Call to Prayer
Search for the LORD and his strength;* continually seek his face.

Psalm 105:4

The Request for Presence
For God alone my soul in silence waits;* truly, my hope is in him.

Psalm 62:6

The Greeting
Out of Zion, perfect in its beauty,* God reveals himself in glory.

Psalm 50:2

The Hymn

Hail, O once despised Jesus!	*Hail, O Once Despised Jesus*
Hail, O Galilean King!	Worship, honor, power, and blessing,
You suffered to release us;	You are worthy to receive;
Free salvation did you bring:	Loudest praises, without ceasing,
Hail, O agonizing Savior,	Right it is for us to give:
Bearer of our sin and shame!	Help, you bright angelic spirits,
By Your merits we find favor;	Bring your sweetest, noblest ways;
Life is given through Your Name.	Help to sing our Savior's merits,
	Help to chant Immanuel's praise.

John Bakewell

Paschal Lamb, by God appointed,
All our sins on You were laid;
By almighty love anointed,
You have full atonement made:
All Your people are forgiven,
Through the virtue of Your blood;
Opened is the gate of heaven,
Made is peace 'tween man and God.

The Refrain for the Vespers Lessons
Let my mouth be full of your praise* and your glory all the day long.

Psalm 71:8

The Vespers Psalm　　　　　　　　*The Law of the LORD Revives the Soul*
The law of the LORD is perfect and revives the soul;* the testimony of the LORD is
　　sure and gives wisdom to the innocent.
The statutes of the LORD are just and rejoice the heart;* the commandment of the
　　LORD is clear and gives light to the eyes.
The fear of the LORD is clean and endures for ever;* the judgments of the LORD are
　　true and righteous altogether.
More to be desired are they than gold, more than much fine gold,* sweeter far than
　　honey, than honey in the comb.
By them also is your servant enlightened,* and in keeping them there is great
　　reward.

Psalm 19:7–11

The Refrain
Let my mouth be full of your praise* and your glory all the day long.

The Cry of the Church
Lord, have mercy upon us. Christ, have mercy upon us. Lord, have mercy upon us.

The Lord's Prayer

The Prayer Appointed for the Week
O God, who before the passion of your only-begotten Son revealed his glory upon
　　the holy mountain: Grant that I, beholding by faith the light of his counte-
　　nance, may be strengthened to bear my cross, and be changed into his likeness

from glory to glory; through Jesus Christ my Lord, who lives and reigns with you and the Holy Spirit, one God, for ever and ever. *Amen.* †

Concluding Prayers of the Church

Almighty God, who has promised to hear the petitions of those who ask in your Son's Name: I beseech you mercifully to incline your ear to me who have made my prayers and supplications to you; and grant that those things which I have faithfully asked according to your will, may effectually be obtained, to the relief of my necessity, and to the setting forth of your glory; through Jesus Christ my Lord. *Amen.* †

May the souls of the faithful departed, through the mercy of God, rest in eternal peace. *Amen.*

The Morning Office   **To Be Observed on the Hour or Half Hour Between 6 and 9 a.m.**

The Call to Prayer

Bless the LORD, you angels of his, you mighty ones who do his bidding,* and hearken to the voice of his word.

Bless the LORD, all you hosts,* you ministers of his who do his will.

Bless the LORD, all you works of his, in all places of his dominion;* bless the LORD, O my soul.

Psalm 103:20–22

The Request for Presence

Give ear to my words, O LORD;* consider my meditation.

Hearken to my cry for help, my King and my God,* for I make my prayer to you.

In the morning, LORD, you hear my voice;* early in the morning I make my appeal and watch for you.

Psalm 5:1–3

The Greeting

Let the words of my mouth and the meditation of my heart be acceptable in your sight,* O LORD, my strength and my redeemer.

Psalm 19:14

The Refrain for the Morning Lessons

The LORD's will stands fast for ever,* and the designs of his heart from age to age.

Psalm 33:11

A Reading

Jesus taught us, saying: "When the Son of Man comes in his Glory, escorted by all the angels, then he will take his seat on his throne of glory. All nations will be assembled before him and he will separate people one from another as the shepherd separates sheep from goats. He will place the sheep on his right hand and the goats on his left. Then the King will say to those on his right hand,

'Come, you whom my Father has blessed, take as your heritage the kingdom prepared for you since the foundation of the world. For I was hungry and you gave me food, I was thirsty and you gave me drink, I was a stranger and you made me welcome, lacking clothes and you clothed me, sick and you visited me.' Then the upright will say to him in reply, 'Lord, when did we see you hungry and feed you, or thirsty and give you drink? When did we see you a stranger and make you welcome, lacking clothes and clothe you? When did we see you sick or in prison and go to visit you?' And the King will answer, 'In truth I tell you, in so far as you did this to one of the least of these brothers of mine, you did it to me.' Then he will say to those on his left hand, 'Go away from me, with your curse upon you, to the eternal fire prepared for the devil and his angels. For I was hungry and you never gave me food, I was thirsty and you never gave me anything to drink, I was a stranger and you never made me welcome, lacking clothes and you never clothed me, sick and in prison and you never visited me.' Then it will be their turn to ask, 'Lord, when did we see you hungry or thirsty, a stranger or lacking clothes, sick or in prison and did not come to your help?' Then he will answer, 'In truth I tell you, in so far as you neglected to do this to one of the least of these, you neglected to do it to me.' And they will go away to eternal punishment, and the upright to eternal life."

Matthew 25:31–46

The Refrain
The LORD's will stands fast for ever,* and the designs of his heart from age to age.

The Morning Psalm   *Who May Abide Upon Your Holy Hill?*
LORD, who may dwell in your tabernacle?* who may abide upon your holy hill?
Whoever leads a blameless life and does what is right,* who speaks the truth from his heart.
There is no guile upon his tongue; he does no evil to his friend;* he does not heap contempt upon his neighbor.
In his sight the wicked is rejected,* but he honors those who fear the LORD.
He has sworn to do no wrong* and does not take back his word.
He does not give his money in hope of gain,* nor does he take a bribe against the innocent.
Whoever does these things* shall never be overthrown.

Psalm 15

The Refrain
The LORD's will stands fast for ever,* and the designs of his heart from age to age.

The Small Verse
The people that walked in darkness have seen a great light; on those who have lived in a land of deep shadow a light has shown.

Isaiah 9:1

The Lord's Prayer

The Prayer Appointed for the Week

O God, who before the passion of your only-begotten Son revealed his glory upon the holy mountain: Grant that I, beholding by faith the light of his countenance, may be strengthened to bear my cross, and be changed into his likeness from glory to glory; through Jesus Christ my Lord, who lives and reigns with you and the Holy Spirit, one God, for ever and ever. *Amen.* †

The Concluding Prayer of the Church

Lord God, almighty and everlasting Father, you have brought me in safety to this new day: Preserve me with your mighty power, that I may not fall into sin, nor be overcome by adversity; and in all I do direct me to the fulfilling of your purpose; through Jesus Christ my Lord. *Amen.* †

The Midday Office   **To Be Observed on the Hour or Half Hour Between 11 a.m. and 2 p.m.**

The Call to Prayer

Let everything that has breath* praise the LORD.

Psalm 150:6

The Request for Presence

LORD, hear my prayer, and in your faithfulness heed my supplications;* answer me in your righteousness.

Psalm 143:1

The Greeting

My eyes are fixed on you, O my Strength;* for you, O God, are my stronghold.

Psalm 59:10

The Refrain for the Midday Lessons

In righteousness shall he judge the world* and the peoples with equity.

Psalm 98:10

A Reading

YAHWEH gives death and life, brings down to Sheol and draws up; YAHWEH makes poor and rich, he humbles and also exalts. He raises the poor from the dust, he lifts the needy from the dunghill to give them a place with princes, to assign them a seat of honor; for to YAHWEH belong the pillars of the earth, on these he has poised the world.

I Samuel 2:6–10

The Refrain

In righteousness shall he judge the world* and the peoples with equity.

The Midday Psalm   *Heal Me, for I Have Sinned*

Happy are they who consider the poor and needy!* the LORD will deliver them in the time of trouble.

The LORD preserves them and keeps them alive, so that they may be happy in the
    land;* he does not hand them over to the will of their enemies.
The LORD sustains them on their sickbed* and ministers to them in their illness.
I said, "LORD, be merciful to me;* heal me, for I have sinned against you."

Psalm 41:1–4

The Refrain
In righteousness shall he judge the world* and the peoples with equity.

The Small Verse
Today if you shall hear his voice, harden not your heart.

The Lord's Prayer

The Prayer Appointed for the Week
O God, who before the passion of your only-begotten Son revealed his glory upon
    the holy mountain: Grant that I, beholding by faith the light of his counte-
    nance, may be strengthened to bear my cross, and be changed into his likeness
    from glory to glory; through Jesus Christ my Lord, who lives and reigns with
    you and the Holy Spirit, one God, for ever and ever. *Amen.* †

The Concluding Prayer of the Church
O God, the source of light: Shed forth your unending day upon all of us who
    watch for you, that our lips may praise you, our lives may bless you, and our
    worship may give you glory; through Jesus Christ our Lord. *Amen.* †

The Vespers Office   **To Be Observed on the Hour or Half Hour**
                                        Between 5 and 8 p.m.

The Call to Prayer
We will bless the LORD,* from this time forth for evermore.

Psalm 115:18

The Request for Presence
Answer me when I call, O God, defender of my cause;* you set me free when I am
    hard-pressed; have mercy on me and hear my prayer.

Psalm 4:1

The Greeting
Be exalted, O LORD, in your might;* we will sing and praise your power.

Psalm 21:14

The Hymn   *O for a Thousand Tongues to Sing*
    O for a thousand tongues to sing my great Redeemer's praise,
    The glories of my God and King, the triumphs of his grace!

    My gracious Master and my God, assist me to proclaim,
    To spread through all the earth abroad the honors of your name.

Jesus! The name that charms our fears, that bids our sorrows cease;
'Tis music in the sinner's ears, 'tis life, and health, and peace.

He breaks the power of canceled sin, he sets the prisoner free;
His blood can make the foulest clean; his blood availed for me.

He speaks, and listening to his voice, new life the dead receive;
The mournful, broken hearts rejoice, the humble poor believe.

In Christ, your head, you then shall know, shall feel your sins forgiven;
Anticipate your heaven below, and own that love in heaven.

Charles Wesley

The Refrain for the Vespers Lessons
. . . I call upon you all the day long.

Psalm 86:3

The Vespers Psalm   My Days Drift Away Like Smoke
LORD, hear my prayer, and let my cry come before you;* hide not your face from
    me in the day of my trouble.
Incline your ear to me;* when I call, make haste to answer me,
For my days drift away like smoke,* and my bones are hot as burning coals.
My heart is smitten like grass and withered,* so that I forget to eat my bread.
Because of the voice of my groaning* I am but skin and bones.
I have become like a vulture in the wilderness,* like an owl among the ruins.
I lie awake and groan;* I am like a sparrow, lonely on a house-top.

Psalm 102:1–7

The Refrain
. . . I call upon you all the day long.

The Cry of the Church
In the evening, in the morning, and at noonday, I will complain and lament,* and
    he will hear my voice.

Psalm 55:18

The Lord's Prayer

The Prayer Appointed for the Week
O God, who before the passion of your only-begotten Son revealed his glory upon
    the holy mountain: Grant that I, beholding by faith the light of his counte-
    nance, may be strengthened to bear my cross, and be changed into his likeness
    from glory to glory; through Jesus Christ my Lord, who lives and reigns with
    you and the Holy Spirit, one God, for ever and ever. *Amen.* †

The Concluding Prayer of the Church
For an angel of peace, faithful guardian and guide of our souls and our bodies, we
    beseech thee, O Lord.

Orthodox

◈

The Morning Office   **To Be Observed on the Hour or Half Hour**
Between 6 and 9 a.m.

The Call to Prayer
Praise God from whom all blessings flow; Praise Him all creatures here below;
    Praise him above, you heavenly hosts; Praise Father, Son, and Holy Ghost.

Traditional Doxology

The Request for Presence
Hear, O Shepherd of Israel, leading Joseph like a flock;* shine forth, you that are
    enthroned upon the cherubim.

Psalm 80:1

The Greeting
The Lord lives! Blessed is my Rock!* Exalted is the God of my salvation!

Psalm 18:46

The Refrain for the Morning Lessons
We have sinned as our forebears did;* we have done wrong and dealt wickedly.

Psalm 108:6

A Reading
Then Jesus was led by the Spirit out into the desert to be put to the test by the
    devil. He fasted for forty days and forty nights, after which he was hungry, and
    the tester came and said to him, 'If you are the Son of God, tell these stones to
    turn into loaves.' But he replied, 'Scripture says: *Human beings live not on bread
    alone but on every word that comes from the mouth of God.*' The devil then took him
    to the holy city and set him upon the parapet of the Temple. 'If you are the Son
    of God,' he said, 'throw yourself down; for scripture says: *He has given his
    angels about you, and they will carry you in their arms in case you trip over a stone.*'
    Jesus said to him, 'Scripture also says: *Do not put the Lord your God to the test.*'
    Next, taking him to a very high mountain, the devil showed him all the king-
    doms of the world and their splendor. And he said to him, 'I will give you all
    these, if you fall at my feet and do me homage.' Then Jesus replied, 'Away with
    you, Satan! For scripture says: *The Lord your God is the one to whom you must do
    homage, him alone you must serve.*' Then the devil left him, and suddenly angels
    appeared and looked after him.

Matthew 4:1–11

The Refrain
We have sinned as our forebears did;* we have done wrong and dealt wickedly.

The Morning Psalm   LORD, *Let My Cry Come Unto You*
LORD, hear my prayer, and let my cry come before you;* hide not your face from
   me in the day of my trouble.
Incline your ear to me;* when I call, make haste to answer me,
For my days drift away like smoke,* and my bones are hot as burning coals.
My heart is smitten like grass and withered,* so that I forget to eat my bread.
Because of the voice of my groaning* I am but skin and bones.
I have become like a vulture in the wilderness,* like an owl among the ruins.
I lie awake and groan;* I am like a sparrow, lonely on a house-top.
My enemies revile me all day long,* and those who scoff at me have taken an oath
   against me.
For I have eaten ashes for bread* and mingled my drink with weeping.
Because of your indignation and wrath* you have lifted me up and thrown me away.
My days pass away like a shadow,* and I wither like the grass.
But you, O LORD, endure for ever,* and your Name from age to age.

Psalm 102:1–12

The Refrain
We have sinned as our forebears did;* we have done wrong and dealt wickedly.

The Small Verse
The people that walked in darkness have seen a great light; on those who live in a
   land of deep shadow a light has shone.

Isaiah 9:1

The Lord's Prayer

The Prayer Appointed for the Week
Almighty God, whose blessed Son was led by the Spirit to be tempted by Satan:
   Come quickly to help us who are assaulted by many temptations; and, as you
   know the weaknesses of each of us, let each one find you mighty to save;
   through Jesus Christ your Son our Lord, who lives and reigns with you and the
   Holy Spirit, one God, now and for ever. *Amen.* †

The Concluding Prayer of the Church
Lord God, almighty and everlasting Father, you have brought me in safety to this
   new day: Preserve me with your mighty power, that I may not fall into sin, nor
   be overcome by adversity; and in all I do direct me to the fulfilling of your purpose; through Jesus Christ my Lord. *Amen.* †

The Midday Office   **To Be Observed on the Hour or Half Hour**
                                    Between 11 a.m. and 2 p.m.

The Call to Prayer
Let all those whom the LORD has redeemed proclaim* that he redeemed them from
   the hand of the foe.

Psalm 107:2

The Request for Presence
May God give us his blessing,* and may all the ends of the earth stand in awe of him.

Psalm 67:7

The Greeting
You, O Lord, are a shield about me;* you are my glory, the one who lifts up my head.
I call aloud upon the Lord,* and he answers me from his holy hill;
I lie down and go to sleep;* I wake again, because the Lord sustains me.

Psalm 3:3–5

The Refrain for the Midday Lessons
May the glory of the Lord endure for ever;* may the Lord rejoice in all his works.

Psalm 104:32

A Reading
Of Christ, the Apostle wrote: ". . . he took to himself *the line of Abraham.* It was essential that he should in this way be made completely like his brothers so that he could become a compassionate and trustworthy high priest for their relationship to God, able to expiate the sins of the people. For the suffering he himself passed through while being put to the test enables him to help others when they are being put to the test."

Hebrews 2:16–18

The Refrain
May the glory of the Lord endure for ever;* may the Lord rejoice in all his works.

The Midday Psalm   *Having You I Desire Nothing Upon Earth*
Whom have I in heaven but you?* and having you I desire nothing upon earth.
Though my flesh and my heart should waste away,* God is the strength of my heart and my portion for ever.
Truly, those who forsake you will perish;* you destroy all who are unfaithful.
But it is good for me to be near God;* I have made the Lord God my refuge.

Psalm 73:25–28

The Refrain
May the glory of the Lord endure for ever;* may the Lord rejoice in all his works.

The Cry of the Church
O God, come to my assistance! O Lord, make haste to help me!

The Lord's Prayer

The Prayer Appointed for the Week
Almighty God, whose blessed Son was led by the Spirit to be tempted by Satan: Come quickly to help us who are assaulted by many temptations; and, as you know the weaknesses of each of us, let each one find you mighty to save; through Jesus Christ your Son our Lord, who lives and reigns with you and the Holy Spirit, one God, now and for ever. *Amen.* †

The Concluding Prayer of the Church
O God, on this first day of the week, I join all creation and people of all ages in praising you. Your kindness and forgiveness flow like a river through the centuries refreshing our faith, our hope and our love. May you be forever praised throughout all the ages. *Amen.*

The Vespers Office   **To Be Observed on the Hour or Half Hour**
                                       Between 5 and 8 p.m.

The Call to Prayer
Bless the LORD, you angels of his, you mighty ones who do his bidding,* and hearken to the voice of his word.
Bless the LORD, all you his hosts,* you ministers of his who do his will.
Bless the LORD, all you works of his, in all places of his dominion;* bless the LORD, O my soul.

Psalm 103:20–22

The Request for Presence
Hear, O Shepherd of Israel, leading Joseph like a flock;* shine forth, you that are enthroned upon the cherubim.

Psalm 80:1

The Greeting
Praise God from whom all blessings flow;
Praise him all creatures here below;
Praise Him above, you heavenly hosts;
Praise Father, Son, and Holy Ghost.
Doxology

The Hymn   *Sing with Gladness*
Sing, you faithful, sing with gladness, wake your noblest, sweetest strain,
With the praises of your Savior let his house resound again;
Him let all your music honor, let your songs exalt his reign.

Sing how he came forth from heaven, bowed himself to Bethlehem's cave,
Stooped to wear the servant's vesture, bore the pain, the cross, the grave,
Passed within the gates of darkness, thence his banished ones to save.

So, he tasted death for mortals, he, of humankind the head,
Sinless one, among the sinful, Prince of life, among the dead;
Thus he wrought the full redemption, and the captor captive led.

Now, on high, yet ever with us, from his Father's throne the Son
Rules and guides the world he ransomed, till the appointed work be done,
Till he sees, renewed, perfected, all things gathered into one.

John Ellerton

The Refrain for the Vespers Lessons
Fight those who fight me, O Lord;* attack those who are attacking me.
. . . say to my soul, "I am your salvation."

Psalm 35:1ff

The Vespers Psalm   *Lift Up Your Heads, O Gates*
Lift up your heads, O gates; lift them high, O everlasting doors;* and the King of
    glory shall come in.
"Who is this King of glory?"* "The Lord, strong and mighty, the Lord, mighty in
    battle."
Lift up your heads, O gates; lift them high, O everlasting doors;* and the King of
    glory shall come in.
"Who is he, this King of glory?"* "The Lord of hosts, he is the King of glory."

Psalm 24:7–10

The Refrain
Fight those who fight me, O Lord;* attack those who are attacking me.
. . . say to my soul, "I am your salvation."

The Cry of the Church
Even so, come Lord Jesus!

The Lord's Prayer

The Prayer Appointed for the Week
Almighty God, whose blessed Son was led by the Spirit to be tempted by Satan:
    Come quickly to help us who are assaulted by many temptations; and, as you
    know the weaknesses of each of us, let each one find you mighty to save;
    through Jesus Christ your Son our Lord, who lives and reigns with you and the
    Holy Spirit, one God, now and for ever. *Amen.* †

The Concluding Prayer of the Church
Lord God, whose Son our Savior Jesus Christ, triumphed over the powers of death
    and prepared for us our place in the new Jerusalem: Grant that I, who have this
    day given thanks for his resurrection, may praise you in the City of which he is
    the light, and where he lives and reigns for ever and ever. *Amen.* †

The Morning Office   **To Be Observed on the Hour or Half Hour**
Between 6 and 9 a.m.

The Call to Prayer
"Come now, let us reason together," says the Lord.
Isaiah 1:18, KJV

The Request for Presence
Be my strong rock, a castle to keep me safe;* you are my crag and my stronghold.
Psalm 71:3

The Greeting
The words of the LORD are pure words,* like silver refined from ore and purified
  seven times in the fire.

Psalm 12:6

The Refrain for the Morning Lessons
"Because the needy are oppressed, and the poor cry out in misery,* I will rise up,"
  says the LORD, "And give them the help they long for."

Psalm 12:5

A Reading
Jesus taught us, saying: "In all truth I tell you, no one can enter the kingdom of
  God without being born through water and the Spirit; what is born of human
  nature is human; what is born of the Spirit is spirit. Do not be surprised when I
  say: You must be born from above. The wind blows where it pleases; you can
  hear its sound, but you cannot tell where it comes from or where it is going. So
  it is with everyone who is born of the Spirit."

John 3:5–8

The Refrain
"Because the needy are oppressed, and the poor cry out in misery,* I will rise up,"
  says the LORD, "And give them the help they long for."

The Morning Psalm   *He Has Shown His People the Power of His Works*
Great are the deeds of the LORD!* they are studied by all who delight in them.
His work is full of majesty and splendor,* and his righteousness endures for ever.
He makes his marvelous works to be remembered;* the LORD is gracious and full
  of compassion.
He gives food to those who fear him;* he is ever mindful of his covenant.
He has shown his people the power of his works* in giving them the lands of the
  nations.
The works of his hands are faithfulness and justice;* all his commandments are
  sure.
They stand fast for ever and ever,* because they are done in truth and equity.
He sent redemption to his people; he commanded his covenant for ever;* holy and
  awesome is his Name.

Psalm 111:2–9

The Refrain
"Because the needy are oppressed, and the poor cry out in misery,* I will rise up,"
  says the LORD, "And give them the help they long for."

The Cry of the Church
Even so, come Lord Jesus!

The Lord's Prayer

The Prayer Appointed for the Week
Almighty God, whose blessed Son was led by the Spirit to be tempted by Satan:
Come quickly to help us who are assaulted by many temptations; and, as you
know the weaknesses of each of us, let each one find you mighty to save;
through Jesus Christ your Son our Lord, who lives and reigns with you and the
Holy Spirit, one God, now and for ever. *Amen.* †

The Concluding Prayer of the Church
Lord God, almighty and everlasting Father, you have brought me in safety to this
new day: Preserve me with your mighty power, that I may not fall into sin, nor
be overcome by adversity; and in all I do direct me to the fulfilling of your purpose; through Jesus Christ my Lord. *Amen.* †

The Midday Office   **To Be Observed on the Hour or Half Hour
                                      Between 11 a.m. and 2 p.m.**

The Call to Prayer
Let Israel rejoice in his Maker;* let the children of Zion be joyful in their King.

Psalm 149:2

The Request for Presence
Restore us, O God of hosts;* show me the light of your countenance, and we shall
be saved.

Psalm 80:7

The Greeting
Not to us, O LORD, not to us, but to your Name give glory;* because of your love
and because of your faithfulness.

Psalm 115:1

The Refrain for the Midday Lessons
Righteousness and justice are the foundations of your throne;* love and truth go
before your face.

Psalm 89:14

A Reading
Ephraim, how could I part with you? Israel, how could I give you up? How could
I make you like Admah or treat you like Zeboiim? My heart within me is over-
whelmed, fever grips my inmost being. I will not give rein to my fierce anger, I
will not destroy Ephraim again, for I am God, not man, the Holy One in your
midst, and I shall not come to you in anger.

Hosea 11:8–9

The Refrain
Righteousness and justice are the foundations of your throne;* love and truth go
before your face.

The Midday Psalm   *He Redeems Your Life from the Grave*

Bless the LORD, O my soul,* and all that is within me, bless his holy Name.

Bless the LORD, O my soul,* and forget not all his benefits.

He forgives all your sins* and heals all your infirmities;

He redeems your life from the grave* and crowns you with mercy and loving-
kindness;

He satisfies you with good things,* and your youth is renewed like an eagle's.

Psalm 103:1-5

The Refrain

Righteousness and justice are the foundations of your throne;* love and truth go
before your face.

The Cry of the Church

O God, come to my assistance! O Lord, make haste to help me!

The Lord's Prayer

The Prayer Appointed for the Week

Almighty God, whose blessed Son was led by the Spirit to be tempted by Satan:
Come quickly to help us who are assaulted by many temptations; and, as you
know the weaknesses of each of us, let each one find you mighty to save;
through Jesus Christ your Son our Lord, who lives and reigns with you and the
Holy Spirit, one God, now and for ever. *Amen.* †

The Concluding Prayer of the Church

God, you have prepared in peace the path I must follow today. Help me to walk
straight on that path. If I speak, remove lies from my lips. If I am hungry, take
away from me all complaint. If I have plenty, destroy pride in me. May I go
through the day calling on you, you, O Lord, who know no other Lord.

Ethiopian

The Vespers Office   **To Be Observed on the Hour or Half Hour**
Between 5 and 8 p.m.

The Call to Prayer

Taste and see that the LORD is good;* happy are those who trust in him!

Psalm 34:8

The Request for Presence

LORD, hear my prayer, and let my cry come before you;* hide not your face from
me in the day of my trouble.

Psalm 102:1

The Greeting

To you, O LORD, I lift up my soul;* my God I put my trust in you; . . .

Psalm 25:1

The Hymn

God, whose almighty word
Chaos and darkness heard
    And took their flight:
Hear us we humbly pray,
And where the gospel day
Sheds not its glorious ray
    Let there be light.

Savior who came to bring
On your redeeming wing
    Healing and sight—
Health to the sick in mind,
Sight to the inly blind—
O now to all mankind
    Let there be light.

Spirit of truth and love,
Life-giving holy dove,
    Speed on your flight;
Move on the waters' face,
Bearing the lamp of grace,
And in earth's darkest place
    Let there be light.

Holy and blessed Three,
Glorious Trinity,
    Wisdom, Love, Might,
Boundless as ocean-tide
Rolling in fullest pride,
Through the world, far and wide
    Let there be light.

John Marriott

The Refrain for the Vespers Lessons
Some put their trust in chariots and some in horses,* but we will call upon the
    Name of the LORD our God.

Psalm 20:7

The Vespers Psalm   *Glorious Things Are Spoken of You*
On the holy mountain stands the city he has founded;* the LORD loves the gates of
    Zion more than all the dwellings of Jacob.
Glorious things are spoken of you,* O city of our God.
I count Egypt and Babylon among those who know me;* behold Philistia, Tyre,
    and Ethiopia: in Zion were they born.
Of Zion it shall be said, "Everyone was born in her,* and the Most High himself
    shall sustain her."
The LORD will record as he enrolls the peoples,* "These also were born there."
The singers and the dancers will say,* "All my fresh springs are in you."

Psalm 87

The Refrain
Some put their trust in chariots and some in horses,* but we will call upon the
    Name of the LORD our God.

The Cry of the Church
Lord, have mercy on us. Christ, have mercy on us. Lord, have mercy on us.

The Lord's Prayer

The Prayer Appointed for the Week
Almighty God, whose blessed Son was led by the Spirit to be tempted by Satan:
    Come quickly to help us who are assaulted by many temptations; and, as you
    know the weaknesses of each of us, let each one find you mighty to save;

through Jesus Christ your Son our Lord, who lives and reigns with you and the Holy Spirit, one God, now and for ever. *Amen.* †

The Concluding Prayer of the Church
Stay, O Lord, with those who wake, or watch, or weep tonight, and give your angels and saints charge over those who sleep.

The Morning Office   **To Be Observed on the Hour or Half Hour Between 6 and 9 a.m.**

The Call to Prayer
Sing praise to the LORD who dwells in Zion;* proclaim to the peoples the things he has done.

Psalm 9:11

The Request for Presence
May God be merciful to us and bless us,* show us the light of his countenance and come to us.

Psalm 67:1

The Greeting
Awesome things will you show us in your righteousness, O God of our salvation,* O Hope of all the ends of the earth and of the seas that are far away.

The Refrain for the Morning Lessons
Your kingdom is an everlasting kingdom;* your dominion endures throughout all ages.

Psalm 145:13

A Reading
Jesus taught us, saying: "The sheep that belong to me listen to my voice; I know them and they follow me. I give them eternal life; they will never be lost and no one will ever steal anything from the Father's hand. The Father and I are as one."

John 10:27–30

The Refrain
Your kingdom is an everlasting kingdom;* your dominion endures throughout all ages.

The Morning Psalm   *O Israel, If You Would But Listen to Me*
Hear, O my people, and I will admonish you:* O Israel, if you would but listen to me!
There shall be no strange god among you;* you shall not worship a foreign god.
I am the LORD your God, who brought you out of the land of Egypt and said,* "Open your mouth wide, and I will fill it."

Psalm 81:8–10

The Refrain
Your kingdom is an everlasting kingdom;* your dominion endures throughout
all ages.

The Cry of the Church
O God, come to my assistance! O Lord, make haste to help me!

The Lord's Prayer

The Prayer Appointed for the Week
Almighty God, whose blessed Son was led by the Spirit to be tempted by Satan:
Come quickly to help us who are assaulted by many temptations; and, as you
know the weaknesses of each of us, let each one find you mighty to save;
through Jesus Christ your Son our Lord, who lives and reigns with you and the
Holy Spirit, one God, now and for ever. *Amen.* †

The Concluding Prayer of the Church
Lord God, almighty and everlasting Father, you have brought me in safety to this
new day: Preserve me with your mighty power, that I may not fall into sin, nor
be overcome by adversity; and in all I do direct me to the fulfilling of your purpose; through Jesus Christ my Lord. *Amen.* †

The Midday Office   **To Be Observed on the Hour or Half Hour**
                               Between 11 a.m. and 2 p.m.

The Call to Prayer
Let the words of my mouth and the meditation of my heart be acceptable in your
sight,* O LORD, my strength and my redeemer.

Psalm 19:14

The Request for Presence
Open my eyes, that I may see* the wonders of your law.

Psalm 119:18

The Greeting
My God, my rock in whom I put my trust,* my shield, the horn of my salvation,
and my refuge; you are worthy of praise.

Psalm 18:2

The Refrain for the Midday Lessons
When I called, you answered me;* you increased my strength within me.

Psalm 138:4

A Reading
When we were still helpless, at the appointed time, Christ died for the godless.

Romans 5:6

The Refrain
When I called, you answered me;* you increased my strength within me.

The Midday Psalm   *Give Me Life in Your Ways*

Teach me, O LORD, the way of your statutes,* and I shall keep it to the end.
Give me understanding, and I shall keep your law;* I shall keep it with all my
      heart.
Make me go in the path of your commandments,* for that is my desire.
Incline my heart to your decrees* and not to unjust gain.
Turn my eyes from watching what is worthless;* give me life in your ways.

Psalm 119:33–37

The Refrain
When I called, you answered me;* you increased my strength within me.

The Cry of the Church
Be, Lord, my helper and forsake me not. Do not despise me, O God, my savior.

THE SHORT BREVIARY

The Lord's Prayer

The Prayer Appointed for the Week
Almighty God, whose blessed Son was led by the Spirit to be tempted by Satan:
      Come quickly to help us who are assaulted by many temptations; and, as you
      know the weaknesses of each of us, let each one find you mighty to save;
      through Jesus Christ your Son our Lord, who lives and reigns with you and the
      Holy Spirit, one God, now and for ever. *Amen.* †

The Concluding Prayer of the Church
Heavenly Father, in you I live and move and have my being: I humbly pray you so
      to guide and govern me by your Holy Spirit, that in all cares and occupations
      of my life I may not forget you, but may remember that I am ever walking in
      your sight; through Jesus Christ my Lord. *Amen.* †

The Vespers Office   **To Be Observed on the Hour or Half Hour**
                                                    Between 5 and 8 p.m.

The Call to Prayer
Taste and see that the LORD is good;* happy are those who trust in him!

Psalm 34:8

The Request for Presence
O Lamb of God, that takes away the sins of the world, have mercy upon me.
O Lamb of God, that takes away the sins of the world, have mercy upon me.
O Lamb of God, that takes away the sins of the world, grant me your peace.

The Greeting
Happy are those whom you choose and draw to your courts to dwell there!* they
      will be satisfied by the beauty of your house, by the holiness of your temple.

Psalm 65:4

The Hymn   *Throw Out the Lifeline*

Throw out the lifeline across the dark wave,
There is a sister whom someone should save;
Or somebody's brother! Oh, who then, will dare
To throw out the lifeline, his peril to share?
Throw out the lifeline!
Throw out the lifeline!
Someone's drifting away.

Throw out the lifeline with hand quick and strong:
Why do you tarry, why linger so long?
Someone is sinking; oh, hasten today,
And out with the lifeboat, away, then, away!
Throw out the lifeline!
Throw out the lifeline!
Someone's drifting away.

Throw out the lifeline to danger fraught kin,
Sinking in anguish where you've never been:
Winds of temptation and billows of woe
Will soon hurl them out where dark waters flow.
Throw out the lifeline!
Throw out the lifeline!
Someone's drifting away.

Soon will the season of rescue be o'er,
Soon will they drift to eternity's shore;
Haste then, you faithful, no time for delay,
But throw out the lifeline and save them today.
Throw out the lifeline!
Throw out the lifeline!
Someone's sinking today.

                                  Edward Ufford

The Refrain for the Vespers Lessons

Light shines in the darkness for the upright;* the righteous are merciful and full of
    compassion.

                                  Psalm 112:4

The Vespers Psalm   *He Gives His Beloved Sleep*

Unless the Lord builds the house,* their labor is in vain who build it.
Unless the Lord watches over the city,* in vain the watchman keeps his vigil.
It is in vain that you rise so early and go to bed so late;* vain, too, to eat the bread
    of toil, for he gives to his beloved sleep.

                                  Psalm 127:1–3

The Refrain
Light shines in the darkness for the upright;* the righteous are merciful and full of compassion.

The Cry of the Church
In the evening, in the morning, and at noonday, I will complain and lament,* and he will hear my voice.

Psalm 55:18

The Lord's Prayer

The Prayer Appointed for the Week
Almighty God, whose blessed Son was led by the Spirit to be tempted by Satan: Come quickly to help us who are assaulted by many temptations; and, as you know the weaknesses of each of us, let each one find you mighty to save; through Jesus Christ your Son our Lord, who lives and reigns with you and the Holy Spirit, one God, now and for ever. *Amen.* †

The Concluding Prayer of the Church
Almighty Father,
you have given me the strength
to work throughout this day.
Receive my evening sacrifice of praise
in thanksgiving for your countless gifts.
I ask this through my Lord Jesus Christ, your Son,
who lives and reigns with you and the Holy Spirit,
one God, for ever and ever.

adapted from THE LITURGY OF THE HOURS, VOL. III

The Morning Office   **To Be Observed on the Hour or Half Hour**
Between 6 and 9 a.m.

The Call to Prayer
Bless our God, you peoples;* make the voice of his praise to be heard;
Who holds our souls in life,* and will not allow our feet to slip.

Psalm 66:7–8

The Request for Presence
Come to me speedily, O God. You are my helper and my deliverer;* LORD, do not tarry.

Psalm 70:5–6

The Greeting
You are my hope, O Lord GOD,* my confidence since I was young.
I have been sustained by you ever since I was born; from my mother's womb you have been my strength;* my praise shall be always of you.

Psalm 71:5–6

The Refrain for the Morning Lessons
"Be still, then, and know that I am God;* I will be exalted among the nations; I will be exalted in the earth."

Psalm 46:11

A Reading
Another said, 'I will follow you, sir, but first let me go and say good-bye to my people at home.' Jesus said to him, 'Once the hand is laid on the plow, no one who looks back is fit for the kingdom of God.'

Luke 9:61–62

The Refrain
"Be still, then, and know that I am God;* I will be exalted among the nations; I will be exalted in the earth."

The Morning Psalm   *A Thousand Years Are Like a Watch in the Night*
Lord, you have been our refuge* from one generation to another.
Before the mountains were brought forth, or the land and the earth were born,* from age to age you are God.
You turn us back to the dust and say,* "Go back, O child of earth."
For a thousand years in your sight are like yesterday when it is past* and like a watch in the night.
You sweep us away like a dream;* we fade away suddenly like the grass.
In the morning it is green and flourishes;* in the evening it is dried up and withered.
For we consume away in your displeasure;* we are afraid because of your wrathful indignation.
Our iniquities you have set before you,* and our secret sins in the light of your countenance.
So teach us to number our days* that we may apply our hearts to wisdom.

Psalm 90:1–8, 12

The Refrain
"Be still, then, and know that I am God;* I will be exalted among the nations; I will be exalted in the earth."

The Small Verse
The Son of Man shall be delivered over to the Gentiles, to be mocked and scourged and crucified.

The Lord's Prayer

The Prayer Appointed for the Week
Almighty God, whose blessed Son was led by the Spirit to be tempted by Satan: Come quickly to help us who are assaulted by many temptations; and, as you know the weaknesses of each of us, let each one find you mighty to save; through Jesus Christ your Son our Lord, who lives and reigns with you and the Holy Spirit, one God, now and for ever. *Amen.* †

The Concluding Prayer of the Church

Lord God, almighty and everlasting Father, you have brought me in safety to this
new day: Preserve me with your mighty power, that I may not fall into sin, nor
be overcome by adversity; and in all I do direct me to the fulfilling of your purpose; through Jesus Christ my Lord. *Amen.* †

The Midday Office

**To Be Observed on the Hour or Half Hour
Between 11 a.m. and 2 p.m.**

The Call to Prayer

Know this: The LORD himself is God;* he himself has made us, and we are his.

Psalm 100:2

The Request for Presence

May God be merciful to us and bless us,* show us the light of his countenance and
come to us.

Psalm 67:1

The Greeting

I will confess you among the peoples, O LORD;* I will sing praise to you among the
nations.
For your loving-kindness is greater than the heavens,* and your faithfulness
reaches to the clouds.

Psalm 57:9–10

The Refrain for the Midday Lessons

Whoever is wise will ponder these things,* and consider well the mercies of
the LORD.

Psalm 107:43

A Reading

As the chosen of God, then, the holy people whom he loves, you are to be clothed
in heartfelt compassion, in generosity and humility, gentleness and patience.

Colossians 3:12

The Refrain

Whoever is wise will ponder these things,* and consider well the mercies of
the LORD.

The Midday Psalm

Behold and Tend This Vine, O God of Hosts

Restore us, O God of hosts;* show the light of your countenance, and we shall be
saved.
You have brought a vine out of Egypt;* you cast out the nations and planted it.
You prepared the ground for it;* it took root and filled the land.
The mountains were covered by its shadow* and the towering cedar trees by its
boughs.
You stretched out its tendrils to the Sea* and its branches to the River.
Why have you broken down its wall,* so that all who pass by pluck off its grapes?

The wild boar of the forest has ravaged it,* and the beasts of the field have grazed
upon it.
Turn now, O God of hosts, look down from heaven; behold and tend this vine;*
preserve what your right hand has planted.

Psalm 80:7–14

The Refrain
Whoever is wise will ponder these things,* and consider well the mercies of
the LORD.

The Small Verse
Truth shall spring up from the earth,* and righteousness shall look down from
heaven.

Psalm 85:11

The Lord's Prayer

The Prayer Appointed for the Week
Almighty God, whose blessed Son was led by the Spirit to be tempted by Satan:
Come quickly to help us who are assaulted by many temptations; and, as you
know the weaknesses of each of us, let each one find you mighty to save;
through Jesus Christ your Son our Lord, who lives and reigns with you and the
Holy Spirit, one God, now and for ever. *Amen.* †

The Concluding Prayer of the Church
Lord God Almighty, you have made all the peoples of the earth for your glory, to
serve you in freedom and in peace: Give to the people of our country a zeal for
justice and the strength of forbearance, that we may use our liberty in accor-
dance with your gracious will; through Jesus Christ our Lord, who lives and
reigns with you and the Holy Spirit, one God, for ever and ever. *Amen.* †

The Vespers Office   **To Be Observed on the Hour or Half Hour
Between 5 and 8 p.m.**

The Call to Prayer
Sing praises to God, sing praises;* sing praises to our King, sing praises.

Psalm 47:6

The Request for Presence
O God, be not far from me;* come quickly to help me, O my God.

Psalm 71:12

The Greeting
For you, O God, have proved us;* you have tried us just as silver is tried.
You brought us into the snare;* you laid heavy burdens upon our backs.
You let enemies ride over our heads; we went through fire and water;* but you
brought us out into a place of refreshment.

Psalm 66:9–11

The Hymn   *On the Crucifixion*
  Behold the Savior of mankind
  Nailed to the shameful tree;
  How vast the love that him inclined
  To bleed and die for me!

  Hark how he groans! While nature shakes,
  And earth's strong pillars bend!
  The temple's veil in sunder breaks,
  The solid marbles rend.

  It's done! The precious ransom's paid!
  "Receive my soul!" he cries;
  See how he bows his sacred head!
  He bows his head and dies!

  But soon he'll break death's envious chain
  And in full glory shine.
  O Lamb of God, was ever pain,
  Was ever love, like thine?

                    Samuel Wesley

The Refrain for the Vespers Lessons
The LORD, the God of gods, has spoken;* he has called the earth from the rising of
  the sun to its setting.

                    Psalm 50:1

The Vespers Psalm   *So That My Ways Were Made So Direct*
Happy are they whose way is blameless,* who walk in the law of the LORD!
Happy are they who observe his decrees* and seek him with all their hearts!
Who never do any wrong,* but always walk in his ways.
You laid down your commandments,* that we should fully keep them.
Oh, that my ways were made so direct* that I might keep your statutes!
Then I should not be put to shame,* when I regard all your commandments.
I will thank you with an unfeigned heart,* when I have learned your righteous
  judgments.
I will keep your statutes;* do not utterly forsake me.

                    Psalm 119:1–8

The Refrain
The LORD, the God of gods, has spoken;* he has called the earth from the rising of
  the sun to its setting.

The Small Verse
Create in me a clean heart, O God,* and renew a right spirit within me.

                    Psalm 51:11

The Lord's Prayer

The Prayer Appointed for the Week
Almighty God, whose blessed Son was led by the Spirit to be tempted by Satan:
Come quickly to help us who are assaulted by many temptations; and, as you
know the weaknesses of each of us, let each one find you mighty to save;
through Jesus Christ your Son our Lord, who lives and reigns with you and the
Holy Spirit, one God, now and for ever. *Amen.* †

The Concluding Prayer of the Church
Protect us, Lord, as we stay awake; watch over us as we sleep, that awake we may
watch with Christ, and asleep, rest in his peace. *Amen.*

The Morning Office   **To Be Observed on the Hour or Half Hour**
Between 6 and 9 a.m.

The Call to Prayer
Open my lips, O LORD,* and my mouth shall proclaim your praise.
Psalm 51:16

The Request for Presence
Send out your light and your truth, that they may lead me,* and bring me to your
holy hill and to your dwelling.
Psalm 43:3

The Greeting
Who is like you, LORD God of hosts?* O mighty LORD, your faithfulness is all
around you.
Righteousness and justice are the foundations of your throne;* love and truth go
before your face.
Psalm 89:8ff

The Refrain for the Morning Lessons
I will walk in the presence of the LORD* in the land of the living.
Psalm 116:8

A Reading
Jesus taught us, saying: "And the judgement is this: though the light has come into
the world people have preferred darkness to the light because their deeds were
evil . . . but whoever does the truth comes out into the light, so that what he is
doing may plainly appear as done in God."
John 3:19, 21

The Refrain
I will walk in the presence of the LORD* in the land of the living.

The Morning Psalm   *It Is God by Whom We Escape Death*
O God, when you went forth before your people,* when you marched through the
wilderness,
The earth shook, and the skies poured down rain at the presence of God, the God
of Sinai,* at the presence of God, the God of Israel.

You sent a gracious rain, O God, upon your inheritance;* you refreshed the land
    when it was weary.
Your people found their home in it;* in your goodness, O God, you have made
    provision for the poor.
The chariots of God are twenty thousand, even thousands of thousands;* the Lord
    comes in holiness from Sinai.
You have gone up on high and led captivity captive; you have received gifts even
    from your enemies,* that the LORD God might dwell among them.
Blessed be the Lord day by day,* the God of our salvation, who bears our burdens.
He is our God, the God of our salvation;* God is the LORD, by whom we escape
    death.

Psalm 68:7–10, 17–20

The Refrain
I will walk in the presence of the LORD* in the land of the living.

The Cry of the Church
In the evening, in the morning, and at noonday, I will complain and lament,* and
    he will hear my voice.

Psalm 55:18

The Lord's Prayer

The Prayer Appointed for the Week
Almighty God, whose blessed Son was led by the Spirit to be tempted by Satan:
    Come quickly to help us who are assaulted by many temptations; and, as you
    know the weaknesses of each of us, let each one find you mighty to save;
    through Jesus Christ your Son our Lord, who lives and reigns with you and the
    Holy Spirit, one God, now and for ever. *Amen.* †

The Concluding Prayer of the Church
Lord God, almighty and everlasting Father, you have brought me in safety to this
    new day: Preserve me with your mighty power, that I may not fall into sin, nor
    be overcome by adversity; and in all I do direct me to the fulfilling of your pur-
    pose; through Jesus Christ my Lord. *Amen.* †

The Midday Office   To Be Observed on the Hour or Half Hour
Between 11 a.m. and 2 p.m.

The Call to Prayer
Open my lips, O Lord,* and my mouth shall proclaim your praise.

Psalm 51:16

The Request for Presence
Bow down your ear, O LORD, and answer me . . .
Keep watch over my life, for I am faithful.

Psalm 86:1–2

The Greeting
I will offer you the sacrifice of thanksgiving* and call upon the Name of the LORD.

Psalm 116:15

The Refrain for the Midday Lessons
The angel of the LORD encompasses those who fear him,* and he will deliver them.

Psalm 34:7

A Reading
YAHWEH said: "Can a woman forget her baby at the breast, feel no pity for the child she has borne? Even if these were to forget, I shall not forget you."

Isaiah 49:15

The Refrain
The angel of the LORD encompasses those who fear him,* and he will deliver them.

The Midday Psalm   *Your Love, O LORD, Upheld Me*
If the LORD had not come to my help,* I should soon have dwelt in the land of silence.
As often as I said, "My foot has slipped,"* your love, O LORD, upheld me.
When many cares fill my mind,* your consolations cheer my soul.

Psalm 94:17–19

The Refrain
The angel of the LORD encompasses those who fear him,* and he will deliver them.

The Cry of the Church
O God, come to my assistance!* O Lord, make haste to help me!

The Lord's Prayer

The Prayer Appointed for the Week
Almighty God, whose blessed Son was led by the Spirit to be tempted by Satan: Come quickly to help us who are assaulted by many temptations; and, as you know the weaknesses of each of us, let each one find you mighty to save; through Jesus Christ your Son our Lord, who lives and reigns with you and the Holy Spirit, one God, now and for ever. *Amen.* †

The Concluding Prayer of the Church
Most gracious God and Father, you are with me as I make my journey throughout this day. Help me to look lovingly upon all people and events that come into my life today and to walk gently upon this land. Grant this through Jesus who lives and walks among us ever present at each moment. *Amen.* †

The Vespers Office   **To Be Observed on the Hour or Half Hour Between 5 and 8 p.m.**

The Call to Prayer
Come, let us bow down, and bend the knee,* and kneel before the LORD our Maker.

Psalm 95:6

The Request for Presence
Accept, O LORD, the willing tribute of my lips,* and teach me your judgments.
Psalm 119:108

The Greeting
O LORD of hosts,* happy are they who put their trust in you!
Psalm 84:12

The Hymn   *Beneath the Cross of Jesus*
Beneath the cross of Jesus I fain would take my stand,
The shadow of a mighty rock within a weary land,
A home within the wilderness, a rest upon the way,
From the burning noontime heat and the burden of the day.

Upon the cross of Jesus my eyes at times can see
The very dying form of one who suffered there for me;
And from my smitten heart with tears two wonders I confess:
The wonders of redeeming love and my unworthiness.

I take, O cross, your shadow for my abiding place;
I ask no other sunshine than the sunshine of his face;
Content to let my pride go by, to know no gain nor loss,
My sinful self my only shame, my glory all the cross.
Elizabeth Clephane

The Refrain for the Vespers Lessons
You have been gracious to your land, O LORD,* you have restored the good fortune
of Jacob.
Psalm 85:1

The Vespers Psalm   *I Will Listen to What the LORD God Is Saying*
Show us your mercy, O LORD,* and grant us your salvation.
I will listen to what the LORD God is saying,* for he is speaking peace to his faithful
people and to those who turn their hearts to him.
Truly, his salvation is very near to those who fear him,* that his glory may dwell in
our land.
Mercy and truth have met together;* righteousness and peace have kissed each
other.
Truth shall spring up from the earth,* and righteousness shall look down from
heaven.
The LORD will indeed grant prosperity,* and our land will yield its increase.
Righteousness shall go before him,* and peace shall be a pathway for his feet.
Psalm 85:7-13

The Refrain
You have been gracious to your land, O LORD,* you have restored the good fortune
of Jacob.

The Small Verse
The Son of man shall be delivered over to the Gentiles to be mocked and scourged
and crucified.

The Lord's Prayer

The Prayer Appointed for the Week
Almighty God, whose blessed Son was led by the Spirit to be tempted by Satan:
Come quickly to help us who are assaulted by many temptations; and, as you
know the weaknesses of each of us, let each one find you mighty to save;
through Jesus Christ your Son our Lord, who lives and reigns with you and the
Holy Spirit, one God, now and for ever. *Amen.* †

The Concluding Prayer of the Church
O holy God, as evening falls remain with us, Remember our good deeds and forgive our failings. Help us to reflect upon and live according to your covenant
of love. Be with our lonely and elderly sisters and brothers in the evening of
their lives. May all who long to see you face to face know the comfort of your
presence. This we ask in union with Simeon and Anna and all who have gone
before us blessing and proclaiming you by the fidelity of their lives. *Amen.*

THE NEW COMPANION TO THE BREVIARY

The Morning Office   **To Be Observed on the Hour or Half Hour**
Between 6 and 9 a.m.

The Call to Prayer
Fear the LORD, you that are his saints,* for those who fear him lack nothing.

Psalm 34:9

The Request for Presence
Be my strong rock, a castle to keep me safe;* you are my crag and my stronghold.

Psalm 71:3

The Greeting
O LORD, I cry to you for help;* in the morning my prayer comes before you.

Psalm 88:14

The Refrain for the Morning Lessons
God is a righteous judge;* God sits in judgment every day.

Psalm 7:12

A Reading
Then, speaking to all, he said, 'If anyone wants to be a follower of mine, let him
renounce himself and take up his cross everyday and follow me.'

Luke 9:23

The Refrain
God is a righteous judge;* God sits in judgment every day.

The Morning Psalm   *Teach Us to Number Our Days*
The span of our life is seventy years, perhaps in strength even eighty;* yet the sum
of them is but labor and sorrow, for they pass away quickly and we are gone.
Who regards the power of your wrath?* who rightly fears your indignation?
So teach us to number our days* that we may apply our hearts to wisdom.

Psalm 90:10–12

The Refrain
God is a righteous judge;* God sits in judgment every day.

The Small Verse
Today if you shall hear his voice, harden not your heart.

The Lord's Prayer

The Prayer Appointed for the Week
Almighty God, whose blessed Son was led by the Spirit to be tempted by Satan:
Come quickly to help us who are assaulted by many temptations; and, as you
know the weaknesses of each of us, let each one find you mighty to save;
through Jesus Christ your Son our Lord, who lives and reigns with you and the
Holy Spirit, one God, now and for ever. *Amen.* †

The Concluding Prayer of the Church
Lord God, almighty and everlasting Father, you have brought me in safety to this
new day: Preserve me with your mighty power, that I may not fall into sin, nor
be overcome by adversity; and in all I do direct me to the fulfilling of your purpose; through Jesus Christ my Lord. *Amen.* †

The Midday Office   **To Be Observed on the Hour or Half Hour**
Between 11 a.m. and 2 p.m.

The Call to Prayer
Come now and look upon the works of the LORD,* what awesome things he has
done on earth.

Psalm 46:9

The Request for Presence
O LORD, I call to you; come to me quickly;* hear my voice when I cry to you.

Psalm 141:1

The Greeting
When I was in trouble, I called to the LORD;* I called to the LORD, and he answered
me.

The Refrain for the Midday Lessons
Let them be put to shame and thrown back,* all those who are enemies of Zion.

Psalm 129:5

A Reading
With so many witnesses in a great cloud all around us, we too, then, should throw off everything that weighs us down and the sin that clings so closely and with perseverance keep running in the race which lies ahead of us.

Hebrews 12:1

The Refrain
Let them be put to shame and thrown back,* all those who are enemies of Zion.

The Midday Psalm   *Your Word Is a Light Upon My Path*
Your word is a lantern to my feet* and a light upon my path.
I have sworn and am determined* to keep your righteous judgments.
I am deeply troubled;* preserve my life, O LORD, according to your word.
Accept, O LORD, the willing tribute of my lips,* and teach me your judgments.
My life is always in my hand,* yet I do not forget your law.
The wicked have set a trap for me,* but I have not strayed from your commandments.
Your decrees are my inheritance for ever;* truly, they are the joy of my heart.
I have applied my heart to fulfill your statutes* for ever and to the end.

Psalm 119:105–112

The Refrain
Let them be put to shame and thrown back,* all those who are enemies of Zion.

The Small Verse
From my secret sins cleanse me, Lord. And from all strange evils deliver me.

The Lord's Prayer

The Prayer Appointed for the Week
Almighty God, whose blessed Son was led by the Spirit to be tempted by Satan: Come quickly to help us who are assaulted by many temptations; and, as you know the weaknesses of each of us, let each one find you mighty to save; through Jesus Christ your Son our Lord, who lives and reigns with you and the Holy Spirit, one God, now and for ever. *Amen.* †

The Concluding Prayer of the Church
Lord Jesus Christ, by your death you took away the sting of death: Grant me to so follow in faith where you have led the way, that I may at length fall asleep peacefully in you and wake in your likeness; for your tender mercies' sake. *Amen.* †

The Vespers Office   **To Be Observed on the Hour or Half Hour**
                                      Between 5 and 8 p.m.

The Call to Prayer
O tarry and await the LORD's pleasure; be strong, and he shall comfort your heart;* wait patiently for the LORD.

Psalm 27:18

The Request for Presence
I have said to the LORD, "You are my God;* listen, O LORD, to my supplication."

Psalm 140:6

The Greeting
I am bound by the vow I made to you, O God;* I will present to you thank-
offerings;
For you have rescued my soul from death and my feet from stumbling,* that I may
walk before God in the light of the living.

Psalm 56:11–12

The Hymn   *Out of My Bondage, Sorrow, and Night*
Out of my bondage, sorrow, and night,
         Jesus, I come, Jesus, I come;
Into Your freedom, gladness, and light,
         Jesus, I come to You;
Out of my sickness into Your health,
Out of my want and into Your wealth,
Out of my sin and into Yourself,
         Jesus, I come to You.

Out of my shameful failure and loss,
         Jesus, I come, Jesus, I come;
Into the glorious gain of Your cross,
         Jesus, I come to You;
Out of earth's sorrows into Your balm,
Out of life's storm and into Your calm,
Out of distress to jubilant psalm,
         Jesus, I come to You;

Out of unrest and arrogant pride,
         Jesus, I come, Jesus, I come;
Into Your blessed will to abide,
         Jesus, I come to You;
Out of myself to dwell in Your love,
Out of despair into raptures above,
Upward for ever on wings like a dove,
         Jesus, I come to You;

Out of the fear and dread of the tomb,
         Jesus, I come, Jesus, I come;
Into the joy and light of Your home,
         Jesus, I come to You;
Out of the depths of ruin untold,
Into the peace of Your sheltering fold,
Ever Your glorious face to behold,
         Jesus, I come to You;

William Sleeper

The Refrain for the Vespers Lessons
Purge me from my sin, and I shall be pure;* wash me, and I shall be clean indeed.

Psalm 51:8

The Vespers Psalm *God Reveals Himself in Glory*
The LORD, the God of gods, has spoken;* he has called the earth from the rising of
the sun to its setting.

Out of Zion, perfect in its beauty,* God reveals himself in glory.

Our God will come and will not keep silence;* before him there is a consuming
flame, and round about him a raging storm.

He calls the heavens and the earth from above* to witness the judgment of his
people.

"Gather before me my loyal followers,* those who have made a covenant with
me* and sealed it with sacrifice."

Let the heavens declare the rightness of his cause;* for God himself is judge.

Psalm 50:1–6

The Refrain
Purge me from my sin, and I shall be pure;* wash me, and I shall be clean indeed.

The Cry of the Church
Lord, have mercy on us. Christ, have mercy on us. Lord, have mercy on us.

The Lord's Prayer

The Prayer Appointed for the Week
Almighty God, whose blessed Son was led by the Spirit to be tempted by Satan:
Come quickly to help us who are assaulted by many temptations; and, as you
know the weaknesses of each of us, let each one find you mighty to save;
through Jesus Christ your Son our Lord, who lives and reigns with you and the
Holy Spirit, one God, now and for ever. *Amen.* †

Concluding Prayers of the Church
Almighty God, who has promised to hear the petitions of those who ask in your
Son's Name: I beseech you mercifully to incline your ear to me who have made
my prayers and supplications to you; and grant that those things which I have
faithfully asked according to your will, may effectually be obtained, to the
relief of my necessity, and to the setting forth of your glory; through Jesus
Christ my Lord. *Amen.* †

May the souls of the faithful departed, through the mercy of God, rest in eternal
peace. *Amen.*

The Morning Office **To Be Observed on the Hour or Half Hour
Between 6 and 9 a.m.**

The Call to Prayer
Praise the LORD, for the LORD is good;* sing praises to his Name for it is lovely.

Psalm 135:1

The Request for Presence
In your righteousness, deliver and set me free;* incline your ear to me and save me.
Psalm 71:2

The Greeting
O LORD I am your servant;* I am your servant and the child of your handmaid.
Psalm 116:14

The Refrain for the Morning Lessons
I was pressed so hard that I almost fell,* but the LORD came to my help.
Psalm 118:13

A Reading
Jesus said: "Jerusalem, Jerusalem, you that kill the prophets and stone those who are sent to you! How often have I longed to gather your children together, as a hen gathers her brood under her wings, and you refused! Look! Your house will be left to you. Yes, I promise you, you shall not see me till the time comes when you are saying: *Blessed is he who comes in the name of the Lord!*"
Luke 13:34–35

The Refrain
I was pressed so hard that I almost fell,* but the LORD came to my help.

The Morning Psalm   *O LORD, I Am Your Servant*
Precious in the sight of the LORD* is the death of his servants.
O LORD, I am your servant;* I am your servant and the child of your handmaid;
    you have freed me from my bonds.
I will offer you the sacrifice of thanksgiving* and call upon the Name of the LORD.
I will fulfill my vows to the LORD* in the presence of all his people,
In the courts of the LORD's house,* in the midst of you, O Jerusalem.
Psalm 116:13–17

The Refrain
I was pressed so hard that I almost fell,* but the LORD came to my help.

The Cry of the Church
O God, come to my assistance! O Lord, make haste to help me!

The Lord's Prayer

The Prayer Appointed for the Week
Almighty God, whose blessed Son was led by the Spirit to be tempted by Satan: Come quickly to help us who are assaulted by many temptations; and, as you know the weaknesses of each of us, let each one find you mighty to save; through Jesus Christ your Son our Lord, who lives and reigns with you and the Holy Spirit, one God, now and for ever. *Amen.* †

The Concluding Prayer of the Church
Lord God, almighty and everlasting Father, you have brought me in safety to this new day: Preserve me with your mighty power, that I may not fall into sin, nor

be overcome by adversity; and in all I do direct me to the fulfilling of your purpose; through Jesus Christ my Lord. *Amen.* †

The Midday Office   **To Be Observed on the Hour or Half Hour**
                                         Between 11 a.m. and 2 p.m.

The Call to Prayer
Ascribe to the LORD the honor due his Name;* bring offerings and come into his courts.

Psalm 96:8

The Request for Presence
Accept, O LORD, the willing tribute of my lips,* and teach me your judgments.

Psalm 119:108

The Greeting
I give you thanks, O God, I give you thanks,* calling upon your Name and declaring all your wonderful deeds.

based on Psalm 75:1

The Refrain for the Midday Lessons
My tongue will proclaim your righteousness all day long.

Psalm 71:24

A Reading
'Come, let us talk this over,' says YAHWEH. 'Though your sins are like scarlet, they shall be white as snow; though they are as red as crimson, they shall be like wool. If you are willing to obey, you shall eat the good things of the earth. But if you refuse and rebel, the sword shall eat you instead—for YAHWEH's mouth has spoken.'

Isaiah 1:18–20

The Refrain
My tongue will proclaim your righteousness all day long.

The Midday Psalm   *We Will Not Let Hide What Our Forefathers Have Told Us*
Hear my teaching, O my people;* incline your ears to the words of my mouth.
I will open my mouth in a parable;* I will declare the mysteries of ancient times.
That which we have heard and known, and what our forefathers have told us,* we will not hide from their children.
We will recount to generations to come the praiseworthy deeds and the power of the LORD,* and the wonderful works he has done.
He gave his decrees to Jacob and established a law for Israel,* which he commanded them to teach their children;
That the generations to come might know, and the children yet unborn;* that they in their turn might tell it to their children;

So that they might put their trust in God,* and not forget the deeds of God, but
keep his commandments;

Psalm 78:1–7

The Refrain
My tongue will proclaim your righteousness all day long.

The Cry of the Church
O God, come to my assistance! O Lord, make haste to help me!

The Lord's Prayer

The Prayer Appointed for the Week
Almighty God, whose blessed Son was led by the Spirit to be tempted by Satan:
Come quickly to help us who are assaulted by many temptations; and, as you
know the weaknesses of each of us, let each one find you mighty to save;
through Jesus Christ your Son our Lord, who lives and reigns with you and the
Holy Spirit, one God, now and for ever. *Amen.* †

The Concluding Prayer of the Church
O God, the source of eternal light: Shed forth your unending day upon all of us
who watch for you, that our lips may praise you, our lives may bless you, and
our worship may give you glory; through Jesus Christ our Lord. *Amen.* †

The Vespers Office   **To Be Observed on the Hour or Half Hour**
Between 5 and 8 p.m.

The Call to Prayer
Proclaim with me the greatness of the LORD;* let us exalt his Name together.

Psalm 34:8

The Request for Presence
. . . Come to me speedily, O God* . . .

Psalm 70:5

The Greeting
And now that I am old and gray-headed, O God, do not forsake me,* till I make
known your strength to this generation and your power to all who are to come.
Your righteousness, O God, reaches to the heavens;*

Psalm 72:18–19

The Hymn   *Lord, I'm Coming Home*
I've wandered far away from God,
Now I'm coming home;
The paths of sin too long I've trod.
Lord, I'm coming home.
Coming home, coming home,
Nevermore to roam,
Open wide Your loving arms,
O Lord, I'm coming home.

I've wasted many precious years,
Now I'm coming home;
I now repent with bitter tears,
Lord, I'm coming home.

I've tired of sin and straying, Lord,
Now I'm coming home;
I'll trust Your love, believe Your word,
Lord, I'm coming home.

My soul is sick, my heart is sore,
Now I'm coming home;
My strength renew, my hope restore,
Lord, I'm coming home.
Now I'm coming home;
Lord, I'm coming home.
Coming home, coming home,
Nevermore to roam,
Open wide Your loving arms,
O Lord, I'm coming home.

William Kirkpatrick

The Refrain for the Vespers Lessons
Let them know that you, whose Name is YAHWEH,* you alone are the Most High
over all the earth.

Psalm 83:18

The Vespers Psalm   *I Meditate on You in the Night Watches*
O God, you are my God; eagerly I seek you;* my soul thirsts for you, my flesh
    faints for you, as in a barren and dry land where there is no water.
Therefore I have gazed upon you in your holy place,* that I might behold your
    power and your glory.
For your loving-kindness is better than life itself;* my lips shall give you praise.
So will I bless you as long as I live* and lift up my hands in your Name.
My soul is content, as with marrow and fatness,* and my mouth praises you with
    joyful lips,
When I remember you upon my bed,* and meditate on you in the night watches.
For you have been my helper,* and under the shadow of your wings I will rejoice.
My soul clings to you;* your right hand holds me fast.

Psalm 63:1–8

The Refrain
Let them know that you, whose Name is YAHWEH,* you alone are the Most High
over all the earth.

The Small Verse
From the rising of the sun to the place of its going down, let the name of the Lord
be praised henceforth and forever more.

Lent Compline

Sunday
The Night Office   **To Be Observed Before Retiring**

The Call to Prayer
May the Lord Almighty grant me and those I love a peaceful night and a perfect
end. *Amen.* †

The Request for Presence
Our help is in the Name of the Lord; the maker of heaven and earth.

The Greeting
Almighty God, my heavenly Father: I have sinned against you, through my own
fault, in thought, and word, and deed, in what I have done and in what I have
left undone. For the sake of your Son our Lord Jesus Christ, forgive me all my
offenses; and grant that I may serve you in newness of life, to the glory of your
Name. *Amen.* †

The Reading
It happened some time later that God put Abraham to the test. 'Abraham,
Abraham!' he called. 'Here I am,' he replied. God said, 'Take your son, your
only son, your beloved Isaac, and go to the land of Moriah, where you are to
offer him as a burnt offering on one of the mountains which I shall point out to
you.' Early next morning Abraham saddled his donkey and took with him two
of his servants and his son Isaac. He chopped wood for the burnt offering and
started on his journey to the place which God had indicated to him. On the
third day Abraham looked up and saw the place in the distance. Then
Abraham said to his servants, 'Stay here with the donkey. The boy and I are
going over there; we shall worship and then come back to you.' Abraham took
the wood for the burnt offering, loaded it on Isaac, and carried in his own
hands the fire and the knife. Then the two of them set out together. Isaac spoke
to his father Abraham. 'Father?' he said. 'Yes my son,' he replied. 'Look,' he
said, 'here are the fire and the wood, but where is the lamb for the burnt offering?' Abraham replied, 'My son, God himself will supply the lamb for the
burnt offering.' And the two of them went on together. When they arrived at
the place which God had indicated to him, Abraham built an altar there, and
arranged the wood. Then he bound his son and put him on the altar on top of
the wood. Abraham stretched out his hand and took the knife to kill his son.
But the angel of YAHWEH called to him from heaven. 'Abraham, Abraham!' he
said. 'Here I am,' he replied. 'Do not raise your hand against the boy,' the angel
said. 'Do not harm him, for now I know you fear God. You have not refused me
your own beloved son.' Then looking up, Abraham saw a ram caught by its
horns in a bush. Abraham took the ram and offered it as a burnt offering in
place of his son. Abraham called this place 'YAHWEH provides,' and hence the
saying today: 'On the mountain YAHWEH provides.' The angel of YAHWEH
called Abraham a second time from heaven. 'I swear by my own self, YAHWEH
declares, that because you have done this, because you have not refused me
your own beloved son, I will shower blessings on you and make your descen-

dants as numerous as the stars of heaven and the grains of sand on the
seashore. Your descendants will gain possession of the gate of their enemies.
All nations on earth will bless themselves by your descendants, because you
have obeyed my command.' Abraham went back to his servants, and together
they set out for Beersheba, and Abraham settled in Beersheba.

Genesis 22:1–19

The Gloria*

The Psalm   *I Put My Trust in You*

To you, O LORD, I lift up my soul; my God, I put my trust in you;* let me not be
humiliated, nor let my enemies triumph over me.

Let none who look to you be put to shame;* let the treacherous be disappointed in
their schemes.

Show me your ways, O LORD,* and teach me your paths.

Lead me in your truth and teach me,* for you are the God of my salvation; in you
have I trusted all the day long.

Psalm 25:1–4

The Gloria*

The Small Verse

Into your hands, O Lord, I commend my spirit; for you have redeemed me, O
Lord, O God of truth. Keep me, O Lord, as the apple of your eye; hide me
under the shadow of your wings. †

The Lord's Prayer

The Petition

Keep watch, dear Lord, with those who work, or watch, or weep this night, and
give your angels charge over those who sleep. Tend the sick, Lord Christ; give
rest to the weary, bless the dying, soothe the suffering, pity the afflicted, shield
the joyous; and all for your love's sake. *Amen.* †

The Final Thanksgiving

Lord, you now have set your servant free to go in peace as you have promised; for
these eyes of mine have seen the Savior, whom you have prepared for all the
world to see: a Light to enlighten the nations, and the glory of your people
Israel. Glory to the Father, and to the Son, and to the Holy Spirit: as it was in the
beginning, is now, and will be for ever. *Amen.*

Monday
The Night Office   **To Be Observed Before Retiring**

The Call to Prayer
May the Lord Almighty grant me and those I love a peaceful night and a perfect
end. *Amen.* †

The Request for Presence
Our help is in the Name of the Lord; the maker of heaven and earth.

The Greeting
Almighty God, my heavenly Father: I have sinned against you, through my own
fault, in thought, and word, and deed, in what I have done and in what I have
left undone. For the sake of your Son our Lord Jesus Christ, forgive me all my
offenses; and grant that I may serve you in newness of life, to the glory of your
Name. *Amen.* †

The Reading
The will of God be done by us;
The law of God be kept by us;
Our evil will controlled by us;
Our sharp tongue checked by us;
Quick forgiveness offered by us;
Speedy repentance made by us;
Temptation sternly shunned by us;
Blessed death welcomed by us;
Angels' music heard by us;
God's highest praises sung by us.
                    from CELTIC PRAYERS

*The Gloria**

The Psalm   *Look on Him and Be Radiant*
I sought the LORD, and he answered me* and delivered me out of all my terror.
Look upon him and be radiant,* and let not your faces be ashamed.
I called in my affliction and the LORD heard me* and saved me from all my
     troubles.
The angel of the LORD encompasses those who fear him,* and he will deliver them.
Taste and see that the LORD is good;* happy are they who trust in him!
                              Psalm 34:4–8

*The Gloria**

The Small Verse
Into your hands, O Lord, I commend my spirit; For you have redeemed me, O
     Lord, O God of truth. Keep me, O Lord, as the apple of your eye; Hide me
     under the shadow of your wings. †

The Lord's Prayer

The Petition

Keep watch, dear Lord, with those who work, or watch, or weep this night, and
give your angels charge over those who sleep. Tend the sick, Lord Christ; give
rest to the weary, bless the dying, soothe the suffering, pity the afflicted, shield
the joyous; and all for your love's sake. *Amen.* †

The Final Thanksgiving

Lord, you now have set your servant free to go in peace as you have promised; for
these eyes of mine have seen the Savior, whom you have prepared for all the
world to see: a Light to enlighten the nations, and the glory of your people
Israel. Glory to the Father, and to the Son, and to the Holy Spirit: as it was in the
beginning, is now, and will be for ever. *Amen.*

Tuesday
The Night Office   **To Be Observed Before Retiring**

The Call to Prayer

May the Lord Almighty grant me and those I love a peaceful night and a perfect
end. *Amen.* †

The Request for Presence

Our help is in the Name of the Lord; the maker of heaven and earth.

The Greeting

Almighty God, my heavenly Father: I have sinned against you, through my own
fault, in thought, and word, and deed, in what I have done and in what I have
left undone. For the sake of your Son our Lord Jesus Christ, forgive me all my
offenses; and grant that I may serve you in newness of life, to the glory of your
Name. *Amen.* †

The Reading   *To His Last Breath*

The brethren asked Abba Agathon: "Amongst all our different activities, father,
which is the virtue that requires the greatest effort?" He answered: "Forgive
me, but I think there is no labor greater than praying to God. For every time a
man wants to pray, his enemies the demons try to prevent him; for they know
that nothing obstructs them so much as prayer to God. In everything else that a
man undertakes, if he perseveres, he will attain rest, but in order to pray a man
must struggle to his last breath."

Sayings of the Desert Fathers

The Gloria*

The Psalm   *You Have Granted Me the Heritage of Those Who Fear Your Name*
Hear my cry, O God,* and listen to my prayer.

I call upon you from the ends of the earth* with heaviness in my heart; set me
   upon the rock that is higher than I.

For you have been my refuge,* a strong tower against the enemy.

I will dwell in your house for ever;* I will take refuge under the cover of your
   wings.

For you, O God, have heard my vows;* you have granted me the heritage of those
   who fear your Name.

Psalm 61:1–5

*The Gloria**

The Small Verse
Into your hands, O Lord, I commend my spirit; For you have redeemed me, O
   Lord, O God of truth. Keep me, O Lord, as the apple of your eye; Hide me
   under the shadow of your wings. †

The Lord's Prayer

The Petition
Keep watch, dear Lord, with those who work, or watch, or weep this night, and
   give your angels charge over those who sleep. Tend the sick, Lord Christ; give
   rest to the weary, bless the dying, soothe the suffering, pity the afflicted, shield
   the joyous; and all for your love's sake. *Amen.* †

The Final Thanksgiving
Lord, you now have set your servant free to go in peace as you have promised; for
   these eyes of mine have seen the Savior, whom you have prepared for all the
   world to see: a Light to enlighten the nations, and the glory of your people
   Israel. Glory to the Father, and to the Son, and to the Holy Spirit: as it was in the
   beginning, is now, and will be for ever. *Amen.*

Wednesday
The Night Office   **To Be Observed Before Retiring**

The Call to Prayer
May the Lord Almighty grant me and those I love a peaceful night and a perfect
   end. *Amen.* †

The Request for Presence
Our help is in the Name of the Lord; the maker of heaven and earth.

The Greeting

Almighty God, my heavenly Father: I have sinned against you, through my own
fault, in thought, and word, and deed, in what I have done and in what I have
left undone. For the sake of your Son our Lord Jesus Christ, forgive me all my
offenses; and grant that I may serve you in newness of life, to the glory of your
Name. *Amen.* †

The Reading   *O Lord, You Have Searched Me and Know Me*

O Lord, you have searched me
And know me;
You know when I sit down
And when I rise up.
You discern my thoughts
From far away,
And are acquainted with all my ways.

If I have raised my hand
Against the orphan,
Or have caused the eye
Of the widow to fail,
Be gracious to me, O Lord,
And forgive all my sins.

If I have seen anyone perish
For lack of clothing,
Or a poor person without covering,
Be gracious to me, O Lord,
And forgive all my sins.

If I have rejoiced at the ruin
Of those who hate me,
Or exulted when evil overtook them,
Be gracious to me, O Lord,
And forgive all my sins.

If I have walked with falsehood,
Or my foot has hurried to deceit,
Be gracious to me, O Lord,
And forgive all my sins.

If my step has turned aside
From the way,
Or my heart has followed
After my eye,
Be gracious to me, O Lord,
And forgive all my sins.

Answer me, O God of my right,
Hear my prayer,

And deliver me
From all my transgressions,
For my hope is in you. ❖

The Gloria*

The Psalm   *Our Hearts Rejoice in Him*
Our soul waits for the LORD;* he is our help and our shield.
Indeed, our heart rejoices in him,* for in his holy Name we put our trust.
Let your loving-kindness, O LORD, be upon us,* as we have put our trust in you.

Psalm 32:20–22

The Gloria*

The Small Verse
Into your hands, O Lord, I commend my spirit; For you have redeemed me, O
    Lord, O God of truth. Keep me, O Lord, as the apple of your eye; Hide me
    under the shadow of your wings. †

The Lord's Prayer

The Petition
Keep watch, dear Lord, with those who work, or watch, or weep this night, and
    give your angels charge over those who sleep. Tend the sick, Lord Christ; give
    rest to the weary, bless the dying, soothe the suffering, pity the afflicted, shield
    the joyous; and all for your love's sake. *Amen.* †

The Final Thanksgiving
Lord, you now have set your servant free to go in peace as you have promised; for
    these eyes of mine have seen the Savior, whom you have prepared for all the
    world to see: a Light to enlighten the nations, and the glory of your people
    Israel. Glory to the Father, and to the Son, and to the Holy Spirit: as it was in the
    beginning, is now, and will be for ever. *Amen.*

Thursday
The Night Office   **To Be Observed Before Retiring**

The Call to Prayer
May the Lord Almighty grant me and those I love a peaceful night and a perfect
    end. *Amen.* †

The Request for Presence
Our help is in the Name of the Lord; the maker of heaven and earth.

The Greeting

Almighty God, my heavenly Father: I have sinned against you, through my own fault, in thought, and word, and deed, in what I have done and in what I have left undone. For the sake of your Son our Lord Jesus Christ, forgive me all my offenses; and grant that I may serve you in newness of life, to the glory of your Name. *Amen.* †

The Reading   *Anima Christi*

Soul of Christ, sanctify me,
Body of Christ, save me,
Blood of Christ refresh me,
Water from the side of Christ, wash me,
Passion of Christ, strengthen me,
O good Jesus, hear me,
Within your wounds, hide me,
Let me never be separated from you,
From the powers of darkness, defend me,
In the hour of my death call me,
And bid me come with you,
That with your saints I may praise you
For ever and ever. Amen.

Brother Roger of Taize

The Gloria*

The Psalm   *Gracious Is the* Lord

Remember, O Lord, your compassion and love,* for they are from everlasting.
Remember not the sins of my youth and my transgressions;* remember me
   according to your love and for the sake of your goodness, O Lord.
Gracious and upright is the Lord;* therefore he teaches sinners in his way.
He guides the humble in doing right* and teaches his way to the lowly.
All the paths of the Lord are love and faithfulness* to those who keep his
   covenant and his testimonies.
For your Name's sake, O Lord,* forgive my sin, for it is great.

Psalm 25:5–10

The Gloria*

The Small Verse

Into your hands, O Lord, I commend my spirit; For you have redeemed me, O
   Lord, O God of truth. Keep me, O Lord, as the apple of your eye; Hide me
   under the shadow of your wings. †

The Lord's Prayer

The Petition

Keep watch, dear Lord, with those who work, or watch, or weep this night, and
   give your angels charge over those who sleep. Tend the sick, Lord Christ; give

rest to the weary, bless the dying, soothe the suffering, pity the afflicted, shield
the joyous; and all for your love's sake. *Amen.* †

The Final Thanksgiving
Lord, you now have set your servant free to go in peace as you have promised; for
these eyes of mine have seen the Savior, whom you have prepared for all the
world to see: a Light to enlighten the nations, and the glory of your people
Israel. Glory to the Father, and to the Son, and to the Holy Spirit: as it was in the
beginning, is now, and will be for ever. *Amen.*

Friday
The Night Office   **To Be Observed Before Retiring**

The Call to Prayer
May the Lord Almighty grant me and those I love a peaceful night and a perfect
end. *Amen.* †

The Request for Presence
Our help is in the Name of the Lord; the maker of heaven and earth.

The Greeting
Almighty God, my heavenly Father: I have sinned against you, through my own
fault, in thought, and word, and deed, in what I have done and in what I have
left undone. For the sake of your Son our Lord Jesus Christ, forgive me all my
offenses; and grant that I may serve you in newness of life, to the glory of your
Name. *Amen.* †

The Reading   *Litany of Penitence*
Most holy and merciful Father:
I confess to you and to the whole communion of saints
in heaven and on earth,
that I have sinned by my own fault
in thought, word, and deed;
by what I have done, and by what I have left undone.

I have not loved you with my whole heart, and mind, and strength. I have not
loved my neighbors as myself. I have not forgiven others, as I have been
forgiven.
Have mercy on me, Lord.

I have been deaf to your call to serve, as Christ served us. I have not been true to
the mind of Christ. I have grieved your Holy Spirit.
Have mercy on me, Lord.

I confess to you, Lord, all my past unfaithfulness: the pride, hypocrisy, and impatience of my life.
I confess to you, Lord.

My self-indulgent appetites and ways, and my exploitation of other people,
I confess to you, Lord.

My anger at my own frustration, and my envy of those more fortunate than I,
I confess to you, Lord.

My intemperate love of worldly goods and comforts, and my dishonesty in daily life and work,
I confess to you, Lord.

My negligence in prayer and worship, and my failure to commend the faith that is in me,
I confess to you, Lord.

Accept my repentance, Lord, for the wrongs I have done: for my blindness to human need and suffering, and my indifference to injustice and cruelty,
Accept my repentance, Lord.

For all false judgments, for uncharitable thoughts toward my neighbors, and for my prejudice and contempt toward those who differ from me,
Accept my repentance, Lord.

For my waste and pollution of your creation, and my lack of concern for those who come after us,
Accept my repentance, Lord.
Restore me, good Lord, and let your anger depart from me,
Favorably hear me for your mercy is great.

Accomplish in me and all of your church the work of your salvation,
That I may show forth your glory in the world.

By the cross and passion of your Son our Lord,
Bring me with all your saints to the joy of his resurrection. †

*The Gloria**

The Psalm   *The LORD Will Deliver Me*
My heart quakes within me,* and the terrors of death have fallen upon me.
Fear and trembling have come over me,* and horror overwhelms me.
And I said, "Oh, that I had wings like a dove!* I would fly away and be at rest.
I would flee to a far-off place* and make my lodging in the wilderness.
I would hasten to escape* from the stormy wind and tempest."
But I will call upon God,* and the LORD will deliver me.
Cast your burden upon the LORD, and he will sustain you;* he will never let the righteous stumble.

Psalm 55:5–9, 17, 24

The Gloria*

The Small Verse
Into your hands, O Lord, I commend my spirit; for you have redeemed me, O
Lord, O God of truth. Keep me, O Lord, as the apple of your eye; hide me
under the shadow of your wings. †

The Lord's Prayer

The Petition
Keep watch, dear Lord, with those who work, or watch, or weep this night, and
give your angels charge over those who sleep. Tend the sick, Lord Christ; give
rest to the weary, bless the dying, soothe the suffering, pity the afflicted, shield
the joyous; and all for your love's sake. *Amen.* †

The Final Thanksgiving
Lord, you now have set your servant free to go in peace as you have promised; for
these eyes of mine have seen the Savior, whom you have prepared for all the
world to see: a Light to enlighten the nations, and the glory of your people
Israel. Glory to the Father, and to the Son, and to the Holy Spirit: as it was in the
beginning, is now, and will be for ever. *Amen.*

Saturday
The Night Office   **To Be Observed Before Retiring**

The Call to Prayer
May the Lord Almighty grant me and those I love a peaceful night and a perfect
end. *Amen.* †

The Request for Presence
Our help is in the Name of the Lord; the maker of heaven and earth.

The Greeting
Almighty God, my heavenly Father: I have sinned against you, through my own
fault, in thought, and word, and deed, in what I have done and in what I have
left undone. For the sake of your Son our Lord Jesus Christ, forgive me all my
offenses; and grant that I may serve you in newness of life, to the glory of your
Name. *Amen.* †

The Reading
May God support us all the day long,
Till the shades lengthen, and the evening comes,
And the busy world is hushed,

And the fever of life is over,
And our work is done.
Then in his mercy may he give us a safe lodging,
And a holy rest, and peace at last.

John Henry Cardinal Newman

The Gloria*

The Psalm   *You Are My Strength*

My God, my God, why have you forsaken me?* and are so far from my cry and
   from the words of my distress?
I am poured out like water;* all my bones are out of joint; my heart within my
   breast is melting wax.
My mouth is dried out like a pot-shard; my tongue sticks to the roof of my
   mouth;* and you have laid me in the dust of the grave.
Packs of dogs close me in, and gangs of evildoers circle around me;* they pierce
   my hands and my feet; I can count all my bones.
They stare and gloat over me;* they divide my garments among them; they cast
   lots for my clothing.
Be not far away, O LORD;* you are my strength; hasten to help me.

Psalm 22:1, 14–18

The Gloria*

The Small Verse
Into your hands, O Lord, I commend my spirit; For you have redeemed me, O
   Lord, O God of truth. Keep me, O Lord, as the apple of your eye; Hide me
   under the shadow of your wings. †

The Lord's Prayer

The Petition
Keep watch, dear Lord, with those who work, or watch, or weep this night, and
   give your angels charge over those who sleep. Tend the sick, Lord Christ; give
   rest to the weary, bless the dying, soothe the suffering, pity the afflicted, shield
   the joyous; and all for your love's sake. *Amen.* †

The Final Thanksgiving
Lord, you now have set your servant free to go in peace as you have promised; for
   these eyes of mine have seen the Savior, whom you have prepared for all the
   world to see: a Light to enlighten the nations, and the glory of your people
   Israel. Glory to the Father, and to the Son, and to the Holy Spirit: as it was in the
   beginning, is now, and will be for ever. *Amen.*

Holy Week and Easter

The Morning Office   To Be Observed on the Hour or Half Hour
Between 6 and 9 a.m.

The Call to Prayer
Let the peoples praise you, O God;* let all the peoples praise you.
Let the nations be glad and sing for joy,* for you judge the peoples with equity and
guide all nations upon the earth.
Let the peoples praise you, O God;* let all the peoples praise you.

Psalm 67:3–5

The Request for Presence
Hear my voice, O LORD, according to your loving-kindness;* according to your
judgments, give me life.

Psalm 119:149

The Greeting
Hosanna, LORD, hosanna!* . . .
Blessed is he who comes in the name of the Lord.

Psalm 118:25a, 26a

The Refrain for the Morning Lessons
God is the LORD; he has shined upon us;* form a procession with branches up to
the horns of the altar.

Psalm 118:27

A Reading
When they were approaching Jerusalem, at Bethphage and Bethany, close by the
Mount of Olives, he sent two of his disciples and said to them, 'Go to the village facing you, and as you enter it you will at once find a tethered colt that no
one has yet ridden. Untie it and bring it here. If anyone says to you, "What are
you doing?" say, "The Master needs it and will send it back here at once." '
They went off and found a colt tethered near a door in the open street. As they
untied it, some men standing there said, 'What are you doing untying that
colt?' They gave the answer that Jesus had told them, and the man let them go.
Then they took the colt to Jesus and threw their cloaks on its back, and he
mounted it. Many people spread their cloaks on the road, and others greenery
which they had cut in the fields. And those who went in front and those who
followed were all shouting, '*Hosanna! Blessed is he who is coming in the name of
the Lord!* Blessed is the coming kingdom of David our father! *Hosanna* in the
highest heavens!' He entered Jerusalem and went into the Temple; and when
he had surveyed it all, as it was late by now, he went out to Bethany with the
Twelve.

Mark 11:1–11

The Refrain
God is the LORD; he has shined upon us;* form a procession with branches up to
the horns of the altar.

The Morning Psalm   *Open the Gates and Form a Procession with Branches*

Open for me the gates of righteousness;* I will enter them; I will offer thanks to the
  LORD.
"This is the gate of the LORD;* he who is righteous may enter."
I will give thanks to you, for you answered me* and have become my salvation.
The same stone which the builders rejected* has become the chief cornerstone.
This is the LORD's doing,* and it is marvelous in our eyes.
On this day the LORD has acted;* we will rejoice and be glad in it.
Hosanna, LORD, hosanna!* LORD, send us now success.
Blessed is he who comes in the name of the Lord;* we bless you from the house of
  the LORD.
God is the LORD; he has shined upon us;* form a procession with branches up to
  the horns of the altar.
"You are my God, and I will thank you;* you are my God, and I will exalt you."
Give thanks to the LORD, for he is good;* his mercy endures for ever.

                                                                    Psalm 118:19–29

The Refrain

God is the LORD; he has shined upon us;* form a procession with branches up to
  the horns of the altar.

The Cry of the Church

Blessed is he who comes in the name of the Lord, Hosanna in the highest.

The Lord's Prayer

The Prayer Appointed for the Day

Assist me mercifully with your help, O Lord God of our salvation, that I may enter
  with joy upon the contemplation of those mighty acts, whereby you have given
  us life and immortality; through Jesus Christ our Lord. *Amen.* †

The Concluding Prayer of the Church

Almighty and everliving God, in your tender love for the human race you sent
  your Son our Savior Jesus Christ to take upon him our nature, and to suffer
  death upon the cross, giving us the example of his great humility: Mercifully
  grant that I may walk in the way of his suffering, and also share in his resurrection; through Jesus Christ my Lord, who lives and reigns with you and the
  Holy Spirit, one God, for ever and ever. *Amen.* †

The Midday Office   **To Be Observed on the Hour or Half Hour**
                               Between 11 a.m. and 2 p.m.

The Call to Prayer

Come, let us sing to the LORD;* let us shout for joy to the Rock of our salvation.
Let us come before his presence with thanksgiving* and raise a loud shout to him
  with psalms.
For the LORD is a great God,* and a great King above all gods.

In his hands are the caverns of the earth,* and the heights of the hills are his also.
The sea is his, for he made it,* and his hands have molded the dry land.

Psalm 95:1–5

The Request for Presence
May God give us his blessing,* and may all the ends of the earth stand in awe of
him.

Psalm 67:7

The Greeting
You, O LORD, are a shield about me;* you are my glory, the one who lifts up my
head.

Psalm 3:3

The Refrain for the Midday Lessons
May the glory of the LORD endure for ever;* may the LORD rejoice in all his works.

Psalm 104:32

A Reading
Pass through, pass through the gates. Clear a way for my people! Level up, level
up the highway, remove the stones! Hoist a signal to the peoples! This is what
YAHWEH has proclaimed to the remotest part of the earth: Say to the daughter
of Zion, 'Look, your salvation is coming; with him comes his reward, his
achievement precedes him!' They will be called 'The Holy People,' 'YAHWEH's
Redeemed,' while you will be called 'Sought after,' 'City-not-forsaken.'

Isaiah 62:10–12

The Refrain
May the glory of the LORD endure for ever;* may the LORD rejoice in all his works.

The Midday Psalm   The Earth Is the LORD's and All That Is in It
The earth is the LORD's and all that is in it,* the world and all who dwell therein.
For it is he who founded it upon the seas* and made it firm upon the rivers of the
deep.
"Who can ascend the hill of the LORD?"* and who can stand in his holy place?"
"Those who have clean hands and a pure heart,* who have not pledged themselves
to falsehood, nor sworn by what is a fraud.
They shall receive a blessing from the LORD* and a just reward from the God of
their salvation."
Such is the generation of those who seek him,* of those who seek your face, O God
of Jacob.

Psalm 24:1–6

The Refrain
May the glory of the LORD endure for ever;* may the LORD rejoice in all his works.

The Cry of the Church
O God, come to my assistance! O Lord, make haste to help me!

The Lord's Prayer

The Prayer Appointed for the Day
Assist me mercifully with your help, O Lord God of our salvation, that I may enter
with joy upon the contemplation of those mighty acts, whereby you have given
us life and immortality; through Jesus Christ our Lord. *Amen.* †

The Concluding Prayer of the Church
Almighty and everlasting God, who willed that our Savior should take upon Him,
our flesh and suffer death upon the Cross, that all mankind should follow the
example of His great humility, mercifully grant that I may both follow the
example of His patience and also partake of His resurrection. Through the
same Jesus Christ. *Amen.*

adapted from THE SHORT BREVIARY

The Vespers Office   **To Be Observed on the Hour or Half Hour**
Between 5 and 8 p.m.

The Call to Prayer
Come, let us bow down, and bend the knee,* and kneel before the LORD our Maker.
For he is our God* and we are the people of his pasture and the sheep of his hand.

Psalm 95:6–7

The Request for Presence
I call upon you, O God, for you will answer me;* incline your ear to me, and hear
my words.

Psalm 17:6

The Greeting
You are God: I praise you;* you are the Lord: I acclaim you;
You are the eternal Father:* all creation worships you.
Throughout the world the holy Church acclaims you:* Father, of majesty
unbounded,
your true and only Son,* worthy of all worship,
and the Holy Spirit,* advocate and guide.
As these have been from the beginning,* so they are now and evermore shall be.
Amen.

based on the Te Deum and Gloria

The Hymn   *Ride On in Majesty*
Ride on! Ride on in majesty!
Hark! All the tribes hosanna cry;
Your humble beast pursues his road
With palms and scattered garments strowed.

Ride on! Ride on in majesty!
In lowly pomp ride on to die;
O Christ, your triumphs now begin
Over captive death and conquered sin.

Ride on! Ride on in majesty!
The angel armies of the sky
Look down with sad and wondering eyes
To see the approaching sacrifice.

Ride on! Ride on in majesty!
Your last and fiercest strife is nigh;
The Father on his sapphire throne
Expects his own anointed Son.

Ride on! Ride on in majesty!
In lowly pomp ride on to die;
Bow your meek head to mortal pain,
Then take, O God, your power and reign.

Henry H. Milman

The Refrain for the Vespers Lessons

Sing to the LORD, you servants of his;* give thanks for the remembrance of his
holiness.

Psalm 30:4

The Vespers Psalm *In the Temple of the LORD All Are Crying, "Glory!"*

Ascribe to the LORD, you gods,* ascribe to the LORD glory and strength.

Ascribe to the LORD the glory due his Name;* worship the LORD in the beauty of
holiness.

The voice of the LORD is upon the waters; the God of glory thunders;* the LORD is
upon the mighty waters.

The voice of the LORD is a powerful voice;* the voice of the LORD is a voice of
splendor.

The voice of the LORD breaks the cedar trees;* the LORD breaks the cedars of
Lebanon;

He makes Lebanon skip like a calf,* and Mount Hermon like a young
wild ox.

The voice of the LORD splits the flames of fire; the voice of the LORD shakes the
wilderness;* the LORD shakes the wilderness of Kadesh.

The voice of the LORD makes the oak trees writhe* and strips the forests
bare.

And in the temple of the LORD* all are crying, "Glory!"

The LORD sits enthroned above the flood;* the LORD sits enthroned as King for
evermore.

The LORD shall give strength to his people;* the LORD shall give his people the
blessing of peace.

Psalm 29

The Refrain

Sing to the LORD, you servants of his;* give thanks for the remembrance of his
holiness.

The Lord's Prayer

The Prayer Appointed for the Day

Assist me mercifully with your help, O Lord God of our salvation, that I may enter
with joy upon the contemplation of those mighty acts, whereby you have given
us life and immortality; through Jesus Christ our Lord. *Amen.* †

The Concluding Prayer of the Church

Almighty and everliving God, in your tender love for the human race you sent
your Son our Savior Jesus Christ to take upon him our nature, and to suffer
death upon the cross, giving us the example of his great humility: Mercifully
grant that I may walk in the way of his suffering, and also share in his resurrection; through Jesus Christ my Lord, who lives and reigns with you and the
Holy Spirit, one God, for ever and ever. *Amen.* †

The Morning Office **To Be Observed on the Hour or Half Hour**
Between 6 and 9 a.m.

The Call to Prayer

Let my mouth be full of your praise* and your glory all the day long.
Do not cast me off in my old age;* forsake me not when my strength fails.

Psalm 71:8–9

The Request for Presence

O LORD, my God, my Savior,* by day and night I cry to you.
Let my prayer enter into your presence.

Psalm 88:1–2

The Greeting

Show me your ways, O LORD,* and teach me your paths.
Lead me in your truth and teach me,* for you are the God of my salvation; in you
have I trusted all the day long.

Psalm 25:3–4

The Refrain for the Morning Lessons

Deliverance belongs to the LORD.* Your blessing be upon your people!

Psalm 3:8

A Reading

Now it happened that when he was near Bethpage and Bethany, close by the
Mount of Olives as it is called, he sent two of the disciples, saying, 'Go to the
village opposite, and as you enter it you will find a tethered colt that no one
has ever yet ridden. Untie it and bring it here. If anyone asks you, "Why are
you untying it?" you are to say this, "The Master needs it." ' The messengers
went off and found everything just as he had told them. As they were untying
the colt, its owner said, 'Why are you untying it?' and they answered, 'The
Master needs it.' So they took the colt to Jesus and throwing their cloaks upon
its back, they lifted Jesus onto it. As he moved off, they spread their cloaks in

the road, and now, as he was approaching the downward slope of the Mount of Olives, the whole group of disciples joyfully began to praise God at the top of their voices for all the miracles they had seen. They cried out: *Blessed is he who is coming* as King *in the name of the Lord!* Peace in heaven and glory in the highest heavens! Some Pharisees in the crowd said to him, 'Master, reprove your disciples,' but he answered, 'I tell you, if these keep silence, the stones will cry out.'

Luke 19:29–40

The Refrain
Deliverance belongs to the LORD.* Your blessing be upon your people!

The Morning Psalm   *Give Me the Joy of Your Saving Health*
Create in me a clean heart, O God,* and renew a right spirit within me.
Cast me not away from your presence* and take not your holy Spirit from me.
Give me the joy of your saving help again* and sustain me with your bountiful Spirit.
I shall teach your ways to the wicked,* and sinners shall return to you.

Psalm 51:11–14

The Refrain
Deliverance belongs to the LORD.* Your blessing be upon your people!

The Gloria*

The Lord's Prayer

The Prayer Appointed for the Week
Almighty God, who through your only-begotten Son Jesus Christ overcame death and opened to us the gate of everlasting life: Grant that I, who celebrate with joy the day of the Lord's resurrection, may be raised from the death of sin by your life-giving Spirit; through Jesus Christ our Lord, who lives and reigns with you and the Holy Spirit, one God, now and for ever. *Amen.* †

The Concluding Prayer of the Church
Lord God, almighty and everlasting Father, you have brought me in safety to this new day: Preserve me with your mighty power, that I may not fall into sin, nor be overcome by adversity; and in all I do direct me to the fulfilling of your purpose; through Jesus Christ my Lord. *Amen.* †

The Midday Office   **To Be Observed on the Hour or Half Hour**
                                          Between 11 a.m. and 2 p.m.

The Call to Prayer
Praise the LORD, O my soul!* I will praise the LORD as long as I live; I will sing praises to God while I have my being.

Psalm 146:1

The Request for Presence
Bow your heavens, O LORD, and come down;* touch the mountains, and they shall smoke.

Hurl the lightning and scatter them;* shoot out your arrows and rout them.
Stretch out your hand from on high;* rescue me and deliver me from the great
    waters, from the hand of foreign peoples.

Psalm 144:5–7

The Greeting
To you I lift up my eyes,* to you enthroned in the heavens.
As the eyes of the servants look to the hand of their masters,* and the eyes of a
    maid to the hand of her mistress,
So our eyes look to the LORD our God,* until he shows us his mercy.

Psalm 123:1–3

The Refrain for the Midday Lessons
Praise the LORD, you that fear him;* stand in awe of him, O offspring of Israel; all
    you of Jacob's line, give glory.

Psalm 22:22

A Reading
Let this mind be in you,
which was also in Christ Jesus:
Who, being in the form of God,
thought it not robbery to be equal with God:
But made himself of no reputation,
and took upon him the form of a servant,
and was made in the likeness of men:
And being found in fashion as a man,
he humbled himself,
became obedient unto death,
even the death of the cross.
Wherefore God also hath highly exalted him,
and given him a name which is above every name:
That at the name of Jesus every knee should bow,
of things in heaven,
and things in earth,
and things under the earth;
And that every tongue should confess that Jesus Christ is LORD,
to the glory of God the Father.

Phillipians 2:5–11, KJV

The Refrain
Praise the LORD, you that fear him;* stand in awe of him, O offspring of Israel; all
    you of Jacob's line, give glory.

The Midday Psalm   *The Sacrifice of God Is a Troubled Spirit*
Deliver me from death, O God,* and my tongue shall sing of your righteousness,
    O God of my salvation.

Open my lips, O Lord,* and my mouth shall proclaim your praise.
Had you desired it, I would have offered sacrifice,* but you take no delight in
 burnt-offerings.
The sacrifice of God is a troubled spirit;* a broken and contrite heart, O God, you
 will not despise.

Psalm 51:15–18

The Refrain
Praise the LORD, you that fear him;* stand in awe of him, O offspring of Israel; all
 you of Jacob's line, give glory.

The Cry of the Church
Lord, have mercy on us. Christ, have mercy on us. Lord, have mercy on us.

The Lord's Prayer

The Prayer Appointed for the Week
Almighty God, who through your only-begotten Son Jesus Christ overcame death
 and opened to us the gate of everlasting life: Grant that I, who celebrate with
 joy the day of the Lord's resurrection, may be raised from the death of sin by
 your life-giving Spirit; through Jesus Christ our Lord, who lives and reigns
 with you and the Holy Spirit, one God, now and for ever. *Amen.* †

The Concluding Prayer of the Church
Almighty and everlasting God, who willed that our Savior should take upon Him,
 our flesh and suffer death upon the Cross, that all mankind should follow the
 example of His great humility, mercifully grant that I may both follow the
 example of His patience and also partake of His resurrection. Through the
 same Jesus Christ. *Amen.*

adapted from THE SHORT BREVIARY

The Vespers Office   **To Be Observed on the Hour or Half Hour**
Between 5 and 8 p.m.

The Call to Prayer
The righteous will be glad . . .
And they will say, "Surely, there is a reward for the righteous;* surely, there is a
 God who rules in the earth."

Psalm 58:10–11

The Request for Presence
Deliver me from death, O God,* and my tongue shall sing of your righteousness,
 O God of my salvation.

Psalm 51:15

The Greeting
To you, O LORD, I lift up my soul;* my God, I put my trust in you.

Psalm 25:1

The Hymn   *Were You There*
    Were you there when they crucified my Lord?
    Were you there when they crucified my Lord?
    Oh! Sometimes it causes me to tremble, tremble, tremble.
    Were you there when they crucified my Lord?

    Were you there when they nailed him to the tree?
    Were you there when they nailed him to the tree?
    Oh! Sometimes it causes me to tremble, tremble, tremble.
    Were you there when they nailed him to the tree?

    Were you there when they pierced him in the side?
    Were you there when they pierced him in the side?
    Oh! Sometimes it causes me to tremble, tremble, tremble.
    Were you there when they pierced him in the side?

    Were you there when they laid him in the tomb?
    Were you there when they laid him in the tomb?
    Oh! Sometimes it causes me to tremble, tremble, tremble.
    Were you there when they laid him in the tomb?

                                 African American Spiritual

The Refrain for the Vespers Lessons
Make me hear of joy and gladness,* that the body you have broken may rejoice.
                                               Psalm 51:9

The Vespers Psalm   *Having You I Desire Nothing Upon Earth*
Whom have I in heaven but you?* and having you I desire nothing upon earth.
Though my flesh and heart should waste away,* God is the strength of my heart
    and my portion for ever.
Truly, those who forsake you will perish;* you destroy all who are unfaithful.
But it is good for me to be near God;* I have made the Lord GOD my refuge.
                                       Psalm 73:25–28

The Refrain
Make me hear of joy and gladness,* that the body you have broken may rejoice.

The Gloria*

The Lord's Prayer

The Prayer Appointed for the Week
Almighty God, who through your only-begotten Son Jesus Christ overcame death
    and opened to us the gate of everlasting life: Grant that I, who celebrate with
    joy the day of the Lord's resurrection, may be raised from the death of sin by
    your life-giving Spirit; through Jesus Christ our Lord, who lives and reigns
    with you and the Holy Spirit, one God, now and for ever. *Amen.* †

The Concluding Prayer of the Church
Save me, O Lord, while I am awake, and keep me while I sleep that I may wake in
  Christ and rest in peace.

adapted from THE SHORT BREVIARY

The Morning Office   **To Be Observed on the Hour or Half Hour**
Between 6 and 9 a.m.

The Call to Prayer
God has gone up with a shout,* the LORD with the sound of the ram's-horn.
Sing praises to God, sing praises;* sing praises to our King, sing praises.
For God is King of all the earth;* sing praises with all your skill.
God reigns over the nation;* God sits upon his holy throne.

Psalm 47:5–8

The Request for Presence
Early in the morning I cry out to you,* for in your word is my trust.

Psalm 119:147

The Greeting
Not to us, O LORD, not to us, but to your Name give glory;* because of your love
  and because of your faithfulness.

Psalm 115:1

The Refrain for the Morning Lessons
For lo, your enemies, O LORD, lo, your enemies shall perish,* and all the workers
  of iniquity shall be scattered.

Psalm 92:8

A Reading
So they reached Jerusalem and he went into the Temple and began driving out the
  men selling and buying there; he upset the tables of the money changers and
  the seats of the dove sellers. Nor would he allow anyone to carry anything
  through the Temple. And he taught them and said, 'Does not scripture say: *My
  house will be called a house of prayer for all peoples?* But you have turned into *a ban-
  dits' den.'* This came to the ears of the chief priests and the scribes, and they
  tried to find some way of doing away with him; they were afraid of him
  because the people were carried away by his teaching. And when evening
  came he went out of the city.

Mark 11:15–19

The Refrain
For lo, your enemies, O LORD, lo, your enemies shall perish,* and all the workers
  of iniquity shall be scattered.

The Morning Psalm   *In Your Light We See Light*
Your love, O LORD, reaches to the heavens,* and your faithfulness to the clouds.
Your righteousness is like the strong mountains, your justice like the great deep;*
  you save both man and beast, O LORD.

How priceless is your love, O God!* your people take refuge under the shadow of
your wings.
They feast upon the abundance of your house;* you give them drink from the
river of your delights.
For with you is the well of life,* and in your light we see light.
Continue your loving-kindness to those who know you,* and your favor to those
who are true of heart.

Psalm 36:5–12

The Refrain
For lo, your enemies, O LORD, lo, your enemies shall perish,* and all the workers
of iniquity shall be scattered.

The Short Verse
'I am the Alpha and the Omega' says the Lord God, 'who is, who was, and who is
to come, the Almighty.'

Revelation 1:8

The Lord's Prayer

The Prayer Appointed for the Week
Almighty God, who through your only-begotten Son Jesus Christ overcame death
and opened to us the gate of everlasting life: Grant that I, who celebrate with
joy the day of the Lord's resurrection, may be raised from the death of sin by
your life-giving Spirit; through Jesus Christ our Lord, who lives and reigns
with you and the Holy Spirit, one God, now and for ever. *Amen.* †

The Concluding Prayer of the Church
Lord God, almighty and everlasting Father, you have brought me in safety to this
new day: Preserve me with your mighty power, that I may not fall into sin, nor
be overcome by adversity; and in all I do direct me to the fulfilling of your purpose; through Jesus Christ my Lord. *Amen.* †

The Midday Office **To Be Observed on the Hour or Half Hour**
Between 11 a.m. and 2 p.m.

The Call to Prayer
I will call upon God,* and the LORD will deliver me.
In the evening, in the morning, and at the noonday, I will complain and lament,*
and he will hear my voice.
He will bring me safely back* . . .
God, who is enthroned of old, will hear me.

Psalm 55:17ff

The Request for Presence
I have gone astray like a sheep that is lost;* search for your servant, for I do not
forget your commandments.

Psalm 119:176

The Greeting
When your word goes forth it gives light;* it gives understanding to the simple.

Psalm 119:130

The Refrain for the Midday Lessons
He will not let your foot be moved* and he who watches over you will not fall
  asleep.

Psalm 121:3

A Reading
We had all gone astray like sheep, each taking his own way, and YAHWEH brought
  the acts of rebellion of all of us to bear on him. Ill-treated and afflicted, he never
  opened his mouth, like a lamb led to the slaughter-house, like a sheep dumb
  before its shearers he never opened his mouth.

Isaiah 53:6–7

The Refrain
He will not let your foot be moved* and he who watches over you will not fall
  asleep.

The Midday Psalm   The LORD Will Not Abandon His People
How long shall the wicked, O LORD,* how long shall the wicked triumph?
They bluster in their insolence;* all evildoers are full of boasting.
They crush your people, O LORD,* and afflict your chosen nation.
They murder the widow and the stranger* and put the orphans to death.
Yet they say, "The LORD does not see,* the God of Jacob takes no notice."
Consider well, you dullards among the people;* when will you fools understand?
He that planted the ear, does he not hear?* he that formed the eye, does he not see?
He who admonishes the nations, will he not punish?* he who teaches all the
  world, has he no knowledge?
The LORD knows our human thoughts;* how like a puff of wind they are.
Happy are they whom you instruct, O Lord!* whom you teach out of your law;
To give them rest in evil days,* until a pit is dug for the wicked.
For the LORD will not abandon his people,* nor will he forsake his own.
For judgment will again be just,* and all the true of heart will follow it.

Psalm 94:3–15

The Refrain
He will not let your foot be moved* and he who watches over you will not fall
  asleep.

The Gloria*

The Lord's Prayer

The Prayer Appointed for the Week
Almighty God, who through your only-begotten Son Jesus Christ overcame death
  and opened to us the gate of everlasting life: Grant that I, who celebrate with
  joy the day of the Lord's resurrection, may be raised from the death of sin by

your life-giving Spirit; through Jesus Christ our Lord, who lives and reigns
with you and the Holy Spirit, one God, now and for ever. *Amen.* †

The Concluding Prayer of the Church

O God, by the passion of your blessed Son you made an instrument of shameful
death to be for us the means of life: Grant me so to glory in the cross of Christ,
that I may gladly suffer shame and loss for the sake of your Son our Savior
Jesus Christ; who lives and reigns with you and the Holy Spirit, one God, for
ever and ever. *Amen.* †

The Vespers Office   **To Be Observed on the Hour or Half Hour Between 5 and 8 p.m.**

The Call to Prayer

O tarry, and await the LORD's pleasure; be strong, and he shall comfort your
heart;* wait patiently for the LORD.

Psalm 27:18

The Request for Presence

Show us your mercy, O LORD,* and grant us your salvation.

Psalm 85:7

The Greeting

For you are my hope, O Lord GOD,* my confidence since I was young.
I have been sustained by you ever since I was born; from my mother's womb you
have been my strength;* my praise shall be always of you.

Psalm 71:5–6

The Hymn

Descend, O Spirit, purging flame,
Brand us this day with Jesus' Name!
Confirm our faith, consume our doubt;
Sign us as Christ's, within, without.

Forbid us not this second birth;
Grant unto us the greater worth!
Enlist us in your service, Lord;
Baptize all nations with your Word.

Scott F. Brenner

The Refrain for the Vespers Lessons

For one day in your courts is better than a thousand in my own room,* and to stand
at the threshold of the house of my God than to dwell in the tents of the wicked.

Psalm 84:9

The Vespers Psalm   *My Eyes Have Failed from Looking for My God*

Save me, O God,* for the waters have risen up to my neck.
I am sinking in deep mire,* and there is no firm ground for my feet.

I have come into deep waters,* and the torrent washes over me.

I have grown weary with my crying; my throat is inflamed;* my eyes have failed from looking for my God.

Those who hate me without a cause are more than the hairs of my head; my lying foes who would destroy me are mighty.*

Psalm 69:1–5

The Refrain

For one day in your courts is better than a thousand in my own room,* and to stand at the threshold of the house of my God than to dwell in the tents of the wicked.

The Gloria*

The Lord's Prayer

The Prayer Appointed for the Week

Almighty God, who through your only-begotten Son Jesus Christ overcame death and opened to us the gate of everlasting life: Grant that I, who celebrate with joy the day of the Lord's resurrection, may be raised from the death of sin by your life-giving Spirit; through Jesus Christ our Lord, who lives and reigns with you and the Holy Spirit, one God, now and for ever. *Amen.* †

The Concluding Prayer of the Church

Grant me and all of your people the gift of your Spirit, that we may know Christ and make him known; and through him, at all times and in all places, may give thanks to you in all things. *Amen.* †

The Morning Office	**To Be Observed on the Hour or Half Hour**
	Between 6 and 9 a.m.

The Call to Prayer

Blessed be the LORD, the God of Israel,* from everlasting and to everlasting;* and let all the people say, "Amen!"

Psalm 106:48

The Request for Presence

O God of hosts,* show the light of your countenance, and we shall be saved.

Psalm 80:7

The Greeting

Let them know that this is your hand, that you, O LORD, have done it.

Psalm 109:26

The Refrain for the Morning Lessons

Send forth your strength, O God;* establish, O God, what you have wrought for us.

Psalm 68:28

A Reading

It was two days before the Passover and the feasts of Unleavened Bread, and the chief priests and the scribes were looking for a way to arrest Jesus by some trick and have him put to death. For they said, 'It must not be during the festivities, or there will be a disturbance among the people.' He was at Bethany in the house of Simon, a man who had suffered from a virulent skin-disease; he was at table when a woman came with an alabaster jar of very costly ointment, pure nard. She broke the jar and poured the ointment on his head. Some who were there said to one another indignantly, 'Why this waste of ointment? Ointment like this could have been sold for over three hundred denarii and the money given to the poor'; and they were angry with her. But Jesus said, 'Leave her alone. Why are you upsetting her? What she has done for me is a good work. You have the poor with you always, and you can be kind to them whenever you wish, but you will not always have me. She has done what she could: she has anointed my body beforehand for its burial. In truth I tell you, wherever throughout all the world the gospel is proclaimed, what she has done will be told as well, in remembrance of her.' Judas Iscariot, one of the Twelve, approached the chief priests with an offer to hand Jesus over to them. They were delighted to hear it, and promised to give him money; and he began to look for a way of betraying him when the opportunity should occur.

Mark 14:1–11

The Refrain

Send forth your strength, O God;* establish, O God, what you have wrought
    for us.

The Morning Psalm   *Your Testimonies Are Very Sure*

The waters have lifted up, O LORD, the waters have lifted up their voice;* the
    waters have lifted up their pounding waves.
Mightier than the sound of many waters, mightier than the breakers of the sea,*
    mightier is the LORD who dwells on high.
Your testimonies are very sure,* and holiness adorns your house, O LORD, for ever
    and for evermore.

Psalm 93:4–6

The Refrain

Send forth your strength, O God;* establish, O God, what you have wrought
    for us.

*The Gloria**

The Lord's Prayer

The Prayer Appointed for the Week

Almighty God, who through your only-begotten Son Jesus Christ overcame death
    and opened to us the gate of everlasting life: Grant that I, who celebrate with
    joy the day of the Lord's resurrection, may be raised from the death of sin by

your life-giving Spirit; through Jesus Christ our Lord, who lives and reigns with you and the Holy Spirit, one God, now and for ever. *Amen.* †

The Concluding Prayer of the Church
Lord God, almighty and everlasting Father, you have brought me in safety to this new day: Preserve me with your mighty power, that I may not fall into sin, nor be overcome by adversity; and in all I do direct me to the fulfilling of your purpose; through Jesus Christ my Lord. *Amen.* †

The Midday Office   **To Be Observed on the Hour or Half Hour**
     Between 11 a.m. and 2 p.m.

The Call to Prayer
Know this: The LORD himself is God;* he himself has made us, and we are his; we are his people and the sheep of his pasture.

Psalm 100:2

The Request for Presence
Hear the voice of my prayer when I cry out to you,* when I lift up my hands to your holy of holies.

Psalm 28:2

The Greeting
The eyes of all wait upon you, O LORD.*

Psalm 145:16

The Refrain for the Midday Lessons
Tell it out among all the nations: "The LORD is King!* he has made the world so firm that it cannot be moved; he will judge all the peoples with equity."

Psalm 96:10

A Reading
Lord YAHWEH has given me a disciple's tongue, for me to know how to give a word of comfort to the weary. Morning by morning he makes my ear alert to listen like a disciple. Lord YAHWEH has opened my ear and I have not resisted, I have not turned away. I have offered my back to those who struck me, my cheeks to those who plucked my beard; I have not turned my face away from insult and spitting. Lord YAHWEH comes to my help, this is why insult has not touched me, this is why I have my face like flint and know that I shall not be put to shame. Which of you fears YAHWEH and listens to his servant's voice? Which of you walks in darkness and sees no light? Let him trust in the name of YAHWEH and lean on his God!

Isaiah 50:3–7, 10

The Refrain
Tell it out among all the nations: "The LORD is King!* he has made the world so firm that it cannot be moved; he will judge all the peoples with equity."

The Midday Psalm　　　　　　　　　　　　*There Is No End to His Greatness*

Great is the LORD and greatly to be praised;* there is no end to his greatness.

One generation shall praise your works to another* and shall declare your power.

I will ponder the glorious splendor of your majesty* and all your marvelous works.

They shall speak of the might of your wondrous acts,* and I will tell of your
greatness.

They shall publish the remembrance of your great goodness;* they shall sing of
your righteous deeds.

Psalm 145:3–7

The Refrain

Tell it out among all the nations: "The LORD is King!* he has made the world so
firm that it cannot be moved; he will judge all the peoples with equity."

The Small Verse

Happy are the people whose strength is in you!* whose hearts are set on the
pilgrims' way,

For one day in your courts is better than a thousand in my own room,* and to stand
at the threshold of the house of my God than to dwell in the tents of the wicked.

Psalm 84:4, 9

The Lord's Prayer

The Prayer Appointed for the Week

Almighty God, who through your only-begotten Son Jesus Christ overcame death
and opened to us the gate of everlasting life: Grant that I, who celebrate with
joy the day of the Lord's resurrection, may be raised from the death of sin by
your life-giving Spirit; through Jesus Christ our Lord, who lives and reigns
with you and the Holy Spirit, one God, now and for ever. *Amen.* †

The Concluding Prayer of the Church

Lord God, whose blessed Son our Savior gave his body to be whipped and his face
to be spit upon: Give me the grace to accept joyfully the sufferings of the
present time, confident of the glory that shall be revealed; through Jesus Christ
your Son my Lord, who lives and reigns with you and the Holy Spirit, one
God, for ever and ever. *Amen.* †

The Vespers Office　　　　　　**To Be Observed on the Hour or Half Hour**
　　　　　　　　　　　　　　　　　　　　　Between 5 and 8 p.m.

The Call to Prayer

The LORD is near to those who call upon him,* to all who call upon him faithfully.

Psalm 145:19

The Request for Presence

Protect me, O God, for I take refuge in you;* I have said to the LORD, "You are my
Lord, my good above all other."

Psalm 16:1

The Greeting
How deep I find your thoughts, O God!* how great is the sum of them!

Psalm 139:16

The Hymn   *In the Cross of Christ I Glory*
In the cross of Christ I glory, towering over the wrecks of time;
All the light of sacred story gathers round its head sublime.

When the woes of life overtake me, hopes deceive, and fears annoy,
Never shall the cross forsake me. Lo! It glows with peace and joy.

When the sun of bliss is beaming light and love upon my way,
From the cross the radiance streaming adds more luster to the day.

Bane and blessing, pain and pleasure, by the cross are sanctified;
Peace is there that knows no measure, joys that through all time abide.

In the cross of Christ I glory, towering over the wrecks of time;
All the light of sacred story gathers round its head sublime.

John Bowring

The Refrain for the Vespers Lessons
I will bear witness that the LORD is righteous;* I will praise the Name of the LORD
    Most High.

Psalm 7:18

The Vespers Psalm   *They Shall Make Known to a People Yet Unborn*
All the ends of the earth shall remember and turn to the LORD,* and all the families
    of the nations shall bow before him.
For kingship belongs to the LORD;* he rules over the nations.
To him alone all who sleep in the earth bow down in worship;* all who go down to
    the dust fall before him.
My soul shall live for him; my descendants shall serve him;* they shall be known
    as the LORD's forever.
They shall come and make known to a people yet unborn* the saving deeds that
    he has done.

Psalm 22:26–30

The Refrain
I will bear witness that the LORD is righteous;* I will praise the Name of the LORD
    Most High.

The Cry of the Church
Even so, come Lord Jesus!

The Lord's Prayer

The Prayer Appointed for the Week
Almighty God, who through your only-begotten Son Jesus Christ overcame death
    and opened to us the gate of everlasting life: Grant that I, who celebrate with

joy the day of the Lord's resurrection, may be raised from the death of sin by your life-giving Spirit; through Jesus Christ our Lord, who lives and reigns with you and the Holy Spirit, one God, now and for ever. *Amen.* †

The Concluding Prayer of the Church
O God, who willed that Your Son should undergo for us the ignominy of the Cross to deliver us from the power of the enemy, grant to me Your servant, that I may obtain the grace of His resurrection. Through the same Jesus Christ. *Amen.*

adapted from The Short Breviary

The Morning Office   **To Be Observed on the Hour or Half Hour Between 6 and 9 a.m.**

The Call to Prayer
Those who trust in the Lord are like Mount Zion,* which cannot be moved, but stands fast for ever.
The hills stand about Jerusalem;* so does the Lord stand round about his people, from this time forth for evermore.

Psalm 125:1–2

The Request for Presence
Make me understand the way of your commandments,* that I may meditate on your marvelous works.

Psalm 119:27

The Greeting
Remember your word to your servant,* because you have given me hope.
This is my comfort in my trouble,* that your promise gives me life.

Psalm 119:49–50

The Refrain for the Morning Lessons
Do not let your hearts be troubled. You trust in God, trust also in me.

John 14:1

A Reading
Before the festival of Passover, Jesus, knowing that his hour had come to pass from this world to the Father, having loved those who were his in the world, loved them to the end. They were at supper, and the devil had already put it into the mind of Judas Iscariot, son of Simon, to betray him. Jesus knew that the Father had put everything into his hands, and that he had come from God and was returning to God, and he got up from the table, removed his outer garments, and, taking a towel, wrapped it around his waist; he poured water into a basin and began to wash the disciples' feet and to wipe them with the towel he was wearing. He came to Simon Peter, who said to him, 'Lord, are you going to wash my feet?' Jesus answered, 'At the moment you do not know what I am doing, but later you will understand.' 'Never!' said Peter, 'You shall never wash my feet.' Jesus replied, 'If I do not wash you, you can have no share with

me.' Simon Peter said, 'Well then, not only my feet, but my hands and my head as well!' Jesus said, 'No one who has had a bath needs washing, such a person is clean all over. You too are clean, though not all of you are.' He knew who was going to betray him, and that was why he said, 'though not all of you are.' When he had washed their feet and put on his outer garments again he went back to the table. 'Do you understand,' he said, 'what I have done to you? You call me Master and Lord, and rightly, so I am. If I then, the Lord and Master, have washed your feet, you must wash each other's feet. I have given you an example so that you may copy what I have done to you.'

John 13:1–15

The Refrain
Do not let your hearts be troubled. You trust in God, trust also in me.

The Morning Psalm   *That the Generation to Come Might Put Their Trust in God*
Hear my teaching, O my people;* incline your ears to the words of my mouth.
I will open my mouth in a parable;* I will declare the mysteries of ancient times.
That which we have heard and known, and what our forefathers have told us,* we will not hide from their children.
We will recount to generations to come the praiseworthy deeds and the power of the LORD,* and the wonderful works he has done.
He gave his decrees to Jacob and established a law for Israel,* which he commanded them to teach their children;
That the generations to come might know, and the children yet unborn;* that they in their turn might tell it to their children;
So that they might put their trust in God,* and not forget the deeds of God, but keep his commandments;
And not be like their forefathers, a stubborn and rebellious generation,* a generation whose heart was not steadfast, and whose spirit was not faithful to God.

Psalm 78:1–8

The Refrain
Do not let your hearts be troubled. You trust in God, trust also in me.

The Cry of the Church
In the evening, in the morning, and at noonday, I will complain and lament,* and he will hear my voice.

Psalm 55:18

The Lord's Prayer

The Prayer Appointed for the Week
Almighty God, who through your only-begotten Son Jesus Christ overcame death and opened to us the gate of everlasting life: Grant that I, who celebrate with joy the day of the Lord's resurrection, may be raised from the death of sin by your life-giving Spirit; through Jesus Christ our Lord, who lives and reigns with you and the Holy Spirit, one God, now and for ever. *Amen.* †

The Concluding Prayer of the Church
Look down, O Lord, I pray, on all of us, Your Family for whom our Lord Jesus
  Christ was content to be betrayed and to be delivered into the hands of wicked
  men, and to suffer the torment of the Cross. *Amen.*

adapted from The Short Breviary

The Midday Office To Be Observed on the Hour or Half Hour
Between 11 a.m. and 2 p.m.

The Call to Prayer
"Come now, let us reason together," says the Lord.

Isaiah 1:18, KJV

The Request for Presence
Awake, O my God, decree justice;* let the assembly of peoples gather around you.
Let the malice of the wicked come to an end, but establish the righteous;* for you
  test the mind and heart, O righteous God.

Psalm 7:7, 10

The Greeting
Deliver me, O Lord, by your hand* from those whose portion in life is this world.

Psalm 17:14

The Refrain for the Midday Lessons
The sacrifice of God is a troubled spirit;* a broken and contrite heart, O God, you
  will not despise.

Psalm 51:18

A Reading
For the tradition I received from the Lord and also handed on to you is that on the
  night he was betrayed the Lord Jesus took some bread, and after he had given
  thanks, he broke it, and he said, 'This is my body, which is slain for you; do this
  in remembrance of me.' And in the same way, with the cup after supper, saying, 'This is the cup of the new covenant in my blood. Whenever you drink it,
  do this in memorial of me.' Whenever you eat this bread, then, and drink this
  cup, you are proclaiming the Lord's death until he comes. Therefore anyone
  who eats the bread or drinks the cup of the Lord unworthily is answerable for
  the body and blood of the Lord. Everyone is to examine himself and only then
  eat of the bread or drink from the cup; because a person who eats and drinks
  without recognizing the body is eating and drinking his own condemnation.

1 Corinthians 11:23–29

The Refrain
The sacrifice of God is a troubled spirit;* a broken and contrite heart, O God, you
  will not despise.

The Midday Psalm *Why, O God, Have You Utterly Cast Us Off*
O God, why have you utterly cast us off?* why is your wrath so hot against the
  sheep of your pasture?

Remember your congregation that you purchased long ago,* the tribe you redeemed to be your inheritance, and Mount Zion where you dwell.

Turn your steps toward the endless ruins;* the enemy has laid waste everything in your sanctuary.

Your adversaries roared in your holy place;* they set up their banners as tokens of victory.

They were like men coming up with axes to a grove of trees;* they broke down all your carved work with hatchets and hammers.

They set fire to your holy place;* they defiled the dwelling-place of your Name and razed it to the ground.

They said to themselves, "Let us destroy them altogether."* They burned down all the meeting-places of God in the land.

There are no signs for us to see; there is no prophet left;* there is not one among us who knows how long.

How long, O God, will the adversary scoff?* will the enemy blaspheme your Name for ever?

Why do you draw back your hand?* why is your right hand hidden in your bosom?

Psalm 74:1–10

The Refrain

The sacrifice of God is a troubled spirit;* a broken and contrite heart, O God, you will not despise.

The Cry of the Church

Lord, have mercy on us. Christ, have mercy on us. Lord, have mercy on us.

The Lord's Prayer

The Prayer Appointed for the Week

Almighty God, who through your only-begotten Son Jesus Christ overcame death and opened to us the gate of everlasting life: Grant that I, who celebrate with joy the day of the Lord's resurrection, may be raised from the death of sin by your life-giving Spirit; through Jesus Christ our Lord, who lives and reigns with you and the Holy Spirit, one God, now and for ever. *Amen.* †

The Concluding Prayer of the Church

Almighty Father, whose dear Son, on the night before he suffered, instituted the Sacrament of his Body and Blood: Mercifully grant that I may receive it thankfully in remembrance of Jesus Christ our Lord, who in these holy mysteries gives us a pledge of eternal life; and who now lives and reigns with you and the Holy Spirit, one God, for ever and ever. *Amen.* †

The Vespers Office　　　　　**To Be Observed on the Hour or Half Hour**
Between 5 and 8 p.m.

The Call to Prayer

Come and listen, all you who fear God,* and I will tell you what he has done for me.

Psalm 66:14

The Request for Presence
O God, be not far from me;* come quickly to help me, O my God.

Psalm 71:12

The Greeting
You have showed me great troubles and adversities,* but you will restore my life
and bring me up again from the deep places of the earth.

Psalm 71:20

The Hymn   Go to Dark Gethsemane
Go to dark Gethsemane, you that feel the tempter's power;
Your Redeemer's conflict see, Watch with him one bitter hour.
Turn not from his griefs away; learn of Jesus Christ to pray.

See him at the judgment hall, beaten, bound, reviled, arraigned;
O the worm-wood and the Gall! O the pangs his soul sustained!
Shun not suffering, shame, or loss; learn of Christ to bear the cross.

Calvary's mournful mountain climb; there, adoring at his feet,
Mark that miracle of time, God's own sacrifice complete.
"It is finished!" hear him cry; learn of Jesus Christ to die.

Early hasten to the tomb where they laid his breathless clay;
All is solitude and gloom. Who has taken him away?
Christ is risen! He meets our eyes; Savior, teach us so to rise.

James Montgomery

The Refrain for the Vespers Lessons
Deliver me, my God, from the hand of the wicked,* from the clutches of the evil-
doer and the oppressor.

Psalm 71:4

The Vespers Psalm   As for Me, I Am Poor and Needy
Be pleased, O God, to deliver me;* O Lord, make haste to help me.
Let those who seek my life be ashamed and altogether dismayed;* let those who
take pleasure in my misfortune draw back and be disgraced.
Let those who say to me "Aha!" and gloat over me turn back,* because they are
ashamed.
Let all who seek you rejoice and be glad in you;* let those who love your salvation
say for ever, "Great is the Lord!"
But as for me, I am poor and needy;* come to me speedily, O God.
You are my helper and my deliverer;* O Lord, do not tarry.

Psalm 70

The Refrain
Deliver me, my God, from the hand of the wicked,* from the clutches of the evil-
doer and the oppressor.

The Gloria*

The Lord's Prayer

The Prayer Appointed for the Week
Almighty God, who through your only-begotten Son Jesus Christ overcame death
and opened to us the gate of everlasting life: Grant that I, who celebrate with
joy the day of the Lord's resurrection, may be raised from the death of sin by
your life-giving Spirit; through Jesus Christ our Lord, who lives and reigns
with you and the Holy Spirit, one God, now and for ever. *Amen.* †

The Concluding Prayer of the Church
Almighty and everlasting God, grant that we may celebrate the mysteries of our
Lord's Passion in such a manner as to deserve Your pardon. Through the same
Jesus Christ. *Amen.*

adapted from THE SHORT BREVIARY

The Morning Office **To Be Observed on the Hour or Half Hour**
Between 6 and 9 a.m.

The Call to Prayer
I cry out to you, O LORD;* I say, "You are my refuge, my portion in the land of the
living."

Psalm 142:5

The Request for Presence
Be my strong rock, a castle to keep me safe;* you are my crag and my stronghold.

Psalm 71:3

The Greeting
O LORD, I cry to you for help;* in the morning my prayer comes before you.

Psalm 88:14

The Refrain for the Morning Lessons
My God, my God, why have you forsaken me?* and are so far from my cry and
from the words of my distress?

Psalm 22:1

A Reading
Pilate then had Jesus taken away and scourged; and after this, the soldiers twisted
some thorns into a crown and put it on his head and dressed him in a purple
robe. They kept coming up to him and saying, 'Hail, king of the Jews!' and
slapping him in the face. Pilate came outside again and said to them, 'Look, I
am going to bring him out to you to let you see that I find no case against him.
The chief priests and the guards shouted, 'Crucify him! Crucify him!' Pilate
said, 'Take him yourselves and crucify him: I find no case against him.' The
Jews replied, 'We have a Law, and according to that Law he ought to be put to
death, because he has claimed to be the Son of God.' . . . They [the soldiers]
then took charge of Jesus, and carrying his own cross he went out to the Place

of the Skull, or as it is called in Hebrew, Golgatha, where they crucified him with two others, one on either side, Jesus being in the middle . . . When the soldiers had finished crucifying Jesus they took his clothing and divided it into four shares, one for each soldier. His undergarment was seamless, woven in one piece from neck to hem; so they said to one another, 'Instead of tearing it, let's throw dice to decide who is to have it.' In this way the words of scripture were fulfilled: *They divide my garments among them and cast lots for my clothes.* That is what the soldiers did. Near the cross of Jesus stood his mother and his mother's sister, Mary the wife of Clopas, and Mary of Magdela. Seeing his mother and the disciple whom he loved standing near her, Jesus said to his mother, 'Woman, this is your son.' Then to the disciple he said, 'This is your mother.' And from that hour the disciple took her into his home. After this, Jesus knew that everything had now been completed and, so that the scripture should be completely fulfilled, he said: *I am thirsty.* A jar full of wine stood there; so putting a sponge in the wine on a hyssop stick, they held it up to his mouth. After Jesus had taken the wine, he said, 'It is fulfilled'; and bowing his head he gave up the spirit.

John 19:1ff

The Refrain
My God, my God, why have you forsaken me?* and are so far from my cry and from the words of my distress?

The Morning Psalm   *I Am Poured Out Like Water*
I am poured out like water;* all my bones are out of joint; my heart within my breast is melting wax.

My mouth is dried out like a pot-shard; my tongue sticks to the roof of my mouth;* and you have laid me in the dust of the grave.

Packs of dogs close me in, and gangs of evildoers circle around me;* they pierce my hands and my feet; I can count all my bones.

They stare and gloat over me;* they divide my garments among them; they cast lots for my clothing.

Be not far away, O Lord;* you are my strength; hasten to help me.

Save me from the sword,* my life from the power of the dog.

Save me from the lion's mouth,* my wretched body from the horns of wild bulls.

I will declare your Name to my brethren;* in the midst of the congregation I will praise you.

Psalm 22:14–21

The Refrain
My God, my God, why have you forsaken me?* and are so far from my cry and from the words of my distress?

The Cry of the Church
O God, come to my assistance! O Lord, make haste to help me!

The Lord's Prayer

The Prayer Appointed for the Week

Almighty God, who through your only-begotten Son Jesus Christ overcame death and opened to us the gate of everlasting life: Grant that I, who celebrate with joy the day of the Lord's resurrection, may be raised from the death of sin by your life-giving Spirit; through Jesus Christ our Lord, who lives and reigns with you and the Holy Spirit, one God, now and for ever. *Amen.* †

The Concluding Prayer of the Church

O God, you sent Christ Jesus to be my shepherd and the lamb of sacrifice. Help me to embrace the mystery of salvation, the promise of life rising out of death. Help me to hear the call of Christ and give me the courage to follow it readily that I, too, may lead others to you. This I ask through Jesus, my shepherd and guide.

from PEOPLE'S COMPANION TO THE BREVIARY, VOL. II

The Midday Office   **To Be Observed on the Hour or Half Hour Between 11 a.m. and 2 p.m.**

The Call to Prayer

The LORD will make good his purpose for me;* O LORD, your love endures for ever; do not abandon the works of your hands.

Psalm 138:9

The Request for Presence

I spread out my hands to you;* my soul gasps to you like a thirsty land.

O LORD, make haste to answer me; my spirit fails me;* do not hide your face from me or I shall be like those who go down to the Pit.

Psalm 143:6–7

The Greeting

Remember your word to your servant,* because you have given me hope.

This is my comfort in my trouble,* that your promise gives me life.

Psalm 119:49–50

The Refrain for the Midday Lessons

For God alone my soul in silence waits;* from him comes my salvation.

Psalm 62:1

A Reading

Forcibly, after sentence, he was taken. Which of his contemporaries was concerned at his having been cut off from the land of the living, at his having been struck dead for his people's rebellion? He was given a grave with the wicked, and his tomb is with the rich, although he had done no violence, had spoken no deceit. It was YAHWEH's good pleasure to crush him with pain; if he gives his life as a sin offering, he will see his offspring and prolong his life, and through him YAHWEH's good pleasure will be done. After the ordeal he has endured, he will see the light and be content. By his knowledge, the upright one, my servant will justify many by taking their guilt on himself. Hence I shall give him a portion with the many, and he will share the body with the mighty, for having exposed himself to death and for being counted as one of the rebellious, whereas he was bearing the sin of many and interceding for the rebellious.

Isaiah 53:8–12

The Refrain
For God alone my soul in silence waits;* from him comes my salvation.

The Midday Psalm   *Be Not Far from Me, for Trouble Is Near*
But as for me, I am a worm and no man,* scorned by all and despised by the people.

All who see me laugh me to scorn;* they curl their lips and wag their heads, saying,

"He trusted in the LORD; let him deliver him;* let him rescue him, if he delights in him."

Yet you are he who took me out of the womb,* and kept me safe upon my mother's breast.

I have been entrusted to you ever since I was born;* you were my God when I was still in my mother's womb.

Be not far from me, for trouble is near,* and there is none to help.

Psalm 22:6–11

The Refrain
For God alone my soul in silence waits;* from him comes my salvation.

The Cry of the Church
Remember me, Lord, when You come into Your kingdom.

Luke 22:42

The Lord's Prayer

The Prayer Appointed for the Week
Almighty God, who through your only-begotten Son Jesus Christ overcame death and opened to us the gate of everlasting life: Grant that I, who celebrate with joy the day of the Lord's resurrection, may be raised from the death of sin by your life-giving Spirit; through Jesus Christ our Lord, who lives and reigns with you and the Holy Spirit, one God, now and for ever. *Amen.* †

The Concluding Prayer of the Church
Almighty God, I pray you graciously to behold those who are your family, for whom our Lord Jesus Christ was willing to be betrayed, and given into the hands of sinners, and to suffer death upon the cross; who now lives and reigns with you and the Holy Spirit, one God, for ever and ever. *Amen.*

The Vespers Office To Be Observed on the Hour or Half Hour
Between 5 and 8 p.m.

The Call to Prayer
I will call upon God,* and the LORD will deliver me.
In the evening, in the morning, and at the noonday, I will complain and lament,*
and he will hear my voice.
He will bring me safely back . . . God, who is enthroned of old, will hear me.

Psalm 55:17ff

The Request for Presence
Teach me your way, O LORD, and I will walk in your truth;* knit my heart to you
that I may fear your Name.

Psalm 86:11

The Greeting
To you, O LORD, I lift up my soul;* my God, I put my trust in you.

Psalm 25:1

The Hymn *When I Survey the Wondrous Cross*
When I survey the wondrous cross on which the Prince of Glory died,
My richest gain I count but loss, and pour contempt on all my pride.

Forbid it, Lord, that I should boast, save in the death of Christ, my God;
All the vain things that charm me most, I sacrifice them to his blood.

See, from his head, his hands, his feet, sorrow and love flow mingled down.
Did ever such love and sorrow meet, or thorns compose so rich a crown?

Were the whole realm of nature mine, that were an offering far too small;
Love so amazing, so divine, demands my soul, my life, my all.

Isaac Watts

The Refrain for the Vespers Lessons
And now, what is my hope?* O Lord, my hope is in you.

Psalm 39:8

The Vespers Psalm *At the Time You Have Set, O LORD*
Surely, for your sake have I suffered reproach,* and shame has covered my face.
I have become a stranger to my own kindred,* an alien to my mother's children.
Zeal for your house has eaten me up;* the scorn of those who scorn you has fallen
upon me.
I humbled myself with fasting,* but that was turned to my reproach.
I put on sack-cloth also,* and became a byword among them.
Those who sit at the gate murmur against me,* and the drunkards make songs
about me.
But as for me, this is my prayer to you,* at the time you have set, O LORD:
"In your great mercy, O God,* answer me with your unfailing help.

Save me from the mire; do not let me sink;* let me be rescued from those who hate
me and out of the deep waters.
Let not the torrent of waters wash over me, neither let the deep swallow me up;*
do not let the Pit shut its mouth upon me.
Answer me, O Lord, for your love is kind;* in your great compassion, turn
to me."

Psalm 69:8–18

The Refrain
And now, what is my hope?* O Lord, my hope is in you.

The Cry of the Church
O God, come to my assistance! O Lord, make haste to help me!

The Lord's Prayer

The Prayer Appointed for the Week
Almighty God, who through your only-begotten Son Jesus Christ overcame death
and opened to us the gate of everlasting life: Grant that I, who celebrate with
joy the day of the Lord's resurrection, may be raised from the death of sin by
your life-giving Spirit; through Jesus Christ our Lord, who lives and reigns
with you and the Holy Spirit, one God, now and for ever. *Amen.* †

The Concluding Prayer of the Church
Almighty and everlasting God, who willed that our Savior should take our flesh
and suffer death upon the Cross, that all mankind should follow the example
of His great humility, mercifully grant that I may both follow the example of
His patience and also be made a partaker of His resurrection. Through the
same Jesus Christ. *Amen.*

adapted from The Short Breviary

The Morning Office　　　　　**To Be Observed on the Hour or Half Hour**
Between 6 and 9 a.m.

The Call to Prayer
Be strong and let your heart take courage,* all you who wait for the Lord.

Psalm 31:24

The Request for Presence
In your righteousness, deliver and set me free;* incline your ear to me and
save me.

Psalm 71:2

The Greeting
O Lord, I am your servant;* I am your servant and the child of your handmaid;
My times are in your hand.*

Psalm 116:14, 31:15a

The Refrain for the Morning Lessons
I said in my alarm, "I have been cut off from the sight of your eyes."*
    Nevertheless, you heard the sound of my entreaty when I cried out to you.

Psalm 31:22

A Reading
It was the Day of Preparation, and to avoid the bodies' remaining on the cross
    during the Sabbath—since that Sabbath was a day of special solemnity—the
    Jews asked Pilate to have the legs broken and the bodies taken away.
    Consequently the soldiers came and broke the legs of the first man who had
    been crucified with him and then of the other. When they came to Jesus, they
    saw that he was already dead, so instead of breaking his legs, one of the sol-
    diers pierced his side with a lance; and immediately there came out blood and
    water. This is the evidence of one who saw it—true evidence, and he knows
    that what he says is true—and he gives it so that you may believe as well.
    Because all this happened to fulfill the words of scripture: *Not one bone of his*
    will be broken; and again, in another place scripture says: *They will look to the one*
    whom they have pierced. After this, Joseph of Arimathaea, who was a disciple of
    Jesus—though a secret one because he was afraid of the Jews—asked Pilate to
    let him remove the body of Jesus. Pilate gave permission, so they came and
    took it away. Nicodemus came as well—the same one who had first come to
    Jesus at night-time—and he brought a mixture of myrrh and aloes, weighing
    about a hundred pounds. They took the body of Jesus and bound it in linen
    cloths with the spices, following the Jewish burial custom. At the place where
    he had been crucified there was a garden, and in this garden a new tomb in
    which no one had yet been buried. Since it was the Jewish Day of Preparation
    and the tomb was near by, they laid Jesus there.

John 19:31–42

The Refrain
I said in my alarm, "I have been cut off from the sight of your eyes."*
    Nevertheless, you heard the sound of my entreaty when I cried out to you.

The Morning Psalm   *Into Your Hands I Commend My Spirit*
In you, O LORD, have I taken refuge; let me never be put to shame;* deliver me in
    your righteousness.
Incline your ear to me;* make haste to deliver me.
Be my strong rock, a castle to keep me safe, for you are my crag and my stronghold;*
    for the sake of your Name, lead me and guide me.
Take me out of the net that they have secretly set for me,* for you are my tower of
    strength.
Into your hands I commend my spirit,* for you have redeemed me, O LORD, O
    God of truth.

Psalm 31:1–5

The Refrain
I said in my alarm, "I have been cut off from the sight of your eyes."*
    Nevertheless, you heard the sound of my entreaty when I cried out to you.

The Gloria*

The Lord's Prayer

The Prayer Appointed for the Week
Almighty God, who through your only-begotten Son Jesus Christ overcame death
and opened to us the gate of everlasting life: Grant that I, who celebrate with
joy the day of the Lord's resurrection, may be raised from the death of sin by
your life-giving Spirit; through Jesus Christ our Lord, who lives and reigns
with you and the Holy Spirit, one God, now and for ever. *Amen.* †

The Concluding Prayer of the Church
O God, at whose passion, according to the prophesy of Simeon, a sword of sorrow
pierced the sweet soul of the glorious Virgin and Mother Mary, grant in Your
mercy that we, when remembering her pierced soul, through the merits and
prayers of all the Saints faithfully standing by Your Cross, may obtain the
blessed result of Your Passion. Through our Lord. *Amen.*

adapted from The Short Breviary

The Midday Office **To Be Observed on the Hour or Half Hour**
Between 11 a.m. and 2 p.m.

The Call to Prayer
My merciful God comes to meet me;* God will let me look in triumph on my
enemies.

Psalm 59:11

The Request for Presence
O Lord, give victory to the king* and answer us when we call.

Psalm 20:9

The Greeting
Lord, hear my prayer, and in your faithfulness heed my supplications;* answer
me in your righteousness.

Psalm 143:1

The Refrain for the Midday Lessons
Blessed be the Lord God of Israel,* from age to age. Amen. Amen.

Psalm 41:13

A Reading
There is always hope for a tree: when felled, it can start its life again; its shoots
continue to sprout. Its roots may have grown old in the earth, its stump rotting
in the ground, but let it scent the water and it buds, and puts out branches like
a plant newly set. But a human being? He dies, and dead he remains, breathes
his last, and then where is he? The waters of the sea will vanish, the rivers stop
flowing and run dry: a human being, once laid to rest, will never rise again, the
heavens will wear out before he wakes up, or before he is roused from his
sleep. Will no one hide me in Sheol, and shelter me there till your anger is past,

fixing a certain day for calling me to mind—can the dead come back to life?—
day after day of my service, I should be waiting for my relief to come. Then
you would call, and I should answer, you would want to see once more what
you have made. Whereas now you count every step I take, you would then
stop spying on my sin; you would seal up my crime in a bag, and put a cover
over my fault. Alas! Just as, eventually, the mountain falls down, the rock
moves from its place, water wears away the stones, the cloudburst erodes the
soil; so you destroy whatever hope a person has. You crush him once and for
all, and he is gone; first you disfigure him, then you dismiss him. His children
may rise to honors—he does not know it; they may come down in the world—
he does not care. He feels no pangs, except for his own body, makes no lament,
except for his own self.

Job 14:7–22

The Refrain
Blessed be the LORD God of Israel,* from age to age. Amen. Amen.

The Midday Psalm   *Out of the Depths Have I Called to You*
Out of the depths have I called to you, O LORD; LORD, hear my voice;* let your ears
    consider well the voice of my supplication.
If you, LORD, were to note what is done amiss,* O Lord, who could stand?
For there is forgiveness with you;* therefore you shall be feared.
I wait for the LORD; my soul waits for him;* in his word is my hope.
My soul waits for the LORD, more than watchmen for the morning,* more than
    watchmen for the morning.
O Israel, wait for the LORD,* for with the LORD there is mercy;
With him there is plenteous redemption,* and he shall redeem Israel from all their
    sins.

Psalm 130

The Refrain
Blessed be the LORD God of Israel,* from age to age. Amen. Amen.

The Gloria*

The Lord's Prayer

The Prayer Appointed for the Week
Almighty God, who through your only-begotten Son Jesus Christ overcame death
    and opened to us the gate of everlasting life: Grant that I, who celebrate with
    joy the day of the Lord's resurrection, may be raised from the death of sin by
    your life-giving Spirit; through Jesus Christ our Lord, who lives and reigns
    with you and the Holy Spirit, one God, now and for ever. *Amen.* †

The Concluding Prayer of the Church
O God, Creator of heaven and earth: Grant that, as the crucified body of your dear
    Son was laid in the tomb and rested on this holy Sabbath, so I may await with
    him the coming of the third day, and rise with him to newness of life; who now
    lives and reigns with you and the Holy Spirit, one God, for ever and ever. *Amen.* †

The Vespers Office **To Be Observed on the Hour or Half Hour**
Between 5 and 8 p.m.

The Call to Prayer
Let the Name of the LORD be blessed,* from this time forth for evermore.
From the rising of the sun to its going down* let the Name of the LORD be praised.

Psalm 113:2–3

The Request for Presence
Let my cry come before you, O LORD;* give me understanding, according to your
  word.
Let my supplication come before you;* deliver me, according to your promise.

Psalm 119:169–170

The Greeting
The Lord is in his holy temple; Let all the earth keep silence before him. *Amen.*

The Hymn *Take Up Your Cross*

Take up your cross, the Savior said,
If you would my disciple be;
Deny yourself, the world forsake,
And humbly follow after me.

Take up your cross, let not its weight
Fill your weak spirit with alarm;
His strength shall bear your spirit up,
Shall brace your heart and nerve your arm.

Take up your cross then in his strength,
And every danger calmly brave,
To guide you to a better home,
And victory over death and grave.

Take up your cross and follow Christ,
Nor think till death to lay it down;
For only he who bears the cross
May hope to wear the glorious crown.

To you, great Lord, the One in three,
All praise for evermore ascend;
O grant us here below to see
The heavenly life that knows no end.

Charles W. Everest

The Refrain for the Vespers Lessons
Those who sowed with tears* will reap with songs of joy.
Those who go out weeping, carrying the seed,* will come again with joy,
  shouldering their sheaves.

Psalm 126:6–7

The Vespers Psalm   *My Help Comes from the* LORD
I lift up my eyes to the hills;* from where is my help to come?
My help comes from the LORD,* the maker of heaven and earth.
He will not let your foot be moved* and he who watches over you will not fall
asleep.
Behold, he who keeps watch over Israel* shall neither slumber nor sleep.

Psalm 121:1–4

The Refrain
Those who sowed with tears* will reap with songs of joy.
Those who go out weeping, carrying the seed,* will come again with joy,
shouldering their sheaves.

The Small Verse
Christ is risen. Alleluia!

The Lord's Prayer

The Prayer Appointed for the Week
Almighty God, who through your only-begotten Son Jesus Christ overcame death
and opened to us the gate of everlasting life: Grant that I, who celebrate with
joy the day of the Lord's resurrection, may be raised from the death of sin by
your life-giving Spirit; through Jesus Christ our Lord, who lives and reigns
with you and the Holy Spirit, one God, now and for ever. *Amen.* †

The Concluding Prayer of the Church
Rejoice now, heavenly hosts and choirs of angels, and let your trumpets shout
salvation for the victory of our mighty King.
Rejoice and sing now, all the round earth, bright with a glorious splendor, for
darkness has been vanquished by our eternal King.
Rejoice and be glad now, Mother Church, and let your holy courts, in radiant light,
resound with the praises of your people.

The Morning Office   **To Be Observed on the Hour or Half Hour
Between 6 and 9 a.m.**

The Call to Prayer
Praise the LORD, all you nations;* laud him, all you peoples.
For his loving-kindness toward us is great,* and the faithfulness of the LORD
endures for ever. Hallelujah!

Psalm 117

The Request for Presence
I will offer you the sacrifice of thanksgiving* and call upon the Name of the Lord.
I will fulfill my vows to the Lord* in the presence of all his people,
In the courts of the Lord's house,* in the midst of you, O Jerusalem. Hallelujah!

Psalm 116:15–17

The Greeting
Hosanna, Lord, hosanna!* Lord, send us now success.
Blessed is he who comes in the name of the Lord;* we bless you from the house of
the Lord.

Psalm 118:25–26

The Refrain for the Morning Lessons
It is better to rely on the Lord* than to put any trust in flesh.
It is better to rely on the Lord* than to put any trust in rulers.

Psalm 118:8–9

A Reading
After the Sabbath, and towards dawn on the first day of the week, Mary of
Magdela and the other Mary went to visit the sepulchre. And suddenly there
was a violent earthquake, for an angel of the Lord, descending from heaven,
came and rolled away the stone and sat on it. His face was like lightning, his
robe white as snow. The guards were so shaken by fear of him that they were
like dead men. But the angel spoke; and he said to the women, 'There is no need
for you to be afraid. I know you are looking for Jesus, who was crucified. He is
not here, for he has risen, as he said he would. Come and see the place where he
lay, then go quickly and tell his disciples, "He has risen from the dead and now
he is going ahead of you to Galilee; that is where you will see him." Look! I have
told you.' Filled with awe and great joy the women came quickly away from the
tomb and ran to tell his disciples. And suddenly, coming to meet them, was
Jesus. 'Greetings,' he said. And the women came up to him and, clasping his
feet, they did him homage. Then Jesus said to them, 'Do not be afraid; go and
tell my brothers that they must leave for Galilee; there they will see me.'

Matthew 28:1–10

The Refrain
It is better to rely on the Lord* than to put any trust in flesh.
It is better to rely on the Lord* than to put any trust in rulers.

The Morning Psalm   *I Shall Not Die, but Live*
There is a sound of exultation and victory* in the tents of the righteous:
"The right hand of the Lord has triumphed!* the right hand of the Lord is exalted!
the right hand of the Lord has triumphed!"
I shall not die, but live,* and declare the works of the Lord.
The Lord has punished me sorely,* but he did not hand me over to death.
Open for me the gates of righteousness;* I will enter them; I will offer thanks to the
Lord.

"This is the gate of the LORD;* he who is righteous may enter."
I will give thanks to you, for you answered me* and have become my salvation.
The same stone which the builders rejected* has become the chief cornerstone.
This is the LORD's doing,* and it is marvelous in our eyes.
On this day the LORD has acted;* we will rejoice and be glad in it.

Psalm 118:15–24

The Refrain
It is better to rely on the LORD* than to put any trust in flesh.
It is better to rely on the LORD* than to put any trust in rulers.

The Cry of the Church
Alleluia. Christ is risen.
The Lord is risen indeed. Alleluia.

The Lord's Prayer

The Prayer Appointed for the Week
Almighty God, who through your only-begotten Son Jesus Christ overcame death
and opened to us the gate of everlasting life: Grant that I, who celebrate with
joy the day of the Lord's resurrection, may be raised from the death of sin by
your life-giving Spirit; through Jesus Christ our Lord, who lives and reigns
with you and the Holy Spirit, one God, now and for ever. *Amen.* †

The Concluding Prayer of the Church
O God, of unchangeable power and eternal light: Look favorably on your whole
Church, that wonderful and sacred mystery; by the effectual working of your
providence, carry out in tranquility the plan of salvation; let the whole world
see and know that things which were cast down are being raised up, and
things which had grown old are being made new, and that all things are being
brought to their perfection by him through whom all things are made, your
Son Jesus Christ our Lord. *Amen.*

The Midday Office
To Be Observed on the Hour or Half Hour Between 11 a.m. and 2 p.m.

The Call to Prayer
Come, let us sing to the LORD;* let us shout for joy to the Rock of our salvation.
Let us come before his presence with thanksgiving* and raise a loud shout to him
with psalms.
For the LORD is a great God,* and a great King above all gods.
In his hands are the caverns of the earth,* and the heights of the hills are his also.
The sea is his, for he made it,* and his hands have molded the dry land.

Psalm 95:1–5

The Request for Presence
May God give us his blessing,* and may all the ends of the earth stand in awe of him.

Psalm 67:7

The Greeting
You, O Lord, are a shield about me;* you are my glory, the one who lifts up my
head.
I call aloud upon the Lord,* and he answers me from his holy hill.

Psalm 3:3–4

The Refrain for the Midday Lessons
May the glory of the Lord endure for ever;* may the Lord rejoice in all his works.

Psalm 104:32

A Reading
The apostle taught us, saying: "We believe that, if we died with Christ, then we
shall live with him too. We know that Christ has been raised from the dead and
will never die again. Death has no power over him any more. For by dying, he
is dead to sin once and for all, and now the life that he lives is life with God. In
the same way, you must see yourselves as being dead to sin, but alive for God
in Christ Jesus."

Romans 6:8–11

The Refrain
May the glory of the Lord endure for ever;* may the Lord rejoice in all his works.

The Midday Psalm   *Let Them Praise the Name of the Lord*
Praise the Lord from the earth,* you sea-monsters and deeps;
Fire and hail, snow and fog,* tempestuous wind, doing his will;
Mountains and all hills,* fruit trees and all cedars;
Wild beasts and all cattle, creeping things and wingèd birds; Kings of the earth
and all peoples,* princes and all rulers of the world;
Young men and maidens,* old and young together.
Let them praise the Name of the Lord,* for his Name only is exalted, his splendor
is over earth and heaven.
He raised up strength for his people and praise for all his loyal servants,* the
children of Israel, a people who are near him. Hallelujah!

Psalm 148:7–14

The Refrain
May the glory of the Lord endure for ever;* may the Lord rejoice in all his works.

The Cry of the Church
Christ has died, Christ has risen, Christ will come again!

The Lord's Prayer

The Prayer Appointed for the Week
Almighty God, who through your only-begotten Son Jesus Christ overcame death
and opened to us the gate of everlasting life: Grant that I, who celebrate with
joy the day of the Lord's resurrection, may be raised from the death of sin by
your life-giving Spirit; through Jesus Christ our Lord, who lives and reigns
with you and the Holy Spirit, one God, now and for ever. *Amen.* †

The Concluding Prayers of the Church

O God, who wonderfully created, and yet more wonderfully restored, the dignity of human nature: Grant that I may share the divine life of him who humbled himself to share our humanity, your Son Jesus Christ our Lord. *Amen.* †

The Vespers Office   **To Be Observed on the Hour or Half Hour Between 5 and 8 p.m.**

The Call to Prayer

Hallelujah! Give praise, you servants of the LORD;* praise the Name of the LORD.

Psalm 113:1

The Request for Presence

I call upon you, O God, for you will answer me;* incline your ear to me, and hear my words.

Psalm 17:6

The Greeting

You are God: I praise you;* you are the Lord: I acclaim you;
You are the eternal Father:* all creation worships you.
Throughout the world the holy Church acclaims you:* Father, of majesty unbounded,
your true and only Son,* worthy of all worship,
and the Holy Spirit,* advocate and guide.
As these have been from the beginning,* so they are now and evermore shall be.
Alleluia.

based on the Te Deum and Gloria

The Hymn   *Christ the Lord Is Risen Today*

Christ the Lord is risen today. Alleluia!
Earth and heaven in chorus say, Alleluia!
Raise your joys and triumphs high, Alleluia!
Sing, you heavens, and earth reply, Alleluia!

Love's redeeming work is done, Alleluia!
Fought the fight, the battle won, Alleluia!
Death in vain forbids him rise, Alleluia!
Christ has opened paradise, Alleluia!

Lives again our glorious King, Alleluia!
Where, O death, is now your sting? Alleluia!
Once he died our souls to save, Alleluia!
Where's your victory, boasting grave? Alleluia!

Soar we now where Christ has led, Alleluia!
Following our exalted Head, Alleluia!
Made like him, like him we rise, Alleluia!
Ours the cross, the grave, the skies, Alleluia!

Hail the Lord of earth and heaven, Alleluia!
Praise to you by both be given, Alleluia!
You we greet triumphant now, Alleluia!
Hail the Resurrection, thou, Alleluia!

King of glory, soul of bliss, Alleluia!
Everlasting life is this, Alleluia!
You to know, your power to prove, Alleluia!
Thus to sing, and thus to love, Alleluia!

Charles Wesley

The Refrain for the Vespers Lessons
We will bless the Lord,* from this time forth for evermore. Hallelujah!

Psalm 115:18

The Vespers Psalm   *An Evening Song*
I will bless the Lord who gives me counsel;* my heart teaches me, night after
   night.
I have set the Lord always before me;* because he is at my right hand I shall not
   fall.
My heart, therefore, is glad, and my spirit rejoices;* my body also shall rest in
   hope.
For you will not abandon me to the grave,* nor let your holy one see the Pit.
You will show me the path of life;* in your presence is fullness of joy, and in your
   right hand are pleasures for evermore.

Psalm 16:7–11

The Refrain
We will bless the Lord,* from this time forth for evermore. Hallelujah!

The Cry of the Church
Alleluia. Christ is risen.
The Lord is risen indeed. Alleluia!

The Lord's Prayer

The Prayer Appointed for the Week
Almighty God, who through your only-begotten Son Jesus Christ overcame death
   and opened to us the gate of everlasting life: Grant that I, who celebrate with
   joy the day of the Lord's resurrection, may be raised from the death of sin by
   your life-giving Spirit; through Jesus Christ our Lord, who lives and reigns
   with you and the Holy Spirit, one God, now and for ever. *Amen.* †

The Concluding Prayer of the Church
O God, who for our redemption gave your only-begotten Son to the death of the
   cross, and by this glorious resurrection delivered us from the power of our
   enemy: Grant me so to die daily in sin, that I may evermore live with him in the
   joy of his resurrection; through Jesus Christ your Son our Lord, who lives and
   reigns with you and the Holy Spirit, one God, now and for ever. *Amen.* †

The Morning Office

**To Be Observed on the Hour or Half Hour
Between 6 and 9 a.m.**

The Call to Prayer
Rejoice in the LORD, you righteous;* it is good for the just to sing praises.
Praise the LORD with the harp;* play to him upon the psaltery and lyre.
Sing for him a new song;* sound a fanfare with all your skill upon the trumpet.

Psalm 33:1–3

The Request for Presence
Let your loving-kindness, O LORD, be upon us,* as we have put our trust in you.

Psalm 33:22

The Greeting
How great is your goodness, O LORD! which you have laid up for those who fear
you;* which you have done in the sight of all for those who put their trust in
you.

Psalm 31:19

The Refrain for the Morning Lessons
. . . the loving-kindness of the LORD fills the whole earth.

Psalm 33:5

A Reading
Now that very same day, two of them were on their way to a village called
Emmaus, seven miles from Jerusalem, and they were talking together about all
that had happened. And it happened that as they were talking together and
discussing it, Jesus himself came up and walked by their side; but their eyes
were prevented from recognizing him. He said to them, 'What are all these
things that you are discussing as you walk along?' They stopped, their faces
downcast. Then one of them, called Cleopas, answered him, 'You must be the
only person staying in Jerusalem who does not know the things that have been
happening there these last few days.' He asked, 'What things?' They answered,
'All about Jesus of Nazareth, who showed himself a prophet powerful in action
and speech before God and the whole people; and how our chief priests and
our leaders handed him over to be sentenced to death, and had him crucified.
Our own hope had been that he would be the one to set Israel free. And this is
not all: two whole days have now gone by since it all happened; and some
women from our group have astounded us: they went to the tomb in the early
morning, and when they could not find the body, they came back to tell us they
had seen a vision of angels who declared he was alive. Some of our friends
went to the tomb and found everything exactly as the women reported, but of
him they saw nothing.' Then he said to them, 'You foolish men! So slow to
believe all that the prophets have said! Was it not necessary that the Christ
should suffer before entering into his glory?' Then, starting with Moses and
going through all the prophets, he explained to them the passages throughout

the scriptures that were about himself. When they drew near to the village to which they were going, he made as if to go on; but they pressed him to stay with them saying, 'It is nearly evening, and the day is almost over.' So he went in to stay with them. Now while he was with them at table, he took the bread and said the blessing; then he broke it and handed it to them. And their eyes were opened and they recognized him; but he had vanished from their sight. Then they said to each other, 'Did not our hearts burn within us as he talked to us on the road and explained the scriptures to us?' They set out that instant and returned to Jerusalem. There they found the Eleven assembled together with their companions, who said to them, 'The Lord has indeed risen and has appeared to Simon.' Then they told their story of what had happened on the road and how they had recognized him at the breaking of bread.

Luke 24:13–35

The Refrain
. . . the loving-kindness of the LORD fills the whole earth.

The Morning Psalm   *Happy the Nation Whose God Is the LORD*
Let all the earth fear the LORD;* let all who dwell in the world stand in awe of him.
For he spoke, and it came to pass;* he commanded, and it stood fast.
The LORD brings the will of the nations to naught;* he thwarts the designs of the peoples.
But the LORD's will stands fast for ever,* and the designs of his heart from age to age.
Happy is the nation whose God is the LORD!* happy the people he has chosen to be his own!

Psalm 33:8–12

The Refrain
. . . the loving-kindness of the LORD fills the whole earth.

The Cry of the Church
Christ has died. Christ has risen. Christ will come again!

The Lord's Prayer

The Prayer Appointed for the Week
Almighty God, who through your only-begotten Son Jesus Christ overcame death and opened to us the gate of everlasting life: Grant that I, who celebrate with joy the day of the Lord's resurrection, may be raised from the death of sin by your life-giving Spirit; through Jesus Christ our Lord, who lives and reigns with you and the Holy Spirit, one God, now and for ever. *Amen.* †

The Concluding Prayer of the Church
Grant, I pray, Almighty God, that we who celebrate with awe the Paschal feast may be found worthy to attain to everlasting joys; through Jesus Christ our Lord, who lives and reigns with you and the Holy Spirit, one God, now and for ever. *Amen.* †

The Midday Office   To Be Observed on the Hour or Half Hour
                                                          Between 11 a.m. and 2 p.m.

The Call to Prayer
Give thanks to the LORD and call upon his Name;* make known his deeds among
the peoples.
Sing to him, sing praises to him,* and speak of all his marvelous works.
Glory in his holy Name;* let the hearts of those who seek the LORD rejoice.

Psalm 105:1–3

The Request for Presence
Teach me your way, O LORD, and I will walk in your truth;* knit my heart to you
that I may fear your Name.
I will thank you, O LORD my God, with all my heart,* and glorify your Name for
evermore.

Psalm 86:11–12

The Greeting
My mouth shall recount your mighty acts and saving deeds all the day long;*
though I can not know the number of them.

Psalm 71:15

The Refrain for the Midday Lessons
I will confess you among the peoples, O LORD;* I will sing praises to you among
the nations.

Psalm 108:3

A Reading
I have been crucified with Christ and yet I am alive; yet it is no longer I, but Christ
living in me. The life that I am now living, subject to the limitation of human
nature, I am living in faith, faith in the Son of God who loved me and gave
himself for me.

Galatians 2:20

The Refrain
I will confess you among the peoples, O LORD;* I will sing praises to you among
the nations.

The Midday Psalm   *In Your Right Hand Are Pleasures for Evermore*
O LORD, you are my portion and my cup;* it is you who uphold my lot.
My boundaries enclose a pleasant land;* indeed, I have a goodly heritage.
I will bless the LORD who gives me counsel;* my heart teaches me, night after
night.
I have set the LORD always before me;* because he is at my right hand I shall not
fall.
My heart, therefore, is glad, and my spirit rejoices;* my body also shall rest in
hope.
For you will not abandon me to the grave,* nor let your holy one see the Pit.

You will show me the path of life;* in your presence there is fullness of joy, and in your right hand are pleasures for evermore.

Psalm 16:5–11

The Refrain
I will confess you among the peoples, O Lord;* I will sing praises to you among the nations.

The Cry of the Church
Alleluia. Christ is risen.
The Lord is risen indeed. Alleluia.

The Lord's Prayer

The Prayer Appointed for the Week
Almighty God, who through your only-begotten Son Jesus Christ overcame death and opened to us the gate of everlasting life: Grant that I, who celebrate with joy the day of the Lord's resurrection, may be raised from the death of sin by your life-giving Spirit; through Jesus Christ our Lord, who lives and reigns with you and the Holy Spirit, one God, now and for ever. *Amen.* †

The Concluding Prayer of the Church
Almighty God, who for our redemption gave your only begotten Son to death on the cross, and by his glorious resurrection delivered us from the power of our enemy: Grant me so to die daily in sin that I may evermore live with him in the joy of his resurrection; through Jesus Christ our Lord, who lives and reigns with you and the Holy Spirit, one God, now and for ever. *Amen.* †

The Vespers Office 　　　　**To Be Observed on the Hour or Half Hour Between 5 and 8 p.m.**

The Call to Prayer
Open my lips, O Lord,* and my mouth shall proclaim your praise.
Had you desired it, I would have offered sacrifice,* but you take no delight in burnt-offerings.
The sacrifice of God is a troubled spirit;* and a broken and contrite heart, O God, you will not despise.

Psalm 51:16–18

The Request for Presence
Protect me, O God, for I take refuge in you;* I have said to the Lord, "You are my Lord, my good above all other."

Psalm 16:1

The Greeting
I give you thanks, O God, I give you thanks,* calling upon your Name and declaring all your wonderful deeds.

adapted from Psalm 75:1

The Hymn   *Welcome, Happy Morning*
"Welcome, happy morning!" age to age shall say:
hell today is vanquished, heaven is won today!
Lo! The dead is living, God for evermore!
Him their true Creator, all his works adore!

Earth her joy confesses, clothing her for spring,
All fresh gifts returned with her returning King:
Bloom in every meadow, leaves on every bough,
Speak his sorrow ended, hail his triumph now.

Months in due succession, days of lengthening light,
Hours and passing moments praise you in their flight,
Brightness of the morning, sky and fields and sea,
Vanquisher of darkness, bring their praise to thee.
                               Venantius Honorius Fortunatus

The Refrain for the Vespers Lessons
For you are my hope, O Lord GOD,* my confidence since I was young.
                                              Psalm 71:5

The Vespers Psalm   *Turn Now, O God of Hosts*
You have brought the vine out of Egypt;* you cast out the nations and planted it.
You prepared the ground for it;* it took root and filled the land.
The mountains were covered by its shadow* and the towering cedar trees by its
     boughs.
You stretched out its tendrils to the Sea* and its branches to the River.
Why have you broken down its wall,* so that all that pass by pluck off its grapes?
The wild boar of the forest has ravaged it,* and the beasts of the field have grazed
     upon it.
Turn now, O God of hosts, look down from heaven; behold and tend your vine;*
     preserve what your right hand has planted.
                                              Psalm 80:8–14

The Refrain
For you are my hope, O Lord GOD,* my confidence since I was young.

The Cry of the Church
Alleluia. Christ is risen.
The Lord is risen indeed. Alleluia.

The Lord's Prayer

The Prayer Appointed for the Week
Almighty God, who through your only-begotten Son Jesus Christ overcame death
     and opened to us the gate of everlasting life: Grant that I, who celebrate with
     joy the day of the Lord's resurrection, may be raised from the death of sin by
     your life-giving Spirit; through Jesus Christ our Lord, who lives and reigns
     with you and the Holy Spirit, one God, now and for ever. *Amen.* †

The Concluding Prayer of the Church
Almighty and everlasting God, who in the Paschal mystery established the new
covenant of reconciliation: Grant that all who are reborn into the fellowship of
Christ's Body may show forth in our lives what we profess by our faith;
through Jesus Christ our Lord. *Amen.* †

*Holy Week and
Easter Compline*

Sunday
The Night Office   **To Be Observed Before Retiring**

The Call to Prayer
May the Lord Almighty grant me and those I love a peaceful night and a perfect
end. *Amen.* †

The Request for Presence
Our help is in the Name of the Lord; the maker of heaven and earth.

The Greeting
Almighty God, my heavenly Father: I have sinned against you, through my own
fault, in thought, and word, and deed, in what I have done and in what I have
left undone. For the sake of your Son our Lord Jesus Christ, forgive me all my
offenses; and grant that I may serve you in newness of life, to the glory of your
Name. *Amen.* †

The Reading
Faith is strengthened, increased and enriched by those very things that escape the
senses; the less there is to see, the more there is to believe. To adore Jesus on the
Mount of Transfiguration, to love the will of God in extraordinary things, does
not show as much faith as loving the will of God in ordinary things and adoring Jesus on the cross.

Jean-Pierre de Caussade

The Gloria*

The Psalm   *The Just Shall See His Face*
The LORD is in his holy temple;* the LORD's throne is in heaven.
His eyes behold the inhabited world;* his piercing eye weighs our worth.
The LORD weighs the righteous as well as the wicked,* but those who delight in
violence he abhors.
For the LORD is righteous; he delights in righteous deeds;* and the just shall see his
face.

Psalm 11:4–6, 8

The Gloria*

The Small Verse
Into your hands, O Lord, I commend my spirit; for you have redeemed me, O
Lord, O God of truth. Keep me, O Lord, as the apple of your eye; hide me
under the shadow of your wings. †

The Lord's Prayer

The Petition
Keep watch, dear Lord, with those who work, or watch, or weep this night, and
give your angels charge over those who sleep. Tend the sick, Lord Christ; give
rest to the weary, bless the dying, soothe the suffering, pity the afflicted, shield
the joyous; and all for your love's sake. *Amen.* †

The Final Thanksgiving
Lord, you now have set your servant free to go in peace as you have promised; for these eyes of mine have seen the Savior, whom you have prepared for all the world to see: a Light to enlighten the nations, and the glory of your people Israel. Glory to the Father, and to the Son, and to the Holy Spirit: as it was in the beginning, is now, and will be for ever. *Amen.*

Monday
The Night Office   **To Be Observed Before Retiring**

The Call to Prayer
May the Lord Almighty grant me and those I love a peaceful night and a perfect end. *Amen.* †

The Request for Presence
Our help is in the Name of the Lord; the maker of heaven and earth.

The Greeting
Almighty God, my heavenly Father: I have sinned against you, through my own fault, in thought, and word, and deed, in what I have done and in what I have left undone. For the sake of your Son our Lord Jesus Christ, forgive me all my offenses; and grant that I may serve you in newness of life, to the glory of your Name. *Amen.* †

The Reading
O Mary, let me always remember when you comprehended that the depth of the love of the Eternal Father toward the human race was so great that in order to save them, He willed the death of His Son; and that on the other hand, the love of the Son lay in wishing to honor His Father perfectly and therefore to die for us: you, in order to conform yourself, who were always and in all things united to the will of God and to this excessive love of both the Father and the Son towards the human race, you also, with your entire will offered, and consented to the death of your Son, in order that we might be saved.

St. Bonaventure

*The Gloria**

The Psalm   *I Put My Trust in Your Mercy*
How long, O LORD? will you forget me for ever?* how long will you hide your face from me?
How long shall I have perplexity in my mind, and grief in my heart, day after day?* how long shall my enemy triumph over me?

Look upon me and answer me, O Lord my God;* give light to my eyes, lest I sleep
in death;
Lest my enemy say, "I have prevailed over him,"* and my foes rejoice that I have
fallen.
But I put my trust in your mercy;* my heart is joyful because of your saving help.
I will sing to the Lord, for he has dealt with me richly;* I will praise the Name of
the Lord Most High.

Psalm 13

*The Gloria**

The Small Verse
Into your hands, O Lord, I commend my spirit; For you have redeemed me, O
Lord, O God of truth. Keep me, O Lord, as the apple of your eye; Hide me
under the shadow of your wings. †

The Lord's Prayer

The Petition
Keep watch, dear Lord, with those who work, or watch, or weep this night, and
give your angels charge over those who sleep. Tend the sick, Lord Christ; give
rest to the weary, bless the dying, soothe the suffering, pity the afflicted, shield
the joyous; and all for your love's sake. *Amen.* †

The Final Thanksgiving
Lord, you now have set your servant free to go in peace as you have promised; for
these eyes of mine have seen the Savior, whom you have prepared for all the
world to see: a Light to enlighten the nations, and the glory of your people
Israel. Glory to the Father, and to the Son, and to the Holy Spirit: as it was in the
beginning, is now, and will be for ever. *Amen.*

Tuesday
The Night Office   **To Be Observed Before Retiring**

The Call to Prayer
May the Lord Almighty grant me and those I love a peaceful night and a perfect
end. *Amen.* †

The Request for Presence
Our help is in the Name of the Lord; the maker of heaven and earth.

The Greeting
Almighty God, my heavenly Father: I have sinned against you, through my own
fault, in thought, and word, and deed, in what I have done and in what I have

left undone. For the sake of your Son our Lord Jesus Christ, forgive me all my offenses; and grant that I may serve you in newness of life, to the glory of your Name. *Amen.* †

The Reading

My devotion to the Holy Face, or rather all my spirituality, has been based on these words of Isaiah: "There is no beauty in him, nor comeliness: and we have seen him, and there was no sightliness [in him] . . . Despised and the most abject of men, a man of sorrows and acquainted with infirmity: and his look is as it were hidden and despised, whereupon we esteemed him not." I, too, desire to be without glory or beauty, to tread the winepress alone, unknown to any creature.

Thérèse of Lisieux

The Gloria*

The Psalm   *When I Awake, I Shall Be Satisfied, Beholding Your Likeness*

Hear my plea of innocence, O LORD; give heed to my cry;* listen to my prayer, which does not come from lying lips.

Let my vindication come forth from your presence;* let your eyes be fixed on justice.

Weigh my heart, summon me by night,* melt me down; you will find no impurity in me.

I give no offense with my mouth as others do;* I have heeded the words of your lips.

My footsteps hold fast to the ways of your law;* in your paths my feet shall not stumble.

I call upon you, O God, for you will answer me;* incline your ear to me and hear my words.

Show me your marvelous loving-kindness,* O Savior of those who take refuge at your right hand from those who rise up against them.

Keep me as the apple of your eye;* hide me under the shadow of your wings,

From the wicked who assault me,* from my deadly enemies who surround me.

They have closed their heart to pity,* and their mouth speaks proud things.

They press me hard, now they surround me,* watching how they may cast me to the ground,

Like a lion, greedy for its prey,* and like a young lion lurking in secret places.

Arise, O LORD; confront them and bring them down;* deliver me from the wicked by your sword.

Deliver me, O LORD, by your hand* from those whose portion in life is this world;

Whose bellies you fill with your treasure,* who are well supplied with children and leave their wealth to their little ones.

But at my vindication I shall see your face;* when I awake, I shall be satisfied, beholding your likeness.

Psalm 17

The Gloria*

The Small Verse

Into your hands, O Lord, I commend my spirit; For you have redeemed me, O
Lord, O God of truth. Keep me, O Lord, as the apple of your eye; Hide me
under the shadow of your wings. †

The Lord's Prayer

The Petition

Keep watch, dear Lord, with those who work, or watch, or weep this night, and
give your angels charge over those who sleep. Tend the sick, Lord Christ; give
rest to the weary, bless the dying, soothe the suffering, pity the afflicted, shield
the joyous; and all for your love's sake. *Amen.* †

The Final Thanksgiving

Lord, you now have set your servant free to go in peace as you have promised; for
these eyes of mine have seen the Savior, whom you have prepared for all the
world to see: a Light to enlighten the nations, and the glory of your people
Israel. Glory to the Father, and to the Son, and to the Holy Spirit: as it was in the
beginning, is now, and will be for ever. *Amen.*

Wednesday
The Night Office   **To Be Observed Before Retiring**

The Call to Prayer

May the Lord Almighty grant me and those I love a peaceful night and a perfect
end. *Amen.* †

The Request for Presence

Our help is in the Name of the Lord; the maker of heaven and earth.

The Greeting

Almighty God, my heavenly Father: I have sinned against you, through my own
fault, in thought, and word, and deed, in what I have done and in what I have
left undone. For the sake of your Son our Lord Jesus Christ, forgive me all my
offenses; and grant that I may serve you in newness of life, to the glory of your
Name. *Amen.* †

The Reading

Jesus keep me near the cross; there a precious fountain,
Free to all, a healing stream flows from Calvary's mountain.
In the cross, in the cross, be my glory ever,
Till my raptured soul shall find rest beyond the river.

Near the cross, a trembling soul, love and mercy found me;
There the bright and morning star sheds its beams around me.
Near the cross! O lamb of God, bring its scenes before me;
Help me walk from day to day with its shadow o'er me.

Near the cross I'll watch and wait, hoping, trusting ever,
Till I reach the golden strand just beyond the river.
In the cross, in the cross, be my glory ever,
Till my raptured soul shall find rest beyond the river.

Fanny Crosby

The Gloria*

The Psalm   *My Cry of Anguish Came to His Ears*

I love you, O LORD my strength,* O LORD my stronghold, my crag, and my haven.
My God, my rock in whom I put my trust,* my shield, the horn of my salvation,
    and my refuge; you are worthy of praise.
I will call upon the LORD,* and so shall I be saved from my enemies.
The breakers of death rolled over me,* and the torrents of oblivion made me
    afraid.
The cords of hell entangled me,* and the snares of death were set for me.
I called upon the LORD in my distress* and cried out to my God for help.
He heard my voice from his heavenly dwelling;* my cry of anguish came to his
    ears.

Psalm 18:1–7

The Gloria*

The Small Verse
Into your hands, O Lord, I commend my spirit; For you have redeemed me, O
    Lord, O God of truth. Keep me, O Lord, as the apple of your eye; Hide me
    under the shadow of your wings. †

The Lord's Prayer

The Petition
Keep watch, dear Lord, with those who work, or watch, or weep this night, and
    give your angels charge over those who sleep. Tend the sick, Lord Christ; give
    rest to the weary, bless the dying, soothe the suffering, pity the afflicted, shield
    the joyous; and all for your love's sake. *Amen.* †

The Final Thanksgiving
Lord, you now have set your servant free to go in peace as you have promised; for
    these eyes of mine have seen the Savior, whom you have prepared for all the
    world to see: a Light to enlighten the nations, and the glory of your people
    Israel. Glory to the Father, and to the Son, and to the Holy Spirit: as it was in the
    beginning, is now, and will be for ever. *Amen.*

Thursday
The Night Office   **To Be Observed Before Retiring**

The Call to Prayer
May the Lord Almighty grant me and those I love a peaceful night and a perfect
end. *Amen.* †

The Request for Presence
Our help is in the Name of the Lord; the maker of heaven and earth.

The Greeting
Almighty God, my heavenly Father: I have sinned against you, through my own
fault, in thought, and word, and deed, in what I have done and in what I have
left undone. For the sake of your Son our Lord Jesus Christ, forgive me all my
offenses; and grant that I may serve you in newness of life, to the glory of your
Name. *Amen.* †

The Reading
When the time came, he took his place at table, and the apostles with him. And he
said to them, 'I have ardently longed to eat this Passover with you before I suffer; because I tell you, I shall not eat it until it is fulfilled in the kingdom of
God.' Then, taking a cup, he gave thanks and said, 'Take this and share it
among you because from now on, I tell you, I shall never again drink wine
until the kingdom of God comes.' Then he took bread, and when he had given
thanks, he broke it and gave it to them, saying, 'This is my body given for you;
do this in remembrance of me.' He did the same with the cup after supper, and
said, 'This cup is the new covenant in my blood poured out for you. But look,
here with me on the table is the hand of the man who is betraying me. The Son
of man is indeed on the path which was decreed, but alas for that man by
whom he is betrayed!' And they began to ask one another which of them it
could be who was to do this. An argument also began between them about
who should be reckoned the greatest; but he said to them, 'Among the gentiles
it is the kings who lord it over them, and those who have authority over them
are given the title Benefactor. With you this must not happen. No; the greatest
among you must behave as if he were the youngest, the leader as if he were the
one who serves. For who is greater: the one at table or the one who serves? The
one at table, surely? Yet here I am among you as one who serves! You are the
men who have stood by me faithfully in my trials; and now I confer a kingdom
on you, just as my Father conferred it on me: you will eat and drink at my table
in my kingdom, and you will sit on thrones to judge the twelve tribes of Israel.'
Luke 22:14–30

The Gloria*

The Psalm   *The Statutes of the* LORD *Rejoice the Heart*

The law of the LORD is perfect and revives the soul;* the testimony of the LORD is
   sure and gives wisdom to the innocent.

The statutes of the LORD are just and rejoice the heart;* the commandment of the
   LORD is clear and gives light to the eyes.

The fear of the LORD is clean and endures for ever;* the judgments of the LORD are
   true and righteous altogether.

More to be desired are they than gold, more than much fine gold,* sweeter far than
   honey, than honey in the comb.

By them also is your servant enlightened,* and in keeping them there is great
   reward.

Psalm 19:7–11

The Gloria*

The Small Verse

Into your hands, O Lord, I commend my spirit; For you have redeemed me, O
   Lord, O God of truth. Keep me, O Lord, as the apple of your eye; Hide me
   under the shadow of your wings. †

The Lord's Prayer

The Petition

Keep watch, dear Lord, with those who work, or watch, or weep this night, and
   give your angels charge over those who sleep. Tend the sick, Lord Christ; give
   rest to the weary, bless the dying, soothe the suffering, pity the afflicted, shield
   the joyous; and all for your love's sake. *Amen.* †

The Final Thanksgiving

Lord, you now have set your servant free to go in peace as you have promised; for
   these eyes of mine have seen the Savior, whom you have prepared for all the
   world to see: a Light to enlighten the nations, and the glory of your people
   Israel. Glory to the Father, and to the Son, and to the Holy Spirit: as it was in the
   beginning, is now, and will be for ever. *Amen.*

Friday
The Night Office   **To Be Observed Before Retiring**

The Call to Prayer

May the Lord Almighty grant me and those I love a peaceful night and a perfect
   end. *Amen.* †

The Request for Presence
Our help is in the Name of the Lord; the maker of heaven and earth.

The Greeting
Almighty God, my heavenly Father: I have sinned against you, through my own
fault, in thought, and word, and deed, in what I have done and in what I have
left undone. For the sake of your Son our Lord Jesus Christ, forgive me all my
offenses; and grant that I may serve you in newness of life, to the glory of your
Name. *Amen.* †

The Reading

Lofty tree, bend down your branches
To embrace your sacred load;
O, relax the natural tension
Of your all too rigid wood.

Tree of all the one most worthy
Time's greatest Victim to sustain;
Arbor in a raging tempest
And ark that saves the world again;
Tree with sacred blood appointed;
Cross of the Lamb for sinners slain;
Gently bear the members
Of your God and dying King.

Lofty tree, bend down your branches
To embrace your sacred load;
O, relax the natural tension
Of your all too rigid wood.

Honor, blessing everlasting
To the immortal Deity:
To the Father, Son and Spirit
Equal praises ever be:
Glory through the earth and heaven
To that sacred Trinity.
Glory through the earth and heaven
To their sacred Unity.

adapted from THE SHORT BREVIARY

The Gloria*

The Psalm   *The* LORD *Gives Victory to His Anointed*
May the LORD answer you in the day of trouble,* the Name of the God of Jacob
    defend you;
Send you help from his holy place* and strengthen you out of Zion;
Remember all your offerings* and accept your burnt sacrifice;
Grant you your heart's desire* and prosper all your plans.
We will shout for joy at your victory and triumph in the Name of our God;* may
    the LORD grant all your requests.
Now I know that the LORD gives victory to his anointed;* he will answer him out
    of his holy heaven, with the victorious strength of his right hand.
Some put their trust in chariots and some in horses,* but we will call upon the
    Name of the LORD our God.
They collapse and fall down,* but we will arise and stand upright.
O LORD, give victory to the king* and answer us when we call.

Psalm 20

The Gloria*

The Small Verse

Into your hands, O Lord, I commend my spirit; for you have redeemed me, O Lord, O God of truth. Keep me, O Lord, as the apple of your eye; hide me under the shadow of your wings. †

The Lord's Prayer

The Petition

Keep watch, dear Lord, with those who work, or watch, or weep this night, and give your angels charge over those who sleep. Tend the sick, Lord Christ; give rest to the weary, bless the dying, soothe the suffering, pity the afflicted, shield the joyous; and all for your love's sake. *Amen.* †

The Final Thanksgiving

Lord, you now have set your servant free to go in peace as you have promised; for these eyes of mine have seen the Savior, whom you have prepared for all the world to see: a Light to enlighten the nations, and the glory of your people Israel. Glory to the Father, and to the Son, and to the Holy Spirit: as it was in the beginning, is now, and will be for ever. *Amen.*

Saturday
The Night Office   **To Be Observed Before Retiring**

The Call to Prayer

May the Lord Almighty grant me and those I love a peaceful night and a perfect end. *Amen.* †

The Request for Presence

Our help is in the Name of the Lord; the maker of heaven and earth.

The Greeting

Almighty God, my heavenly Father: I have sinned against you, through my own fault, in thought, and word, and deed, in what I have done and in what I have left undone. For the sake of your Son our Lord Jesus Christ, forgive me all my offenses; and grant that I may serve you in newness of life, to the glory of your Name. *Amen.* †

The Reading   *I Would Not Live Forever*

Surely now, O God,
You have worn me out;
You have made desolate
All my company.

You lift me up on the wind
And toss me about
In the roar of the storm.

My eye has grown dim,
And all my members
Are like a shadow.

The night racks my bones,
And the pain that gnaws me
Takes no rest.

Is my strength
The strength of stones,
Or is my flesh bronze?

My heart throbs,
My strength fails me;
My soul is forlorn.

I would choose death
Rather than this body;
I loathe my life;
I would not live forever. ❖

The Gloria*

The Psalm   *All the Ends of the Earth Shall Remember*
All the ends of the earth shall remember and turn to the LORD,* and all the families
    of the nations shall bow before him.
For kingship belongs to the LORD;* he rules over the nations.
To him alone all who sleep in the earth bow down in worship;* who go down to
    the dust fall before him.
My soul shall live for him; my descendants shall serve him;* they shall be known
    as the LORD's for ever.
They shall come and make known to a people yet unborn* the saving deeds that
    he has done.

Psalm 22:26–30

The Gloria*

The Small Verse
Into your hands, O Lord, I commend my spirit; For you have redeemed me, O
    Lord, O God of truth. Keep me, O Lord, as the apple of your eye; Hide me
    under the shadow of your wings. †

The Lord's Prayer

The Petition

Keep watch, dear Lord, with those who work, or watch, or weep this night, and
give your angels charge over those who sleep. Tend the sick, Lord Christ; give
rest to the weary, bless the dying, soothe the suffering, pity the afflicted, shield
the joyous; and all for your love's sake. *Amen.* †

The Final Thanksgiving

Lord, you now have set your servant free to go in peace as you have promised; for
these eyes of mine have seen the Savior, whom you have prepared for all the
world to see: a Light to enlighten the nations, and the glory of your people
Israel. Glory to the Father, and to the Son, and to the Holy Spirit: as it was in the
beginning, is now, and will be for ever. *Amen.*

Acknowledgments

"Brigid's Feast" from *Celtic Prayers* by Robert Van De Weyer. Copyright 1997 by Hunt and Thorpe. Used by permission.

"For We Are the Rind and the Leaf" from *Rilke's Book of Hours: Love Poems to God* by Ranier Maria Rilke, translated by Anita Barrows and Joanna Macy, Translation copyright © 1996 by Anita Barrows and Joanna Macy. Used by permission of Putnam Berkley, a division of Penguin Putnam, Inc.

"God, You Have Prepared in Peace the Path" from *An African Prayer Book* by Desmond Tutu. Copyright 1997 by Doubleday. Used by permission.

"Help Each One of Us, Gracious Father" Prayer from China, from *Another Day: Prayers of the Human Family* compiled by John Carden. Copyright 1986 by Church Missionary Society.

"How Majestic Is Your Name" from *Awake My Heart* by Fred Bassett. Copyright 1998 by Paraclete Press. Used by permission.

"I Would Not Live Forever" from *Awake My Heart* by Fred Bassett. Copyright 1998 by Paraclete Press. Used by permission.

"Morning Prayer" from *Celtic Prayers* by Robert Van De Weyer. Copyright 1997 by Hunt and Thorpe. Used by permission.

Excerpts from *A Short Breviary* edited by The Monks of St. John's Abbey. Copyright 1949 by St. John's Abbey. Used by permission of The Liturgical Press.

All verses, other than Psalms, are excerpted from *The New Jerusalem Bible* unless otherwise noted.

All verses from Psalms are excerpted from *The Book of Common Prayer* unless otherwise noted.

KJV refers to verses excerpted from the King James Version of the Bible.

© Peter Murphy

PHYLLIS TICKLE is Contributing Editor in Religion for *Publishers Weekly*. One of America's most respected authorities on religion, she is frequently interviewed for both print and electronic media and is a regular guest on PBS's *Religion & Ethics NewsWeekly*. The author of more than two dozen books, including the recently published *The Divine Hours*, she lives in Lucy, Tennessee.

Printed in the United States
by Baker & Taylor Publisher Services